COSMOPOLITANISMS

Cosmopolitanisms

Edited by Bruce Robbins and Paulo Lemos Horta
With an Afterword by Kwame Anthony Appiah

NEW YORK UNIVERSITY PRESS
New York

NEW YORK UNIVERSITY PRESS
New York
www.nyupress.org

© 2017 by New York University
All rights reserved

References to Internet websites (URLs) were accurate at the time of writing. Neither the author nor New York University Press is responsible for URLs that may have expired or changed since the manuscript was prepared.

ISBN: 978-1-4798-2968-2 (hardback)
ISBN: 978-1-4798-6323-5 (paperback)

For Library of Congress Cataloging-in-Publication data, please contact the Library of Congress.

New York University Press books are printed on acid-free paper, and their binding materials are chosen for strength and durability. We strive to use environmentally responsible suppliers and materials to the greatest extent possible in publishing our books.

Manufactured in the United States of America

10 9 8 7 6 5 4 3 2 1

Also available as an ebook

CONTENTS

ACKNOWLEDGMENTS

We are grateful to Hilary Ballon for several texts that originated as talks in a series she organized at 19 Washington Square, given by Craig Calhoun, David A. Hollinger, Walter Benn Michaels, and Jeremy Waldron. And we are indebted to Robert Young for the contributions by Homi Bhabha, Achille Mbembe, and Emma Dabiri. Errol Elshtain graciously granted permission for us to include Jean Bethke Elshtain's essay. Leela Gandhi's essay grew out of a collaboration with Practice International, a group of artists and curators.

Many thanks to Eric Zinner at NYU Press for championing this volume and his formidable team, in particular Alicia Nadkarni. We would also like to thank Carmen Germaine and Katherine Delia James for their editorial work on this volume. We would like to acknowledge the support of the NYU Abu Dhabi Institute, in particular Reindert Falkenburg, Philip Kennedy, and Gila Bessarat-Waels. Special thanks to Amanda Anderson, Kerry Barrett, Martin Klimke, Nils Lewis, Isabella Peralta, and Helen Small.

This publication is supported by a grant from the NYU Abu Dhabi Institute, a major hub of intellectual and creative activity, and advanced research. The institute hosts academic conferences, workshops, cultural events, and other public programs, and is a center of scholarly life in Abu Dhabi, bringing together faculty and researchers from institutions of higher education throughout the region and the world.

Introduction

BRUCE ROBBINS AND PAULO LEMOS HORTA

"When I was growing up, strangers would ask me, 'Where are you from?'" Thus begins Cyrus Patell's *Emergent U.S. Literatures: From Multiculturalism to Cosmopolitanism in the Late Twentieth Century* (2014).[1] Patell's hesitation to give any of the usual answers to this somewhat intrusive question is characteristic of what historian David Hollinger taught us to call the "new" cosmopolitanism.[2] The old cosmopolitanism was a normative ideal. Less an ideal than a description, the new cosmopolitanism merely assumes that wherever and whenever history has set peoples in transnational motion, sometimes very forcibly, it is to be expected that many of them and their descendants will show signs of hybrid identity and interestingly divided loyalty. In cosmopolitan circles, self-identification is increasingly assumed to be optional rather than mandatory. Cosmopolitan politeness discourages strangers from demanding to know where one is from.

The shift Hollinger described was from cosmopolitanism in the singular—an overriding loyalty to and concern with the welfare of humanity as a whole—to cosmopolitanisms, plural, which were now seen to be as various as the sociohistorical sites and situations of multiple membership from which they emerged and which were therefore the business of social sciences like anthropology, sociology, and history rather than a topic reserved for political theory and moral philosophy. By this point, one might almost say that cosmopolitanism would look naked without that final "s."[3] Instead of an unhealthily skinny ethical abstraction, we now have many blooming, fleshed-out particulars. And yet the triumph of the descriptive plural over the normative singular opens up as many questions as it answers. First of all, it forces us to ask what or how much these variants have in common with each other. Second and more pressing, especially as we move away from the culture wars of the 1990s that inspired Hollinger and further into the twenty-first century, there is the question of how much of the concept's old normative sense is preserved or transformed by these empirical particulars. What is it exactly that makes them interesting, makes them valuable? To put this another way: can we really separate the new from the old, the plural from the singular? If the new protocols of cosmopolitan politeness discourage questions about identity in metropolitan centers, the populism of Brexit and Donald Trump bring these questions to the fore once more. And the controversies send us back to some of the most ancient thinking on the subject.

Where are you from? The word cosmopolitan was first used as a way of evading exactly this question, which can of course be underhandedly confrontational and even dangerous. When Diogenes the Cynic called himself a "kosmo-polites," or citizen of the world, he was preferring not to say that he was from Sinope, a distant Greek colony on the Black Sea from which he had been banished, as the questioner perhaps knew, for alleged misconduct involving the local coinage.

In its founding moment, then, one might say that cosmopolitanism was already plural. Any given version would display a distinct mixture of two impulses, negative and positive. The negative impulse asserts detachment from one's place of origin or residence, a refusal of the jurisdiction of local authorities, a stepping outside of conventions, prejudices, obligations. The positive impulse asserts membership in some larger, stronger, or more compelling collective. For Diogenes, this seems to have been the "kosmos," meaning perhaps the world or the universe. An obvious logic links the two impulses: my chances of squirming out of the grip of local interrogators increase if I can declare myself subject to a higher authority, ideally an authority they recognize. But the logic may only be latent; it is unclear that a higher authority is always necessary. Since Diogenes's works were lost, it is not known whether he ever clarified what he meant by "kosmos." Perhaps it meant something like "nature." Anecdotes about the Cynic philosopher tend to dramatize his cheery noncompliance. They offer no evidence that his disobedience relied upon metaphysical accreditation, human or divine.

Traditional definitions may tend more to the positive or negative, but they usually agree on some degree of synthesis: cosmopolitanism as a commitment to the good of humans as a whole that overrides all smaller commitments and creates a habitual detachment from the values of the locality. Perhaps inevitably, cosmopolitanism has been or at least has looked like a badge of privilege. As mentioned above, this singular, normative account has been gradually if only partially displaced since the late 1980s by a plural, descriptive understanding. According to the new understanding, cosmopolitanism can be defined as any one of many possible modes of life, thought, and sensibility that are produced when commitments and loyalties are multiple and overlapping, no one of them necessarily trumping the others. This shift from a normative to a descriptive register has meant that there are more kinds of cosmopolitanism out there to be observed and explored, both in the present and in the past, and perhaps also a greater absolute quantity of cosmopolitanism. It has meant that social scientists, cultural critics, and historians could stake claims to a concept that had seemed to belong largely to philosophers and political theorists. And most important, it has meant that instead of being the prerogative of a few heroic figures like Diogenes, cosmopolitanism has come to be seen as a characteristic and possession of substantial social collectivities, often nonelite collectivities that had cosmopolitanism thrust upon them by traumatic histories of dislocation and dispossession. It became possible to speak, in Silviano Santiago's resonant phrase, of the cosmopolitanism of the poor.

Sociologists and ethnographers who have been drawn to the concept in its new plural guise generally continue to use it as a term of praise, claiming for their diverse, hybrid, diasporic subjects something like the honor that the singular, normative, philosophical concept was held to confer. Yet in the new context this honor can no longer be taken for granted. As it is pluralized and democratized, becoming a larger part of the status quo, cosmopolitanism can less comfortably serve as a criterion by which the status quo is judged. If one gets to be a cosmopolitan by becoming a refugee or economic migrant, what is there to celebrate? If the status quo is nationalist, then cosmopolitans may be nationalists as well. (A less flattering designation for the same phenomenon might be "long-distance nationalism.") In that case, would we still be talking about the same idea? In any particular instance, cosmopolitanism's value must it seems be named, shown, and argued for. And the argument will lead back to debate about the general meaning of the idea and the general history which can or cannot be built up around it.

The older, singular, normative understanding tends to generate a relatively schematic and linear history: humble beginnings in ancient Cynicism and Stoicism, when the world was not as tightly woven together in actuality as it was starting to be in thought; modern coming of age in the humanism of the Renaissance and the Enlightenment; an interruption in the nineteenth century, when imperial nationalism rose to dominance; then full flowering in the twentieth and twenty-first centuries, when the actual interconnectedness of the world's peoples brings with it for the first time the possibility that the ideal might be realized in some sort of world community. Distinguishing between old and new cosmopolitanisms, as Hollinger suggests, does not necessarily entail a less optimistic narrative. Hollinger himself applauds the blossoming of a multitude of adjectivally modified cosmopolitanisms: rooted, discrepant, vernacular, critical, subaltern, and so on. But a more severe and perhaps more dialectical narrative would have to recognize that alongside nature, reason, secularism, and humanity, the list of authorities that have sponsored cosmopolitanism also includes colonialism, God, the free market, and collective experiences of divided loyalty that may not be conducive to critical distance. It would have to recognize that cosmopolitanisms in the plural may call for plural histories and that the setting of these histories will not always be Europe. The question thus arises whether a single history of cosmopolitanism that remains responsible for so much diversity is even conceivable.

Assuming that the ancient and modern versions of colonialism refer to roughly the same object—not an assumption on which everyone will agree—there has probably never been a cosmopolitanism that did not have colonialism lurking somewhere in the vicinity. Sinope was a colony, and it spawned colonies of its own. Defenders of Diogenes have claimed that he was indicted and exiled only because he was caught up in a local power struggle between supporters of Persia and Athens, each the center of a regional empire. Students of postcolonialism may be tempted to conclude, therefore, that cosmopolitanism's leap beyond the local became a possibility only because of the existence of empire, that cosmopolitanism could have been inspired or authorized only by the imperial scale, that it therefore takes its very meaning from conquest and colonialism. The argument has been made, for example, by Timothy Brennan: "[I]f we wished to capture the essence of cosmopolitanism in a single formula, it would be this. It is a discourse of the universal that is inherently local—a locality that is always surreptitiously imperial."[4] This transhistorical hypothesis will elicit arguments both pro and con. On the one hand, Diogenes's Cynicism was an influence on the Stoics, several centuries later, who rendered cosmopolitanism hugely popular under the Roman Empire and made it the explicit philosophy of one of its emperors, Marcus Aurelius. On the other side of the ledger is Diogenes's lack of awe in the presence of Alexander the Great. When the latter asked what he could do for the philosopher at his feet, the celebrated reply was, roughly translated, "You can stop blocking my sunlight." It is not hard to show that cosmopolitanism has never been restricted to sunlit emperors or those who look up to them.

For Hegel, Stoicism was the exemplary philosophy of slavery: it taught people to feel free in their minds without obliging them to emancipate their bodies. In spite of the example of Marcus Aurelius, it was less interested in teaching people how to rule than in teaching them how to be ruled. Yes, it flourished during the Roman Empire, but it did so in large part by developing cosmopolitanism's negative drive toward detachment—what Paul Gilroy calls, approvingly, "the principled and methodical cultivation of a degree of estrangement from one's own culture and history" (*Postcolonial Melancholia*, 67). The good life, according to the Stoics, involved learning not to invest too much importance in those people and things that are closest to us simply because they are close rather than far away. This entailed an ability to perceive "adiaphora," or things to which you can properly be indifferent. It also called for practice in cultivating toward such things what the Stoics called "apathy."

There is a stark contrast here with the Enlightenment's characteristic cultivation of empathy, which involved strenuous outreach to people far away. Modern cosmopolitanism is often associated with Kantian ethics, which rejects simple obedience to doctrine and instead sends the moral imagination on a long, exhausting, and perhaps endless journey toward invisible others. But it could also be dated from Adam Smith's *Theory of the Moral Sentiments*. According to Luc Boltanski, the demand for emotional attachment to distant people who are unconnected to you by anything but your common humanity, as posited by Smith, is the invention and distinguishing feature of modern humanitarianism.[5] To its adherents at least, the defining achievement of empathetic cosmopolitanism in its Enlightenment-humanitarian form is the nineteenth-century abolition of the slave trade. So cosmopolitanism might be said to stand on both sides of the slavery question.

There also exist viable claims to cosmopolitanism that are located between the 300s and the 1700s. By one reckoning, almost everything premodern would count. If nationalism, like colonialism, is as modern as the nation-state (again, not a statement with which all scholars would concur), and if cosmopolitanism is nationalism's antithesis, then it is tempting to see most and perhaps all premodern thought as in some sense cosmopolitan. This would be a sort of cosmopolitanism by default, aimed more at the everyday cohabitations and negotiations of diverse groups than at the conceptual goal of transcending cultural differences and producing a universal concept of humanity. But there are examples that are far from minimalist. The most salient instance of a culturally rich, hybrid, intellectually productive cosmopolitanism in the premodern era is perhaps El Andaluz, or Spain between the Islamic conquest and the expulsion of the Moors and Jews by the Christians in 1492.

Premodern and medieval cosmopolitanisms echo postmodern versions in 1) setting themselves against nationalism, seen as distinctively modern, and 2) basing themselves on a combination of imperial conquest and apolitical commerce. In her resounding critique of "Alexandrian cosmopolitanism," Hala Halim accuses European myth makers of celebrating both a Hellenistic and a pre-Nasser cosmopolitanism that in each case forgot about conquest and ignored or scorned the presence of native Arab and Egyptian civilization.[6] Yet it is hard to avoid the narrative that associates the decline of cosmopolitanism with the rise of nationalism. Much the same story has been told about the impact of Egyptian nationalism on Alexandria and about the impact of Greek nationalism on the equally cosmopolitan commercial port city of Thessaloniki. In Amitav Ghosh's *In an Antique Land*, the cosmopolitanism that is honored is underwritten by the circulation of commodities and their agents between medieval South Asia and North Africa.[7] These two social bases can of course also overlap, with imperial power doing the (not always acknowledged) work of facilitating intercontinental exchange. Commerce disguising empire: the formula echoes contemporary globalization.

An alternative, noncommercial origin for modern cosmopolitanism is offered by Walter Mignolo.[8] For Stoicism and the Enlightenment, cosmopolitanism overlaps considerably with secularism. If cosmopolitanism need not be secular, however, then theological debates in sixteenth-century Spain over the status of New World Indians would be an earlier point of emergence than Kant and the northern European Enlightenment—earlier and also better, in the sense that the brief for the indigenous peoples of the Americas received a more detailed and sympathetic hearing in Spain, Mignolo suggests, than it did in Kant's Germany. We assume, with Mignolo, that cosmopolitanism cannot be identified with secularism. It seems plausible that the basic recognition of loyalties divided between the local and the translocal begins with or is strongly encouraged by the advent of monotheism. Instead of "I have my God and you have yours," meaning that I have no obligation to treat you and yours as I treat myself and mine, the premise would be that since there is one God for all, the same moral law should also be applied to all. In theory at least, it would therefore become less acceptable to give preference to compatriots and hold oneself to a lower standard of conduct toward foreigners.

In practice, monotheistic faith has neither been a reliable source of cosmopolitan behavior nor a guarantee of cosmopolitan status. If both anti-Semites and philo-Semites have often taken cosmopolitan as a code word for Jew, whether or not it is preceded by "rootless," the term has not been widely applied to Muslims—for example, those from other countries who crossed borders to fight the Russians in Chechnya or the Americans in Afghanistan. This suggests that usage remains in the residual grip of a secular humanism that has been more covertly particularist—that is, Judaeo-Christian—than it pretends. The same inequity is visible in accounts of the Muslim residents of the European Union, who arguably offer a better illustration than the Jewish diaspora of cosmopolitanism as multiple and overlapping affiliation. In its association with secularism in the political sense, however, cosmopolitanism can also be taken to indicate zones and practices of peaceful coexistence, as between Hindus and Muslims in early modern India or between Muslims, Christians, and Jews under the Ottoman Empire, without any necessary recourse to a universal, transfaith theory of humanity like that posited by monotheism and by the European Enlightenment.

Since the beginning of the twentieth century, witnesses have reported a great leap forward in the objective conditions permitting the development of cosmopolitanisms on a new and larger scale: economic and political interconnectedness reaching further down into society, improvements in the technology of transportation and communication transmitting news of distant places and allowing dispersed populations to stay in contact, and so on. How far and wide these sociotechnical forces have propelled cosmopolitanism remains a question, as does its value when it assumes these putatively democratic, exponentially expanded forms. Many would claim, for example, that human rights have become the dominant version of cosmopolitanism, one that in the period since World War II has seized the hearts and minds of the majority and become, in effect, a secular religion. In that case, it would be vulnerable to the charge of being nothing but Western liberalism, marketed for export. The effective bearers of rights always seem to be individuals, not collectivities. Thus cosmopolitanism sinks back into ethics. It cannot bring about the global economic and political justice that it helps us envisage, which necessarily depends on the action of collectivities and indeed demands preference for members over nonmembers. A similar critique might target a cosmopolitanism that is satisfied with individual acts of consumption, whether of exotic information or exotic food.

Critics have explicitly associated cosmopolitanism with liberalism in two further senses: a downplaying of the present importance of past atrocities (including those perpetrated by colonialism), and a relative disregard for the economic structures that produce inequality. But cosmopolitanism being irreducibly plural, all such associations are in perpetual flux. Since the refugee crisis of 2015, it has seemed less plausible to associate cosmopolitanism with the European Union, once seen complacently as a zone where successful globalization ensured both pacifism and hospitality to outsiders. The cost of claiming to be cosmopolitan in today's Europe is clearly higher than many liberal Europeans are willing to pay. To the extent that cosmopolitanism remains identified with the ideology of the Great Powers, it has come to suggest an excuse for old-fashioned military interventions, now cloaked in the robes of humanitarian disinterestedness. Paul Gilroy speaks of an "armored cosmopolitanism" (63) that "makes the improvement of a resentful and unappreciative world into a matter of morals" (62). David

Harvey worries that cosmopolitanism may become "an ethical mask for hegemonic neoliberal practices of class domination and financial and militaristic imperialism" (84).[9] Yet both Harvey and Gilroy speak in the name of a better cosmopolitanism, one that can choose to reject such high-minded belligerence as a distortion.

The perennial charge that cosmopolitanism is fundamentally elitist has been met with a host of empirical studies exposing the existence of a "cosmopolitanism from below" or (to cite again Silviano Santiago's contribution to this volume) a "cosmopolitanism of the poor." This leveling impulse, which was already at the heart of James Clifford's attention to the native servants, guides, and translators who accompanied and educated European travelers and explorers, has thrived in books like *The Many-Headed Hydra*, by Peter Linebaugh and Marcus Rediker, about the cosmopolitan culture of multiethnic sailors crossing the North Atlantic in the seventeenth and eighteenth centuries.[10] Labor migrants, such as Filipina domestic workers, are now favored objects of empirical research on cosmopolitanism. Though many writers question the possibility of being "outside" the system, almost no one questions the possibility of being below it.

The turn to a descriptive, empirical, plural understanding of cosmopolitanism also invites social scientific argument as to its observable effects on large populations. Responding to a widespread tendency to celebrate diaspora, Benedict Anderson has pointed to many instances where a diaspora actively supported positions within the homeland that were more nationalist and racist than those who had not left home: Hindus living in Canada who supported the destruction of the Babri Mosque in Ayodhya, India; Irish Americans funding the bombing campaign of the IRA in Northern Ireland; Jewish Americans who took more uncompromising stances vis-à-vis the Palestinians than Jews residing in Israel. Migration can intensify ugly emotions rather than inducing detachment from them. Solidarity at a distance is not always a good thing. Anderson calls this phenomenon "long-distance nationalism."[11] But that term has also been adopted without the negative connotations in anthropology, for example in the study of the strenuous and self-sacrificing but generally constructive citizenly role played by Haitian Americans in Haiti.

As long as literature was associated with romantic particulars and cosmopolitanism with ethical universals, relations between them, while not nonexistent, could not be entirely comfortable. Cosmopolitanism's pluralization and particularization help explain the density of literary reference below, whether in Jean Bethke Elshtain's use of Milan Kundera's *The Unbearable Lightness of Being* to illustrate thin and thick belonging, or Elleke Boehmer's exposition of what membership in an international public sphere of readers could mean to postcolonial women, or Ashleigh Harris's reading of Brian Chikwava's *Harare North* as a rejoinder to Afropolitanism. Afropolitanism, a recent coinage (2005), is also the center of this volume's most intense controversy, argued over as it is by Mbembe, Quayson, Harris, and Dabiri. In some ways, the argument is specific to Africa; in others, it gives an African twist to issues that resonate whenever and wherever the concept comes up. To demand "awareness of the interweaving of here and there, the presence of the elsewhere in the here and vice versa, the relativization of primary roots and memberships," as Mbembe so eloquently does: must this be to speak in the voice of the privileged, to close one's eyes to the poverty and homelessness that mobility so often entail for migrants and asylum seekers, to play up cultural inclusiveness and creativity at the expense of economic deprivation? Walter Benn Michaels and Kwame Anthony Appiah, two of the strongest voices in this very much ongoing discussion, offer critical contributions to this volume.

How should we feel about the tendency for cosmopolitanism to overlap with or even take over the function of literariness? Cosmopolitanism, in its recent forms, posits a rich multiplicity of identities and loyalties. Literariness, in its recent forms, has posited for literature an irreducible multiplicity of meanings, hence indeterminacy or (in an older formulation) ambiguity. Cosmopolitanism can thus give literariness a grounding in social reality, or vice versa. Mixed cultural belonging signifies cultural detachment, which in turn signifies literary self-estrangement or disinterestedness: never having to say once and for all where you are from.

As our title suggests, the contributors to this volume do not assume that there is a single cosmopolitan idea, and they privilege multiple types of difference in formulating their ideas of cosmopolitanism. Differences are most often seen as cultural, racial, national. What about economic differences—in other words, inequalities? Writing in the Luso-Brazilian context, Silviano Santiago again calls for a cosmopolitanism from below. In Portugal, he writes, elite cosmopolitanism is bound up with the legacy of empire and empire-returned captains of commerce; it tends to be found in private schools and luxury hotels. For the poor who leave Portugal for Paris, by contrast, cosmopolitanism is more likely to register as an experience of loss—perhaps most poignantly, among second-generation migrants, a loss of the Portuguese language itself, a closing off rather than an expansion of familial and cultural connections. On the other hand, Santiago also contrasts the Europhile and state-sanctioned cosmopolitanism of Brazilian diplomats with the vibrancy of more popular modes of cosmopolitanism that emerge from the favelas and draw upon Afro-Brazilian histories and South-South resonances.

Economic inequality has never been closely associated with cosmopolitanism, but of late the two have been frequently seen in each other's company. Drawing on the works of George Orwell, Bruce Robbins asks how cosmopolitanism might become a force for a more democratic redistribution of global resources. Orwell himself had this goal in mind but saw it as requiring considerable sacrifice on the part of the more prosperous. Examining Orwell's BBC broadcasts to India during World War II, Robbins suggests that Orwell saw wartime rationing as surprising evidence that people were willing to deny themselves material goods for some greater good, hence might be capable of doing so again in the interest of greater global equality.

How much should cultural difference count when weighed against economic difference? This old question comes alive again in rethinking cosmopolitanism. Considering different frameworks for engaging difference, Walter Benn Michaels argues that the salient issue should not be the debate between cosmopolitanism and multiculturalism, but rather the preference for cultural difference over economic difference that for him is implied in both. On university campuses, Michaels contends, cultural difference is considered a positive opportunity while economic difference—that is, poverty—does not define a useful identity. Cosmopolitanism cannot afford to invest in cultural difference at the expense of concern for class difference and social justice.

Though cultural difference may be privileged over economic difference, David Hollinger notes that in the United States the existing apparatus for dealing with cultural diversity itself feels increasingly anachronistic. Differences within communities defined by race, like those that separate the historical experiences of African Americans from African and Caribbean immigrants, have subverted the crude working categories of an older multiculturalism. The result is a questioning of duties to "our own kind"—whatever that has come to mean—and a pressure to think of identity in cosmopolitan terms: less as something to be preserved and perpetuated than as the voluntary formation of new and wider solidarities. If race can be too broad to define a cultural community, it can also be too narrow, as Achille Mbembe suggests. Mbembe discusses the difficulty of defining "who is African" based on race given the continent's long history as both the starting and ending point of population movements and cultural transmissions. Addressing the formation of new solidarities within the transformations taking place across African cultures and identities, Mbembe draws upon that history to posit the possibility of a transnational "Afropolitan" culture that embraces difference as it engages with the world at large. Urban identities based on transnational imaginings also generate solidarity, as Elleke Boehmer's discussion of the virtual cosmopolitanism experienced by colonial and postcolonial readerships in India suggests.

If cosmopolitanism involves developing new, broader senses of solidarity with others, is the cosmopolitan someone who is at home wherever she or he goes? Thomas Bender turns this question upside down: the cosmopolitan is someone who is at least slightly uncomfortable everywhere, even at home. For Bender, cosmopolitanism is an unsettling experience that provokes inquiry into difference. Its demand is not only to come to an understanding of the other, but also to come to a new understanding of oneself. Self-reflexivity inspired by the encounter with difference is difficult, Bender acknowledges, and increasingly rare as public spaces change and human interaction is increasingly digital. So cosmopolitanism remains to a significant degree aspirational; it cannot be taken for granted as what our ordinary social spaces already give us. Jean Bethke Elshtain considers whether a cosmopolitan ethics can be compatible with the solidarity of faith and the strong, particular claims of religion. Elshtain reminds her reader that all moral development begins with the particular and suggests that rather than being opposed to it, cosmopolitanism can be seen as a way of connecting the particular and universal claims of ethics and identity.

What bearing do our cosmopolitan aspirations have on structures of power and vice versa? Robert Young, whose incisive remarks provoked much of the thinking in the lectures from which some of these essays emerged, focuses on the unfinished business that remains between cosmopolitanism and national sovereignty. Can the nation-state, which is still relied on to guarantee the rights of individuals, stretch itself to protect the mobile, migratory, multiply-loyal subjects that nationalism has excluded but that are now so characteristic of our time? It is only in such embodiments, Young suggests, that the cosmopolitan idea truly exists—if indeed cosmopolitanism exists today as such an idea rather than a pressing series of unanswered and perhaps unanswerable questions.

"It is injustice, not justice, which brings us into normative politics," as Avishai Margalit remarks. Homi Bhabha takes this observation as his point of departure for snapshots of what he calls spectral sovereignty, vernacular cosmopolitanism, and cosmopolitan memory. The nation-state persists in spectral or compromised form, Bhabha argues, long after it has been declared dead. It remains an object of desire for those who don't have it, like the Kashmiris, the Palestinians, and many indigenous peoples. It is not a holdover from the past but absolutely contemporary, part of any properly cosmopolitan aspiration in the digital era. Like migrants, they need to settle down. But settlement is not the affirmation of an authentic, already existing identity. The vernacular cosmopolitanism that accompanies the desire introduces into their identity a primordial indefiniteness—one might say, a refusal to be pinned down by the question, "Where are you from?" For Bhabha, this indefiniteness parallels the role of dignity in the discourse of human rights: it is the proper basis for a cosmopolitan ethics.

For better or worse, another form of sovereignty that has shaped cosmopolitanism as a concept and a historical experience is empire. Paulo Lemos Horta provides a novel perspective on cosmopolitanism in the service of empire through the works of the famous Richard Francis Burton, self-described "cosmopolite" and Kwame Anthony Appiah's prime example of his cosmopolitan imperative to be open to cultural difference. The Victorian explorer, diplomat, and translator considered cosmopolitan experience—his conception of which was somewhat similar to Bender's—essential to the success of the British Empire, both politically and culturally. Yet, as Horta argues, Burton and his notion of a properly cosmopolitan empire bring into focus the role of prejudice in cosmopolitan self-fashioning, for Burton failed to fulfill a key element in Appiah's definition: to recognize a responsibility for every human being. Through Burton, Horta suggests the difficulty of disentangling cosmopolitan from counter-cosmopolitan impulses in the context of empire.

Also taking empire as his guiding thread, Phillip Mitsis offers a polemical corrective to the uses of ancient philosophy in the influential reformulations of cosmopolitanism by Kwame Anthony Appiah and Martha Nussbaum. Appiah and Nussbaum deploy the Stoics in the service of liberal and progressive conceptions of cosmopolitanism. According to Mitsis, however, their readings reverse the Stoics' original meaning. Plutarch's biography of Alexander the Great displays an admiration for Alexander as conqueror, who accomplished, he thought, what the philosophers could not, bringing different peoples under the same system of law. Those who see cosmopolitanism today as Western imperialism in liberal disguise would recognize the precedent. Indeed, Emma Dabiri critiques mainstream modes of Afropolitanism as a type of imperialism of cultural consumerism capitalized upon by Western markets and as primarily concerned with commodifying "African flavored" versions of Western conventions and forms. She contemplates the alternative of an Afropolitanism beyond such elite consumerism that would be guided by African precolonial modernity, epistemologies, and forms of creativity.

Cosmopolitanism as a privileged style of consumerism is not only inaccessible to most—an old complaint that, as we see here, haunts new cosmopolitanisms—but, as Craig Calhoun explains, it is also incapable of engaging with the ethical and political issues that the new global interconnectedness brings in its wake. And cosmopolitanism as a universalistic ethics which asserts our basic moral obligation to other humans can confront differences only as problems. Calhoun asks, shouldn't differences be seen as opportunities? For him, cosmopolitanisms are plural and particular, "communities of fate" bound together by particular sets of historically grounded relationships and institutions. The key to a robust cosmopolitanism, Calhoun contends, is attention to the specificity of social and historical connectedness.

Attention to the spaces of cosmopolitanism can also give rise to novel modes of analysis. Ato Quayson grounds his analysis of cosmopolitanism in urban social space, where he finds cosmopolitanism visible in the streets—in the self-fashioning of the youth of Accra, for example, defined by the overlapping histories manifest in the city's signs and slogans, the music, the food, the architecture, the shape of the streets themselves. While Silviano Santiago points out the influence on Brazilian popular cosmopolitanism of the cultures brought over by slaves from Africa, Quayson symmetrically reveals the influence of former slaves from Brazil who settled in Accra. The Tabon were former slaves who migrated to Ghana in 1836, probably in the aftermath of the 1835 Muslim slave rebellion in Bahia. They brought with them both a Portuguese language, which served them well when Portuguese pidgin was still prevalent in mercantile networks, and skills and trades vital for developing the urban street culture of Accra and tapping into transnational networks of commerce.

While Quayson writes of the cosmopolitan impact of the return of African populations to the continent, Ashleigh Harris critiques the tendency to locate Afropolitanism in African expatriate and diaspora culture, particularly as a culture of elite consumerism. Asking if "Afropolitanism" is a useful term, Harris argues that without it, the ways in which economic inequalities shape Africans' experience of worldliness would largely remain invisible. Beyond the consumer culture of the elite, she contends, Africans do not enjoy equal cosmopolitan freedoms as citizens of the world. In her analysis of Brian Chikwava's novel *Harare North* as a dramatization of the cosmopolitan experience of being African in the world, Harris arrives at a conclusion that seems similar to Bender's conception of the cosmopolitan as someone who is at home nowhere rather than everywhere, but is more literal: the Afropolitanism Chikwava expresses in his novel is an actual state of homelessness, rather than the possibility of being at home in the world.

Recovering the cosmopolitanism of the medieval Catholic university, Jeremy Waldron offers an eloquent update of what Hollinger would call the "old" cosmopolitanism that is both particular and universal. For him, differences have been overvalued. Whatever their usefulness to a grade school teacher introducing children to the larger world, differences may not define how actual people around the world see themselves or experience the world. Monotheisms link very diverse societies. Scientific knowledge is universal: there is no Swedish physics or

Namibian chemistry, just chemistry and physics. World trade has made many commodities universal. These are the real material basis for a cosmopolitanism that need not after all deny its founding universalism. The critics of Martha Nussbaum are wrong to think that cosmopolitanism requires a world state. Religion, science, and commerce are doing the job of grounding it and making it concrete.

A cosmopolitan space may also be aspirational, as in Kang Youwei's *Book of Great Harmony*, a utopian portrait of the peoples of the earth living together without racial, national, or cultural divides that emerged, almost miraculously, at the height of Chinese resistance to the Japanese invasion of the 1930s. Placing the book into its tormented historical context, Yan Haiping takes her departure from the idea that cosmopolitanism as universalism can echo rather than supersede nationalism. Arguing that figures previously conceived as nationalist can also be thought of as cosmopolitans, she lays out a tradition of cosmopolitanism that is both Chinese and cross-cultural.

Does this mean that there is no one cosmopolitan idea? Not necessarily. It is also arguable that cosmopolitanism properly speaking is the idea that makes room for these multiple and overlapping conceptions, forced by the imperative of inclusiveness to change its own rules. An alternate title for this volume might have been imperfect cosmopolitanisms. Leela Gandhi insists on this sense of imperfection, playing upon the grammatical import of the imperfect verb form: "Unlike the preterit form, which implies an already completed past action, the imperfective aspect renders an apparently concluded (perfected) action unfinished and suddenly infinitive. In this way the imperfectionism at the core of disapparation makes the subject of ethics into a perpetual—restless— work in progress." Robert Young in turn asks, "How can we translate the cosmopolitan idea into a transformative reality?" The question presupposes that, even as we seek to describe its actually existing shapes and spaces, cosmopolitanism remains for us a strenuous aspiration.

NOTES

1 Cyrus R. K. Patell, *Emergent U.S. Literatures: From Multiculturalism to Cosmopolitanism in the Late Twentieth Century* (New York: NYU Press, 2014).
2 David A. Hollinger, "Not Universalists, Not Pluralists: The New Cosmopolitans Find Their Own Way," *Constellations* 8, 2 (June 2001): 236–248.

3 Some examples include Gita Rajan and Shailja Sharma, eds., *New Cosmopolitanisms: South Asians in the US* (Stanford: Stanford University Press, 2006); Robert J. Holton, *Cosmopolitanisms: New Thinking and New Directions* (Basingstoke, Hampshire: Palgrave Macmillan, 2009); and John C. Hawley, ed., *India in Africa, Africa in India: Indian Ocean Cosmopolitanisms* (Bloomington: Indiana University Press, 2008).

4 Timothy Brennan, *At Home in the World: Cosmopolitanism Now* (Cambridge: Harvard University Press, 1997), 81.

5 Luc Boltanski, *Distant Suffering: Morality, Media and Politics*, trans. Graham Burchell (Cambridge: Cambridge University Press, 1999).

6 Hala Halim, *Alexandrian Cosmopolitanism: An Archive* (New York: Fordham University Press, 2013).

7 Amitav Ghosh, *In an Antique Land* (New York: Vintage, 1994).

8 Walter Mignolo, "The Many Faces of Cosmo-Polis: Border Thinking and Critical Cosmopolitanism," *Public Culture* 12, 3 (Fall 2000): 721–748.

9 Paul Gilroy, *Postcolonial Melancholia* (New York: Columbia University Press, 2005); David Harvey, *Cosmopolitanism and the Geographies of Freedom* (New York: Columbia University Press, 2009).

10 James Clifford, *The Predicament of Culture* (Cambridge: Harvard University Press, 1988); and Peter Linebaugh and Marcus Rediker, *The Many Headed Hydra: Sailors, Slaves, Commoners, and the Hidden History of the Revolutionary Atlantic* (Boston: Beacon Press, 2000).

11 Benedict Anderson, "Long-Distance Nationalism," in *The Spectre of Comparisons: Nationalism, Southeast Asia and the World* (London: Verso, 1998).

PART I

Justice

1

The Cosmopolitanism of the Poor

SILVIANO SANTIAGO

Translated by Magdalena Edwards and Paulo Lemos Horta

I.

As Manoel de Oliveira's 1997 film *Voyage to the Beginning of the World* unfolds, the camera's focus gets confused with the car's rearview mirror.[1] The camera, or the rearview mirror, determines the point of view that will guide the viewer's perception of the voyage from Lisbon to a distant town embedded in the mountains of northern Portugal. For the characters in transit, distance from the past and the future holds the same dramatic weight. The arrival at their destination will take even longer due to the rhetorical effect—and the experience that awaits the characters in the future is an unknown that will unfurl without warning, as opposed to what happens in David Lynch's films where the camera's gaze follows the road taken and a climate of suspense dominates. Here, as the car gains ground, the camera shows us the signage that has already been obeyed, the asphalt path already traveled, and the landscape unveiled. The viewer enters into a time machine. By filling up the heart of the past twice consecutively, the present becomes a throughway to the future.

Four people travel along the modern Portuguese highway, not counting the fifth, the unknown figure of the driver. Two by two. The old film director, Manoel, and the starlet in love with him. And two more actors—one is Portuguese and the other French, the son of a Portuguese father who at the age of fourteen crossed the poor mountains of northern Portugal, fleeing by foot to Spain and from there emigrating to France. He abandoned his native village to earn a living and start a family. The famous French actor Afonso, who arrives in Lisbon to star in a big film production, plans a voyage to the beginning of the world. He wants to meet his rural relatives who still live in northern Portugal.

The group is transnational in its ease with national languages. Everyone is of Portuguese origin and, with the exception of the actor Afonso who speaks only French, bilingual.

Two films unfold and are contrasted in *Voyage to the Beginning of the World*. The first is in the hands of Manoel, the film director. The French Portuguese actor Afonso, who is the son of another Manoel, drives the second. In the first, the director, played by Marcello Mastroianni, commandeers the voyage's original impetus, namely, the curiosity and anxiety of the exile, from the French actor. The old director steals the desire to walk his family's past from the son of the alien (*meteco* or *métèque*). Unlike the actor, who eagerly anticipates his first meeting with the Portuguese family he lost due to his father's emigration in the 1930s, the director only intends to revisit the aristocratic past of the Portuguese nation, which includes his ancestors' achievements, and more recently, his own. In a predictable and tiring monologue, he seeks the attention of his three fellow travelers so he can recall his own memories. His courtly youth, Portugal's history, and the nation-state become muddled in memory's landscape. In an attempt to free his memory from the anguish of *saudade*, he makes the driver take a detour three times, thus imposing his particular past's images on that route's place and putting them ahead of the images of the second film.

The car first stops in front of the renowned aristocratic Jesuit school where the director began his early studies. The camera abandons the position dictated by the rearview mirror in order to capture the car and the characters in profile, as if to say that it is now narrating a story at the margins of the voyage's trajectory. The car stops a second time. While the director weaves additional reminiscences, the group wanders through the abandoned gardens of a former luxury hotel. Still catering to the director, the car stops for a third and final time, now in front of a house with a statue of Pedro Macau, a paternal image for the director. Pedro Macau represents the Portuguese who, having enriched themselves in the colonies, returned wealthy to their country of origin and brought to its shores "the white man's burden," to use a classic expression from Rudyard Kipling. Notice the log Pedro carries on his back, immobilizing him; read the metaphor of Pedro's adventures: the Portuguese present moment is torment, and the future arrives gnawed by remorse. A country of sailors, the Portuguese ended up exiling themselves in their own land, in maturity or in old age.

The film director's story is no different from so many others depicted in modern national literatures since the beginning of the twentieth century. Marcel Proust's branding iron both laid bare and universally marked the individual literary memory of the past century. All the great artists and intellectuals of Western modernity, including the Marxists, went through the *madeleine* experience. There is a shared past—in most cases cosmopolitan, aristocratic, stately—that can be drawn from each one of the subsequent autobiographies of various authors. In the preface of Sérgio Buarque de Holanda's *Raízes do Brasil* (Roots of Brazil), Antonio Candido was sensitive to the disappearance of the *individual* from the socio-literary texts of the decade in question. The memory's text transforms what seemed to be different and multiple into one and the same. He observes: "[O]ur particular witness accounts become a register for the experience of the many, all of whom, belonging to what dominates a generation, deem themselves different from one another in the beginning and become, little by little, so similar they end up disappearing as individuals."

The passengers' attention, and the spectators', is diverted three times from the second film's images and dialogue, which hold more interest than the first. The French actor, as much as he tries to counterattack the usurper, only manages to confiscate the narrative thread from him late in the film. The film director does not have the right to impose the memories that fill the void of the aristocracy's *saudade* on the other two Portuguese travelers and on the son of the *meteco* (alien), now a *rastaqüera* or *rastaquouère* (good-for-nothing). The Portuguese language in Brazil appropriated the words *meteco* and *rastaqüera*, which have pejorative meanings in modern France, which we use here to characterize the French actor, the son of Portuguese emigrants.[2] Consider this passage from *Mocidade no Rio e Primeira viagem à Europa* (Youth in Rio and First Voyage to Europe) (1956), the memoirs of the author, lawyer, and diplomat Gilberto Amado (1887–1969): "I began, naturally, to be delighted by the masterworks of French cuisine. I raised my already reasonable aptitude for opining knowingly, and not approximately like a *rastaqüera* or *meteco*, on these matters of sauces and condiments." In French lands, the diplomat, a member of the Brazilian elite, did not want to be confused with the immigrants, from whom he also distances himself back home.

When the actor overtakes the film's narrative thread—an opportunity the up-to-that-point costar seizes in order to take the spotlight from the director and to command, as the star, the continuity of the narrative until the end—his action does not operate as a mere cut within the film. The seizure signals more: it has to do with a true *epistemological cut*. The words and the images of memory, in Manoel the film director's hands, follow the experience of one day in the life of the French actor, son of another Manoel, the Portuguese émigré we have already discussed. The first name of the director and of any and all Portuguese émigrés is the same—Manoel. What differentiates and distances the two is the family name and the place each occupies in Portuguese society. On this day, which is to be experienced by the four fellow travelers, the Portuguese past of all those other Manoeís (plural of Manoel in Portuguese) will be unveiled, in every way different from the past of the Manoeís who were being represented by the film director's autobiographical and elitist speech. The actor says to his fellow traveler:

"I liked listening to him, but what he said does not pertain to me."

The actor's interest in the voyage is another, his anxiety is another, and his memories are other—dictated by the life experience of that other Manoel, his father. He was a "very willful" boy, the son of poor farmers from northern Portugal. Without documentation or money, he climbed the mountains of Felpera with only the clothes on his back. He made it to Spain during the Civil War. He was imprisoned. In jail, he learned the rudiments of mechanics. He went cold and hungry and often did not have a roof over his head. He crossed the Pyrenees, who knows how, made it to France, and settled in Toulouse, where he became an employee at an auto shop and later the owner. He married a French woman, had two children with her, and bedded many other women. In that other Manoel's past, his son wants to discover the misery of life in the countryside as much as the taste of adventure in distant lands. From his father, the son inherited nostalgia, translated by the guitar he carried and the *fado* he sang. In the father's future, in a most unexpected way, a son appeared who—through who knows how much effort and tenacity—belongs to the elite of French cinema.

Achievements are not the only things in the life of Manoéis good-for-nothings (*rastaqüeras*). The cosmopolitanism of the poor Portuguese man brought *losses* for the son that only the voyage at hand—the opposite of the emigrant father's voyage by foot—can reveal and recompense. The main loss is that of the maternal language. In the win-or-lose of cosmopolitan life, the actor ended up without control over the indispensable tool for communicating directly with his forefathers. Having a father who abandoned his original nationality, the son ended up suffering the violent process of becoming a citizen of France. In the film director's speech, during the first film within the film, Portuguese is a language as exotic for the French actor as the autobiographical material it carries. The other two travelers take on the role of interpreters. The Portuguese spoken in the car has nothing to do with him, the son of the *meteco* (alien) in France.

In the second film, when everyone sits around the table in the dining room of the house where Afonso's father was born, the actor realizes that he has lost his relatives less in memory than in the linguistic hiatus that isolates them in the present. The lack of a shared language brings about a lack of communication and creates distrust in the home, dominated by the black color of the clothing. The actor feels exiled in his father's land for a different reason than the one raised by the film director's narrative. As he gets closer to those who are distant, the inverse voyage undertaken by the son distances him, in another way, from the relatives who should be close. The inverse transforms the anxious and happy reunion scene among relatives into an afflicted game dominated by misalignment and distrust. In the process of *hybridization*, typical in the lives of *metecos* who don't reset their family values to a blank slate, the actor commits an irreparable omission: the failure of continuity with the mother tongue, having forgotten it.

We can bring some originality to the debate in vogue today by introducing the idea of the stable and anachronistic *Portuguese village* into the discussion about the unstable and postmodern *global village* constituted in transit by the economic circuits of the globalized world. *Voyage to the Beginning of the World* dramatizes two types of poverty that are minimized in analyses about the processes of the transnational economy.

The first type of poverty dramatized in the second film predates the Industrial Revolution and presents man in his condition as a worker of the land and herder of animals, a romantic and autochthonous representation. Faced with the powerful machines that till, plant, harvest, and satisfy the needs of the transnational economy of grains, faced with the extremely modern processes of breeding and raising domestic birds and animals, faced with the mysteries of cloning animals, the emblematic figure of the Portuguese peasant is anachronistic—an individual lost in time and space in the twentieth century, without ties to the present and, for this reason, destitute of any idea of the future. He can't even relate to modern electronic gadgets like television, which are within reach thanks to the perverse tricks of consumer society.

The days that follow are confused with the return voyage to the "beginning of the world." The image of the actor's aunt is as mineral in quality as the stony landscape where survival unfolds for those who remain to till the land and raise the livestock. Her husband has the snout of an animal, which the director character points out crudely by making faces to imitate him. Both are timely through the revanchist metaphors they carry: the aunt, a stone in the middle of economic globalization's road; the uncle, a wolf on the lookout for failures in the computerized sheepfolds so he can pounce.

In the case of Brazil, the two revanchist metaphors find their political redemption in the *Movimento dos Trabalhadores Rurais Sem-Terra* (the Brazilian Landless Workers Movement—MST).[3] They fight for agrarian reform on the legislative level and for the ownership of unproductive lands on the judicial level. They fight for the permanence of peasants in a motorized and technocratic world that excludes them, reducing them to the condition of global society's pariahs. These days, due to police persecution that is compounded by interminable judicial processes, many activists survive as the accused.

The other type of poverty dramatized by the second film occurred after the Industrial Revolution. Thanks to the democratization of transportation methods, the horizons of the farmer disinherited from the land and animal rearing were broadened. He was beckoned by the possibility of easy migration to the big urban centers, which had become devoid of cheap workers. The poor are anachronistic in another way now, in contrast to the grandiloquent postmodern spectacle that summoned them to its lands for manual labor and housed them in the metropolises' miserable neighborhoods. This new ruse of transnational capital with the peripheral countries anchors the peasant in foreign lands, where his descendants will lose the weight and strength of their original traditions little by little. A few, like the actor in the film, arrive at the condition of a recognized agent, a French national, but many experience a future they do not participate in except through manual labor, which has been disqualified and rejected by the citizens of the country in question.

A new and thus far unknown form of social *inequality* has been created, which cannot be understood in the legal landscape of a single nation-state, nor through the official ties between national governments, since the economic reason that brings the new poor to the postmodern metropolis is transnational and, in the majority of cases, is also clandestine. The flow of its new inhabitants is determined in large part by the need to recruit the world's disadvantaged, who are willing to perform the so-called domestic and cleaning services and to transgress the national laws established by immigration services. They are predetermined by necessity and by postmodern profit. Kwame Anthony Appiah highlights this in the preface to Saskia Sassen's book: "[T]he highly qualified employees of the management sectors, like finance, see their salaries grow scandalously while the remuneration given to those who clean the offices or make photocopies stagnate or sink at once."

Between the two poverties—the one prior to and the one following the Industrial Revolution—there exists a revealing and intriguing *silence* in Manoel de Oliveria's film. In the universe of *Voyage to the Beginning of the World* there are neither factories nor workers. There is, if anything, the national entertainment industry, represented by the director and the actor, which today is totally globalized. In truth this is the industry that is being questioned by the film's multicultural strategy. For the miserable and willful farmer, just as for the unemployed workers in the urban world, social inequality in the motherland suggests a *leap* into the very rich and transnational world, a leap that appears somewhat enigmatic but which is concrete in reality. That leap is propelled by the lack of options for economic and social betterment in their own villages and often in the small urban centers of their own countries, as is the case of the Governador Valadares region in Minas Gerais. The world's unemployed unite in Paris, London, Rome, New York, and São Paulo.

Long gone is the time described in Graciliano Ramos's *Vidas secas*, a time dominated by the *pau-de-arara* transportation trucks. Long gone is the time of the *retirantes* (refugees, literally people who retire from the land) from the *latifúndio*'s monoculture and the Northeastern drought. Today Brazil's *retirantes*, many of them natives of Brazilian states that are relatively rich, follow the flow of transnational capital like a sunflower. Still young and strong, they want to enter the postindustrial world's metropolises. To obtain a passport, they form long lines at the doors of the consulates. Without getting a visa, they travel to bordering countries like Mexico or Canada in relation to the United States of America, or Portugal and Spain in relation to the European Union, and there they come together with fellow travelers of all nationalities. The peasant today leaps over the Industrial Revolution and lands on his feet, midswim, by train, ship, or airplane, directly in the postmodern metropolis, often without the necessary intermediacy of a consular visa. Rejected by the powerful national states, avoided by the traditional bourgeoisie, incited by the unionized working class, and coveted by the transnational entrepreneurs, the migrant farmer is today the "very brave" *clandestine* passenger in the postmodern ship of crazies.

Fortunately, *Voyage to the Beginning of the World* is a film with a *happy ending.*

The French Portuguese actor requests an interpreter again, in order to speak with his relatives. The old aunt, his father's sister, played admirably by Isabel de Castro, does not recognize her nephew in the French words he employs. She looks into his eyes while speaking to the interpreter:

"For whom should I speak? He does not understand what I say."

As she continues to question the situation, she is harsh, intolerant, and agitated:

"Why doesn't he speak our language?"

Because of the actor's successive requests for recognition as her nephew, translated into Portuguese by the interpreter(s), she repeats the same question to the point of exhaustion: "Why doesn't he speak our language?" The actor realizes too late that in the economy of family love, the work of linguistic interpreters has no value. Their goodwill does not compensate for the loss of the mother tongue.

Scrutinizing the enigma of rustic ignorance that confronts the good manners and *savoir faire* of metropolitans, the actor arrives at the possibility of a common language that transcends words—the language of affection. The aunt enters into a wordless dialogue established by her nephew's gestures. She begins to recognize him through his gaze and likeness. The son looks like his father; they have the same eyes. Immediately the language of affection employs the vocabulary of skin-to-skin contact. The actor takes off his jacket, gets close to his aunt, rolls up his sleeves, and asks her, through the interpreter, to embrace him. Arms and hands cross, tightening family bonds. The actor says to her:

"Language is not what matters, what matters is blood."

The blood dictionary holds the etymology of the language of affection's elements. The aunt finally recognizes him as her brother's son. They embrace. The nephew asks her to go to the cemetery, to visit his grandparents' tomb. The language of affection becomes complete at the moment when the aunt seals the meeting by giving the nephew a piece of peasant bread. Nevertheless, the aunt's bitter conclusion remains:

"Look, Afonso, if your father did not teach you our language, he was a bad father."

We cannot ask the poor and cosmopolitan Manoéis to abdicate their conquests in the global village, far from the native village, but each nation-state in the First World can provide them, in spite of the absence of responsibility on social and economic levels, the possibility of not losing touch with the social values that sustain them in the cultural isolation they must endure in the postmodern metropolis.

II.

If we are all in favor of multiculturalism, we have to define at least two of its modes—one already quite old, and the other more than contemporary.

There is an old multiculturalism—of which Brazil and the remaining nations of the New World are an example—the illustrious reference of which in each postcolonial nation is Western civilization as defined by the conquistadors and as built by the original colonizers and the groups that followed them. Despite preaching peaceful coexistence among various ethnic and social groups that enter into contact in each national *melting pot*, theory and practice are the responsibility of white men of European origin, tolerant or not, Catholic or Protestant, speakers of one of the various languages of the Old World. The multicultural action is the work of white men so that everyone, without exception, will be Europeanized in a disciplined way like them.

Nowadays, the old multiculturalism has been forsaken by the leaders of the recently formed African and Asian nations and valued by the nations of the Old World, such as Germany, France, and England, where violent pockets of intolerance, not to mention racism, still exist in broad daylight. The boomerang that multiculturalism threw to the New World in the nineteenth century, in order for it to remain an appendage of Europe in the postcolonial period, in recent years flew over the targets of Africa and Asia and returned to where it was first launched. The spell turns against the sorcerer in his own house. Outside its place of origin, today the old multiculturalism works to resolve conflictual and apocalyptic situations that crop up in the nations belonging to the first version of the European Union.

Among the most credible theorists of the old multiculturalism is the North American William G. Summer who, in 1906, coined and defined the term *ethnocentrism*. In his book *Folkways*, published in 1906, Summer defines ethnocentrism as "the technical term that designates the vision of things according to our own group being at the center of things, such that all other groups are mediated and evaluated in reference to the first." And he continues: "Each group thinks that its own customs (*folkways*, in the original) are the only good ones, and if it observes that other groups have other customs, these provoke disdain."

Among the theorists of multiculturalism is also the Brazilian Gilberto Freyre, author of *Casa-grande & senzala*; the scholars from the Social Science Research Council in the United States, who since the 1930s have defended cultural diversity; and the anthropologist Margaret Mead. Faced with the scandal triggered by the draft of "second class citizens" (blacks, to be precise) by the U.S. government during World War II, she coined the famous phrase that grew to include *citizens* without distinction: "we are all third generation." The fundamental principles of that multiculturalism rest on a key concept, *acculturation*. Robert Redfield, Ralph Linton, and Melville Herskovits defined acculturation in 1936: "[A]cculturation is the set of phenomena that results in continuous and direct contact between groups of individuals of different cultures and that brings on transformations in the initial cultural models (*patterns*, in the original) of one or both groups." The old concept of multiculturalism rests on that concept and on the work that, anachronistically and with the help of Jacques Derrida, we will call *deconstructing ethnocentrism*. In Brazil, as we know, the multiculturalist landscape was strengthened by the ideology of *cordiality*.

The examples of cordial multiculturalism in Latin American literature are old and numerous. Let us cite a few from Brazilian literature. Let us begin with *Iracema* (1865) by José de Alencar, then move on to *O cortiço* (1888) by Aluísio Azevedo, and end with *Gabriela, cravo e canela* (1958) by Jorge Amado. The impersonal and sexual voice of the nation-state that, in retrospect, had been formed in the melting pot's interior speaks through that multiculturalism. Now, under the empire of the governmental and entrepreneurial elites and the country's laws, various and different ethnic groups, various and different national cultures, intersect in a patriarchal and fraternal manner (the terms are dear to Gilberto Freyre). They mix in order to constitute another, different national culture that is sovereign and whose dominant characteristics, in the Brazilian case include the extermination of the native population, the *escravocrata* (slave-ocrat) model of colonization, and the silencing of women and sexual minorities.

Immigrants who did not fit the principles defined by the nation-state that generously welcomed them would be decisively excluded from the agenda of planned immigration, or would not be accepted in national territory. One of the most illustrative historical debates regarding the rejection of immigrants who might not submit to the national organization dictated by the *establishment* of the Second Brazilian Reign is the case of Chinese emigration at the end of the nineteenth century. In 1881, a little before the abolition of black slavery in our country, Salvador de Mendonça defined his ideological position, which ended up being countersigned by the Brazilian government: "To use [the Chinese population] during half a century, without permanent conditions, without allowing settlement in our land, with the periodic renewal of staffing and contracts, seems the best step that we can make towards vanquishing the present challenges and preparing auspiciously for the nation's future." The wolf's reason is clear: to count on Chinese agricultural labor, without, meanwhile, welcoming them definitively into the national territory. Fortunately, the positivists reacted to this intolerant reasoning, subordinating the political exercise to the moral. They declared that it amounted to replacing a slave arm with a quasi-slave arm. The Chinese did not emigrate to Brazil for two complementary reasons.

The words dictated by the nation-state's intolerance when faced with the *difference* presented by the foreign are not absent from many of the recent declarations of U.S. politicians. During a discussion in the U.S. Senate regarding the advantages and disadvantages of a shared American market, a prominent senator uttered this pearl that accentuates the impossibility of the balanced welding of the continent's nations: "If the other [countries of the American continent] are too slow, we will go ahead without them." We know what the unbridled and selfish advance of a single nation-state can lead to. After the events of September 11, 2001, in which ethnic and religious differences were aggravated by the biases of mutual fundamentalism, the possibilities of multiculturalism, as it had been practiced since the great discoveries of the sixteenth century and theoretically determined in the first half of the twentieth century, were thrown in the trash can of the new millennium. At the same time, groups of emigrants (or those who are already immigrants) in the United States suffer from the restrictions and annoyances that all the newspapers and televisions report.

The multiculturalism that reorganizes the disparate elements that are found in any particular colonial or postcolonial region, or that supports immigration planned by the nation-state according to a system of quotas, has invariably referred to the rhetoric of strengthening "imagined communities," to use Benedict Anderson's well-known expression. For Anderson, the nation is imagined as a *limited and sovereign community*. Let us cite the definitions that he gives us of the three italicized terms. First: "the nation is imagined as *limited*, because even the largest of them, which encompasses perhaps a billion human beings, possesses finite borders, even though elastic, beyond which are found other nations. No nation considers itself coextensive with humanity." Second:

"It is imagined as *sovereign*, because the concept emerged at a time when the Enlightenment and Revolution were destroying the legitimacy of the hierarchical dynastic reign that is divinely put in place. (. . .) The pledge and symbol of that liberty is the sovereign State." Third: "the nation is imagined as a *community* because, without taking into account the inequality and exploitation that currently prevail in all of them, the nation is always conceived of as deep and horizontal fellowship."

Through persuasion of a patriotic ilk, the multiculturalists of the imagined community have freed the dominant elite of the social, political, and cultural demands that overflow from the narrow circle of economic citizenship. If you want to wash your dirty laundry, you will have to do it at home. The ethnic, linguistic, religious, and economic differences, roots of internal conflicts or possible future conflicts, were discarded in favor of a united national *whole*, patriarchal and brotherly, republican and disciplined, apparently cohesive, and sometimes democratic. The shards and remnants of the construction material that helped to elevate the building of nationality are thrown in the trash of subversion, which should be combated at whatever cost by the police and military. According to the rules of this multiculturalism, the construction of the state had as a priority its aggrandizement through the destruction of the marginalized population's individual memory and the favoring of collective memory's artificiality.

In these times of the transnational market economy, would it be fair to preach the theoretical principles developed within multicultural research and practice as they were defined in the past?

The structure of the old multiculturalism—whether attested within the new economic order by the most diverse national hegemonic governments or not—is at odds with today's need for a new theorization that would base itself on an understanding of the dual process set in relentless motion by the global economy—that of the "denationalizing of the urban space" and of the "denationalizing of politics," to use Saskia Sassen's expressions from *Globalization and Its Discontents*. She goes on, characterizing the social agents seduced by the process: "And many of the unprivileged workers in the global cities are women, immigrants, and people of color, whose political sense of individuality and whose identities are not necessarily immersed in the 'nation' or the 'national community.'"

The constitutive principles of the imagined community are being harnessed by the multiracial fountain and by the transnational economy from which it drinks and from which the marginal, and also hegemonic, nation-states still drink. First, the nation-state becomes coextensive with humanity. As an example, we can cite the polemical essay by Vaclav Havel, "Kosovo and the End of the Nation-State," in which he sounds the alarm that the bombing of Yugoslavia by NATO forces puts human rights above the rights of the state (which was responsible, let us remember, for the "ethnic cleansing" of Kosovo). Havel favors the desire to put into play a law greater than that which safeguards the sovereignty of each nation-state. Visibly inspired by a Christian ethic, he writes: "[H]uman rights have their deepest roots in a place that is outside the world we see [. . .]. While the state is a human creation, human beings are God's creation." Second, the sovereignty of the nation-state is questioned in connection to the law and social models. Third, the "deep and horizontal fellowship" is left shipwrecked in the very rhetorical figures that constituted it.

A new form of multiculturalism seeks to first take into account the influx of poor migrants in the postmodern megalopolises, mostly former farmers who make up the majority of legal and illegal migrants, and second to take in poor ethnic and social groups marginalized by the marked process of multiculturalism in service of the nation-state.

Today transnational political movements, notably NGOs working together with the civil society of each nation-state, support the political struggle of migrants in postmodern megalopolises and those marginalized in nation-states. Consider the case of the black women's movement in Brazil and the role of the website *criola*, whose stated objective is the mobilization of young black women to confront racism, sexism, and homophobia.[4] The transnational form of NGOs can be adapted to the economic margins thanks to Brazil's abandonment of classic modes of communication—the postal service, telegrams, and fax—in favor of the increasingly less expensive, faster, and more global Internet. A civil society in the periphery is paradoxically inconceivable without the technological advances of information science.

The nation loses a utopian condition that has barely been imagined, it is worth reiterating, by its intellectual, political, and business elite. It begins to demand a cosmopolitan reconfiguration of its new dwellers as much as its old marginalized inhabitants. Contemporary economists and politicians pragmatically reconfigure national culture in order to make it conform to the determinations of the flow of transnational capital that drives the diverse market economies into conflict on the world stage. With regard to marginalized groups in countries on the periphery of the global market, the national culture would be, or rather should be, newly configured in a way that would lead to the unprecedented manifestation of a cosmopolitan attitude among economically disadvantaged cultural actors.

The indigenous Brazilian population is one of the ethnic groups with the greatest difficulty in articulating itself locally, nationally, and internationally. The demographic weight of the indigenous population in Brazil does not compare with the presence of similar groups in the national population of Bolivia (57 percent) or of Peru (40 percent). A relatively diverse and diffuse population base proves an obstacle to stable and less volatile forms of representation, the Social-Environmental Institute explains.[5] Indigenous organizations, legitimated by the 1988 Federal Constitution, nonetheless represent the use of mechanisms that make it possible to deal with the institutional world of national and international society.

A notable example of that cosmopolitan turn, now by Afro-Brazilians, is the official webpage of Martinho da Vila, composer and singer, son of farmers.[6] Compared by many to the hero of black Brazilian resistance, Zumbi dos Palmares, the artist also makes sure he includes a list and biographies of several other black leaders on his website. The list includes: Manoel Congo, Amílcar Cabral, Samora Moisés Machel, João Cândido, Winnie Mandela, Martin Luther King, Agostinho Neto, and Malcolm X. The recent cultural closeness between Brazil and African nations has little or nothing to do with the official policy of the Brazilian government, which since the presidency of Jânio Quadros has tended to bring postcolonial Africa to industrialized Brazil and to take industrialized Brazil to postcolonial Africa, in order to strengthen the export system for consumer goods.

The Afro-Brazilian cultural movement was set off by another singer from the blue-collar heartland, Clara Nunes, who described herself as a "Minas Gerais warrior daughter of Ogum with Yansã." Carmen Miranda ceased being the model of the sambista; instead of a "tutti-frutti hat," a cowbell. In 1979–80, the former textile factory worker in Belo Horizonte appeared on Brazilian television dressed in the style of a black woman from Angola. She sang the song "Morena de Angola," by Chico Buarque (included in the album *Brasil mestiço*, 1980): "Morena de Angola who has the cowbell tied to her leg / Does she shake the cowbell or does the cowbell shake her up?"

Within the same landscape created by Clara Nunes, while also pushing its boundaries, Martinho da Vila organized international gatherings of black art from 1984 until 1990, which he baptized as *Kizomba*, an African word meaning an encounter of identities, a celebration of confraternity. Martinho explains:

> I decided to do the Kizombas because I felt that the Brazilian people were very curious and had little information about mother Africa. In addition to not having much information about black culture in the diaspora. To give you an idea, Angola, so influential in the formation of Brazilian culture, only came to Brazil for the first time when we organized the Primeiro Canto Livre, in January of 1983. It goes without saying that, until the first Kizomba, Brazil was practically disconnected from the anti-apartheid protests. 30 countries had already participated, including Angola, Mozambique, Nigeria, Congo, French Guinea, the United States, and South Africa.

The redefinition of Afro-Brazilian culture as cosmopolitan and poor has polarized Brazil as much as Africa, and former French colonizers as much as the United States. The basic principle is challenging the inefficiency and injustice caused by the intellectual and political elite's discourse of national citizenship for centuries. As for the marginalized, the radical critique of the national state's disorder no longer appears in terms of the official policy of the government nor in terms of the economic agenda taken on by the Central Bank in accordance with the coercive influence of international financial mechanisms, as the current critique is being reconstituted in a period of globalization. The radical critique appears in terms of the dialogue between similar cultures that were equally unaware of each other until today. Although their subversive mode is soft, their political stock may be strong and little influenced by the festivities generated by the governmental machine.

In Latin America, where cosmopolitanism was always the possession and the afterthought of the rich and idle, of diplomats and intellectuals, intercultural relations of an international variety flourished principally in the realm either of embassies or the institutions of higher learning. There are sad cases. There are extraordinary cases, like that of the Brazilian modernists of the 1920s. Now is not the moment to trace their history. Invitations extended to foreign professors and scholars to help educate new generations also became common currency during the late creation of the university in Brazil. An example of this is the extraordinary story of Claude Lévi-Strauss's *Tristes trópicos*, in particular Chapter XI, "São Paulo." There, the French anthropologist defines the national interlocutors he and his wife entertained:

Our friends were not truly people, they were more functions whose intrinsic importance, less so than their availability, seems to have determined the list. In this way, there was the Catholic, the liberal, the legitimist, the communist; or, on other planes, the foodie, the bibliophile, the lover of purebred dogs (or horses), of classical painting, of modern painting; also the local erudite, the surrealist poet, the musicologist, the painter.

Since the 1960s, the establishment of agencies for the advancement of research (CAPES and CNPq) has made it possible for young researchers and instructors in higher education to enrich their knowledge at foreign universities and for foreign professors and researchers to continue visiting Brazil. More recently, major Brazilian states have created their respective Foundations for Research Support (*Fundações de Amparo à Pesquisa*, or FAPEs).

Over the last few years, many of our illustrious foreign visitors have traveled to other parts of the land and established new connections. They leave the asphalt, climb to the favelas and interact with cultural groups located there. Conversely, many of the young artists living in underprivileged communities have traveled to foreign countries and presented their work on international stages.

A wonderful example of this kind of partnership is found in the theater group *Nós do Morro* (Us from the Hill), which emerged in the favela known as Vidigal in 1986.[7] Today the group's cultural and artistic activities transcend the limits of the favela and of the theater language of their origin. The group's participants hold a place of distinction both in the world of theater and in national cinema. The detailed history composed by the group's members highlights their participation in *Outros olhares, outras vozes* (Other Views, Other Voices), a short film project from 1988 that included young people from five countries and their respective organizations. The members of "Nós do Morro" also took part in the Shakespeare Forum and thus attended classes with Cicely Berry from the Royal Shakespeare Company. The production of *Cidade de Deus* (City of God) directed by Fernando Meirelles, which recruited more than 110 nonprofessional actors from the poor communities of Rio de Janeiro as cast members, included acting workshops coordinated by Guti Fraga, the director of the theater group "Nós do Morro," which produced performances praised by critics and the audience at the Cannes Festival in 2002.

As an exception to the rule, anthropologists and missionaries have long worked with indigenous people. But these new partnerships are unprecedented. A few decades ago this kind of contact between professionals from a hegemonic culture and young representatives from the cultures of the poor from a country like Brazil would have been unthinkable.

NOTES

This chapter was first published as "O Cosmopolitanismo do Pobre" in *Margens/ Márgenes—Revista de Cultura*, Belo Horizonte/Buenos Aires/Mar del Plata/Salvador, n. 2 (December 2002): 4–13.

1 *Voyage to the Beginning of the World*, Manoel de Oliveira's 1997 film starring Marcello Mastroianni in his final production before his death in 1996, is a quasi-reconstructed documentary/biography based on the real-life experience of the actor Yves Afonso, who filmed a French Portuguese coproduction in Portugal in 1987. *Voyage*, whose main character is a filmmaker named Manoel played by Mastroianni, won the FIPRESCI Prize at the Cannes Film Festival in 1997.

2 *Meteco* (*métèque*) and *rastaquera* (*rastaquouère*) are two common Gallicisms used in the speech of bourgeois literary Brazilians. These words have an evident pejorative meaning and refer to, respectively, the condition of the foreign, poor immigrant in European society and the undisguisable presumption of being on the level with cosmopolitan values.

3 More information can be found on the Internet at www.mst.org.br (the site is in Portuguese and six other foreign languages, and serves as a good example of what,

concretely, we are characterizing as the cosmopolitanism of the poor). There you can read that, since 2001, the MST's fight has been marked by its internationalist character.

4 Lúcia Xavier, Jurema Werneck, Luciane O. Rocha, Maria Aparecida de Assis Patroclo, Sonia Beatriz dos Santos, "Criola," accessed December 22, 2016, www.criola.org.br.

5 Fany Pantaleoni Ricardo, Bruno Bevilaqua Aguiar, Tatiane Klein, and Isabel Hariri, "Povos Indígenas no Brasil," accessed December 22, 2016, www.socioambiental.org.

6 Martinho da Vila, "Movimentos Negros," accessed December 22, 2016, www.martinhodavila.com.br.

7 Luciana Bezerra, "Nós do Morro Comemora 30 Anos de Atividades com ocupação no Teatro Serrador," November 1, 2016, www.nosdomorro.com.br.

2

George Orwell, Cosmopolitanism, and Global Justice

BRUCE ROBBINS

In the middle of his book *The Road to Wigan Pier* (1936), which described the effects of the Great Depression in the mining towns of northern England, George Orwell suddenly looked away from the poverty and squalor in front of him and spoke instead about inequality and deprivation on a global scale. "Under the capitalist system," he declared memorably, "in order that England may live in comparative comfort, a hundred million Indians must live on the verge of starvation—an evil state of affairs, but you acquiesce in it every time you step into a taxi or eat a plate of strawberries and cream. The alternative is to throw the Empire overboard and reduce England to a cold and unimportant little island where we should all have to work very hard and live mainly on herrings and potatoes."[1]

I want to reflect on this proposition, which is both compelling and also (for a champion of plain speech like Orwell) devious and even emotionally contorted. It is not a truth that the capitalist system universally acknowledges about itself. Perhaps it is not a "truth" in the strongest sense at all. Nevertheless, it now has a place within progressive and liberal common sense. Consider some famous words by George F. Kennan from Policy Planning Study 23, a confidential document circulated within the U.S. State Department in 1948 and published to the world at large only in the 1970s: "We have about 50% of the world's wealth, but only 6.3% of its population. . . . In this situation, we cannot fail to be the object of envy and resentment. Our real task in the coming period is to devise a pattern of relationships which will permit us to maintain this position of disparity." It is a remarkable fact that Kennan's statement had to be kept secret and, when it was ultimately leaked, was considered scandalous. Why should it be scandalous? After all, Kennan does not admit to theft; he does not say, as Orwell does, that our wealth depends on their deprivation. Yet his words were and are embarrassing, and the embarrassment deserves to be thought of as an intriguing historical phenomenon in its own right. It implies the existence of a cosmopolitan norm which, without necessarily going as far as Orwell, nonetheless agrees with him that access to the world's resources ought to be better aligned with population—ought to be subject to something like global democracy perhaps, or at any rate ought not to be simply a matter of each nation trying to seize as much for itself as it can.

If such a cosmopolitan norm exists and has entered into our common sense, one would like to know where it came from and what can be done to encourage it.

In the humanities, these questions are not often raised about cosmopolitanism. Cosmopolitanism as it is currently conceived has to do with "a receptive and open attitude towards the other," to quote one of many recent books on the subject; it does not have to do with economic redistribution between rich and poor.[2] Further evidence to this effect can be found in Kwame Anthony Appiah's eloquent and insightful book *Cosmopolitanism*, which is probably the single most quoted source on the subject. Appiah spends a great deal of time on respect for differences, and very little time on obligations to distant others, in particular material obligations. Indeed, one of the most visible impulses of the book is to fend off appeals like Peter Singer's for the citizens of the rich countries to ensure that citizens of poor countries get what Appiah himself calls "their fair share."[3] If some people these days tend to feel a certain sinking of the heart when the word cosmopolitanism is pronounced, or at least a diminishment of intellectual expectation and excitement, I think it is only partly because the word is now being overused. As another recent book says, "At the present cosmopolitan moment in anthropology there is a temptation to label almost anyone—African labour migrants, urbanites, Pentecostals, traders, diasporics—'cosmopolitan.'"[4] The deeper reason is that cosmopolitanism is not sufficiently demanding. As one reviewer of Appiah's book objected, "[M]ost of us [are] already the 'partial cosmopolitans' Appiah wants us to be."[5] This means that invocations of the concept tend to be a bit complacent, and certainly not strenuous in the way the Kennan quote would urge us to be.

One might well object that, rather than being too satisfied with things as they are, today's cosmopolitanism is asking for a great deal more than it can expect to get: namely, an end to war making. For Kant and for a majority of its champions since, peace has been cosmopolitanism's primary aim and measure. The best incentive to take the concept seriously has been the fact that wars and the rumor of further wars are still everywhere you look. As U.S. hegemony declines, this logic will probably get even more pertinent. If our "city on a hill" days are over, if America is already a fatally wounded giant, as some pundits have proposed, liable to flail militarily in all directions as its economic and political power ebbs, then it may be that cosmopolitan humanists should start training themselves for a different, a more defensive role: not seeking a better distribution of global resources, but merely tempering the destruction the giant is likely to cause to those around it as it thrashes and totters and perhaps falls, especially destruction outside its borders. That role would certainly be taxing enough. At any rate, this idea seems worth adding to conversations about the value of the humanities.

At the risk of stating the obvious, however, I will add that economic inequalities are one of the main causes of war. It follows that cosmopolitanism cannot do even its traditional job without paying serious attention to those inequalities. This it has largely failed to do. Here I am as guilty as anyone. I was first inspired to use the term by the historian of anthropology James Clifford.[6] Around 1990, I noticed that Clifford, whose work I have always found instructive, had done an interesting about-face. In 1980, in an influential review of Edward Said's *Orientalism*, Clifford had used the term cosmopolitan to describe the "humanist" side of Said, of which he strongly disapproved. This was the side that claimed "the privilege of standing above cultural particularism, of aspiring to the universalist power that speaks for humanity," a privilege "invented by a totalizing Western liberalism."[7] Ten years later, in Clifford's essay "Traveling Cultures," the term cosmopolitan had migrated from Western anthropologists and travelers to "the host of servants, helpers, companions, guides, bearers, etc. [who had] been discursively excluded from the role of proper travelers because of their race and class."[8] These too, Clifford now said, had "their specific cosmopolitan viewpoints,"[9] viewpoints that were very much worth retrieving.

This positing of a "cosmopolitanism from below" was an inspiration to me and to many others. In the cultural disciplines in particular, it opened up what turned out to be a very fruitful program of work, some of it empirical research into the transnational subjectivity of the new, less privileged cast of cosmopolitan characters, and some of it reflection on the moral and pedagogical goals of the humanities. This is the "new" rather than the "old" cosmopolitanism, where the "new" is also described as "full" rather than "empty" (as David Hollinger puts it) and as empirical rather than normative.[10] If Appiah is the poster boy for the new, full, empirical cosmopolitanism, Martha Nussbaum seems the most widely cited representative of the old, empty, normative version. The question that gradually came to trouble me was crystallized by the opposition between empirical and normative. Thinking back to Clifford, it was suddenly unclear to me exactly how much of a change in course his two statements marked. In 1990, was he assigning to different characters the same normative, Nussbaumian task—implying, in other words, that the nonelite cosmopolitans were also, like Said, speaking for humanity? Or was he assuming that Said's task of speaking for humanity, which Clifford had criticized in 1980, would be repudiated by the new, nonelite cosmopolitans in favor of particular experiences of border crossing that could not or should not be generalized? If this was all about particular experiences, then interrogating "guides, assistants, translators, carriers, etc." (107) might not have anything at all to do with Said's themes of imperialism and global justice.[11] The same was true about the rest of us who enthusiastically joined Clifford in building up a new, nonelite cast of characters to fill in the category of "cosmopolitanism from below," modifying cosmopolitan's universalism with adjectives like "vernacular" or "rooted" or "actually existing." The cause of planetary justice could not be satisfied merely by including more voices. Adding the poor and disadvantaged to cosmopolitanism certainly did not in itself mean that we were pushing directly for a more equitable distribution of the world's material resources. It was even possible to make these additions while resisting a redistribution of resources. That's arguably what happens in Appiah's book.

The question that follows is this: is it possible to see the new cosmopolitanism as also a redistributive cosmopolitanism?

If so—and that is what I will be suggesting here—it will be thanks in part to one valuable thing that Appiah accomplished: subverting the antithesis between cosmopolitanism and the nation-state. The gesture was not unprecedented, but for thinkers of the past two decades, it has been decisive. Most recent champions of cosmopolitanism have assumed, I think rightly, that the nation-state as such is not their perpetual or fore-ordained enemy. Cosmopolitanism has even reappeared as an updated form of American patriotism. The formula is now both/and: multiple and overlapping loyalties. This both/and cannot be taken as some sort of guarantee that one will be spared a choice between loyalty to one's country and loyalty to humanity in general—that a moment of either/ or can never arise. Again, that seems to me what Appiah proposes. The quotation from Kennan was intended to suggest that this is simply not good enough, at least not for residents of the wealthy global North. But it prods us to scan for certain possibilities that might not otherwise have been visible.

Why is it so significant that nationalism and cosmopolitanism need not always contradict each other? Because historically the nation-state has been a somewhat successful agent of economic redistribution. When it works, to the extent that it works, that agency is what we mean by the welfare state. When the welfare state is allowed to fail, as it largely has been in the period of neoliberalism that began roughly with Ronald Reagan's election in 1980, under Democrats as well as Republicans, what is missing is arguably a sufficient quantity of national solidarity. That remains in itself a political goal worth fighting for. Recent theorists of cosmopolitanism, myself included, have suggested that national solidarity and international solidarity are not different in kind. At least in theory, then, it is possible to imagine building international solidarity out of national solidarity, extending the ideas and institutions of the welfare state so as also to include noncitizens in need. Here I could offer the example of the transnational struggle against the big pharmaceutical companies to secure the right to produce low-cost, generic antiretroviral drugs for HIV/AIDS. This struggle, though led by nongovernmental organizations, also required the help of states like Brazil and India, which afforded the technical competence and political will to produce generic versions of brand-name drugs. It also required the good offices of European governments. And it was a success, though a limited and provisional one.[12]

In this sense, celebrations of the demise of the nation-state would not necessarily be good news for the project of a redistributive cosmopolitanism. Which brings me back to George Orwell and the role the

British state played in permitting him to link cosmopolitanism to global economic justice.

"Orwell may or may not have felt guilty about the source of his family's income—an image that recurs in his famous portrait of England itself as a family with a conspiracy of silence about its finances—but he undoubtedly came to see the exploitation of the colonies as the dirty secret of the whole enlightened British establishment."[13] Christopher Hitchens is referring here to the origins of the Blair family fortune (long gone by the time Eric Blair/George Orwell was born) in Jamaican sugar, hence in slavery, as well as his father's role as a minor functionary in the opium trade. Hitchens is one of many critics who have both raised the theme of guilt in Orwell and explicitly used self-blame to account for Orwell's unusual attention to injustice at a cosmopolitan scale. It's as if there were a peculiar mystery about the emphasis Orwell gives to the economic well-being of distant foreigners, especially but not exclusively the subjects of the British Empire, in contrast to a more natural concern for the domestic working class, and something personal had to be said to account for it.

The psychologizing of Orwell's political commitments tends of course to cast doubt on their usefulness and validity. So, for example, Louis Menand writes: "The guilt [his term] that he felt about his position as a member of the white imperialist bourgeoisie preceded his interest in politics as such."[14] If you start from guilt, nothing good can follow. Orwell says

that if what he calls political speech—by which he appears to mean political clichés—were translated into plain, everyday speech, confusion and insincerity would begin to evaporate. It is a worthy, if unrealistic, hope. But he does not stop there. All politics, he writes, "is a mass of lies, evasions, folly, hatred and schizophrenia." And by the end of the essay he has damned the whole discourse: "Political language—and with variations this is true of all political parties, from Conservatives to Anarchists—is designed to make lies sound truthful and murder respectable."

Drawing his political commitments from self-blame, Menand suggests, Orwell can only finish by repudiating politics as such.

Orwell in fact remained a socialist to the end of his life, even through the dark years when the Cold War was beginning to dictate the terms in which his writing would henceforth be interpreted. This does not mean that Menand is mistaken. But what we tend to recognize as politics is politics at the scale of the nation. Hence cosmopolitanism or internationalism or any pretense of politics beyond the scale of the nation will always look not like socialism but like mere personal psychology or like a repudiation of politics, whether we are talking about Orwell or about anyone else.

And there are plausible reasons for this. Sustaining political commitment beyond the scale of the nation does seem to be a challenge. Certainly it was for Orwell. Consider the extraordinary sentences with which I began:

> Under the capitalist system, in order that England may live in comparative comfort, a hundred million Indians must live on the verge of starvation—an evil state of affairs, but you acquiesce in it every time you step into a taxi or eat a plate of strawberries and cream. The alternative is to throw the Empire overboard and reduce England to a cold and unimportant little island where we should all have to work very hard and live mainly on herrings and potatoes.

Did Orwell include himself among the "left-wingers" of the final sentence, who do not wish England to become a cold and unimportant little island? It's not clear. It's equally unclear that he himself was committed to ending the injustice he so forcefully laid out. It seems likely that he was speaking as one of the taxi-takers and strawberry-and-cream eaters, though there is room for doubt: for better or worse, Orwell's class politics were fueled in part by a vigorous personal asceticism. To assume that Orwell spoke not as a renunciate but as a fellow beneficiary, which would help explain why the passage is so at odds with itself, would not clarify other issues. If Orwell did not want England to give up its empire and go back to eating herrings and potatoes, then what did he want? If he too "acquiesces" in this "evil state of affairs" while continuing to insist on how evil it is, then where does he place himself, where does he belong? Assuming that he were to be successful in persuading a certain number of readers that this state of affairs is indeed evil, as he seems to be attempting to do, to what category would those readers who agree with him then belong? What kind of membership is available to a European or Northerner who would take up the cause of ending inequality between global North and global South, a cause that is not in his or her self-interest but that also does not require face-to-face communication or collaboration with actual global Southerners, let alone the autonomous activity of those Southerners? If action creates membership just as membership creates action, what hypothetical action and what hypothetical membership does an indictment like Orwell's aim at? What might be done, and who might do it, about the global injustice that Orwell describes?

The clause "you acquiesce in it" seems very provocative, very tough on the (presumably English) reader. But does it have an impact that could be properly described as political? Does it lead anywhere? It would not appear to be designed to. Unlike tea or opium, the taxi, strawberries, and cream are (or were at that time) recognizably domestic products. This leaves the non-Indian reader a little farther from seeing, in the desired sudden flash of insight, what exactly India might have to do with his or her little luxuries. The choice of domestic over exotic goods can perhaps be read as symptomatic. Perhaps the strawberries and cream are there so that tea and especially opium (which made the tea trade possible) can be absent. In any case, their absence makes it easier to hide the mediations, the visible causal steps that would lead from comfort here to starvation there. Enumerating these steps would allow them to be retraced, thus indicating what we might be able to do about this situation—consumer boycotts, or whatever. By omitting them, Orwell gives us nothing to do, no possible deliverance from the universal culpability.

That's precisely the point of his next sentence: neither he nor the British left can see any eligible option. "The alternative is to throw the Empire overboard and reduce England to a cold and unimportant little island where we should all have to work very hard and live mainly on herrings and potatoes. That is the very last thing that any left-winger wants."[15] By making the alternative so ineligible, Orwell makes the clash of interests between Indians and Englishmen seem total and inescapable. Extreme self-blame begets an equally extreme sense of necessity. There is no possible overlap of interests, no room for negotiation. Simply because we are who we are and they are who they are, our guilt too becomes total and inescapable. The logic, both paradoxical and utterly familiar, combines provocation and backlash in one sentence. And the result is that the guilt disappears. If this exploitation is really as inevitable as you say it is, I reason, then I will refuse to feel guilty about it. After all, I have to get on with my life; that is, I have to try to change what can be changed. If this can't be changed, if there is really no alternative, then it's not my business any more. Poof—my guilt is gone. And cosmopolitanism disappears along with it.

The standard reading of Orwell's career suggests that he followed something like this trajectory himself. In the run-up to World War II, he was radically cosmopolitan enough to question the value of fighting on the side of the British Empire even against an enemy like the Nazis. But he reversed himself, becoming a patriot and, as if to leave no doubt about it, berating other intellectuals for their supposed lack of patriotism. After the war, this patriotic and anti-cosmopolitan turn became part of the larger, depressing story of the Cold War binary and its chilling effect on intellectual life. In some ways, to put it this way is to understate the case. Even as a cosmopolitan, Orwell had been a bit of a cultural conservative. One of his favorite terms was "decency." He relied on decency to make his case against imperialism: "no modern man, in his heart of hearts, believes that it is right to invade a foreign country and hold the population down by force." On the other hand, the decent heart of hearts tended to be oblivious to economic injustice:

> Foreign oppression is a much more obvious, understandable evil than economic oppression. Thus in England we tamely admit to being robbed in order to keep half a million worthless idlers in luxury, but we would fight to the last man sooner than be ruled by Chinamen; similarly, people who live on unearned dividends without a single qualm of conscience, see clearly enough that it is wrong to go and lord it in a foreign country where you are not wanted.[16]

Here national identity is destiny. And if so—given what had not yet come to be called the international division of labor—then economic identity is also destiny. Schemes for economic justice, whether at the domestic level or, even more so, beyond it, founder on the unchangeability of human nature.

In the "you acquiesce in it" passage, however, Orwell's eventual point, arrived at only after a lengthy detour about attitudes toward class, is that, like the abolition of class distinctions, the abolition of the Empire (and the abolition of unearned income from overseas investments, which Orwell characteristically and prophetically adds) will mean, for the average middle-class person, "abolishing a part of yourself."[17] In some moods, he says this means "they are asking us to commit suicide."[18] In other moods, it merely suggests a need for "uncomfortable changes" in one's habits.[19] Surprisingly, Orwell does not seem sure after all that this is too much to ask.

Just as surprisingly, these uncomfortable changes are what he has on his mind in the midst of World War II. After the 1941 publication of *The Lion and the Unicorn*, with its attack on cosmopolitan intellectuals, Orwell found himself working for the BBC Eastern Service, writing and supervising pro-Allied broadcasts to India. Critical discussions of this episode have tended to focus on whether, by making himself an instrument of propaganda—something he never denied—he was contradicting his trademark ideal of absolute truth telling. But the episode raises a more interesting point. In his unpromising effort to talk his Indian listeners into taking the side of their colonizers, Orwell obviously could not content himself with reciting the litany of Axis atrocities, though he does devote airtime to them. In India, the atrocities committed by the British Empire were all too well known. Atrocities alone could not push Indians into taking one side against the other. So what could? Orwell hoped that Britain would promise India its independence, but he also knew that he could not be persuasive unless he could address the economic factors working against this alliance. In "Not Counting Niggers," he refused what he called the "first duty of a 'good anti-Fascist,'" which was "to lie about" the disparity in income between England and India, a disparity so great that, Orwell asserts, an Indian's leg is commonly thinner than an Englishman's arm.[20] "One mightn't think it when one looks round the back streets of Sheffield, but the average British income is to the Indian as twelve to one. How can one get anti-Fascist and anti-capitalist solidarity in such circumstances? . . . Indians refuse to believe that any class-struggle exists in Europe. In their eyes the underpaid, downtrodden English worker is himself an exploiter."[21] If he was going to make his case, Orwell would have to find a way of speaking to the point he had raised in *The Road to Wigan Pier* five years earlier: the dependence of the ordinary Englishman on Indian poverty—not just the taxi-taking, strawberry-and-cream eating member of the middle class, but also those well below them on the social ladder. This would mean producing evidence that the British as a nation were prepared to live on less on a less important island.

Amazingly, that is the inconvenient prospect he brings up, beginning on his first day on the job. His first weekly news broadcast for the BBC, on January 20, 1942, notifies his Indian audience that consumption in Britain has been restricted.

> Once war has started, every nation must choose between guns and butter . . . since England is an island and shipping is very precious, they [the working population] must make do with amusements that do not waste imported materials . . . the luxuries which have to be discarded are the more elaborate kinds of food and drink, fashionable clothes, cosmetics and scents—all of which either demand a great deal of labor or use up rare imported materials. . . . If you have two hours to spare, and if you spend it in walking, swimming, skating, or playing football, according to the time of year, you have not used up any material or made any call on the nation's labor power. On the other hand, if you use those two hours in sitting in front of the fire and eating chocolates, you are using up coal which has to be dug out of the ground and carried to you by road, and sugar and cocoa beans which have to be transported half across the world.[22]

The next sentence makes it clear that, though bananas have disappeared and even sugar is "none too plentiful," Orwell genuinely approves of rationing: "In the case of a good many unnecessary luxuries, the government diverts expenditure in the right direction by simply cutting off supplies."[23] In his second broadcast, on January 22, he announces: "There is a great deal of evidence that food rationing has not so far done any harm to public health in Britain—rather the contrary, if anything. English people before the war usually ate too much sugar and drank too much tea."[24] It's not exactly a call for England to go on a herring-and-potato diet, but his enthusiasm does seem to exceed what is strictly necessary in order to maintain wartime morale. Three weeks later, his approval of wartime rationing has become even more intense: "The ordinary people who have to put up with these restrictions do not grumble, and are even heard to say that they would welcome greater sacrifices, if these would set free more shipping for the war effort, since they have a clear understanding of the issue, and set much more store by their liberty than by the comforts they have been accustomed to in peacetime."[25] W. J. West, the editor of the BBC broadcasts, finds this evocation of an uncomplaining multitude almost unbearable. He comments in a note: "The resemblance between Orwell's writing here and the voice screeching about rationing over the telescreens in Nineteen Eighty-Four is striking. 'The ordinary people' who 'would welcome greater sacrifices' are very clearly the basis for Orwell's creation in that book, the 'Proles.'"[26]

The leap to *Nineteen Eighty-Four* may be inevitable, but it is also misleading. Orwell no doubt came to feel revulsion for much of what he did for the Ministry of Information, but he could not help but know that in working there he had also served purposes he had believed in before the war, continued to believe in after it, and freely announced when he did not have the government looking over his shoulder. In talking up austerity, Orwell was not simply talking up the war effort or saying what his bosses wanted him to say. On the contrary, his broadcasts on rationing were among those most severely censored by the government. The following passage (from March 14, 1942) is one of many that were cut by the censors: "The British people are disciplining themselves yet harder for the demands of total war. The penalties against those who operate the Black Market in food have been stiffened up, so that offenders can now get as much as fourteen years imprisonment. White flour is to be withdrawn from the market shortly, and only wheatmeal flour allowed. This alone will save half a million tons of shipping space every year. It is probable also that the use of petrol for mere pleasure or convenience will shortly be prohibited. No one complains of these restrictions—on the contrary, the general public are demanding that they be made even stricter, so that the selfish minority who behave as though Britain were not at war can be dealt with once and for all."[27]

Though the government was not fully enthusiastic about what Orwell was saying, it had already performed one absolutely crucial service for him: it had demonstrated and was continuing to demonstrate the existence of an alternative to the apparently iron laws of the market. Rationing showed that demand was not omnipotent. It could be successfully interfered with, and with the assent of the consumers. In interfering with it, the state too was acting under pressure, of course; it was the war that made regulation of the market both militarily necessary and politically possible. Yet the collision of necessities resulted in a freedom that, however provisional, taught Orwell a very useful lesson. For motives of his own, Orwell needed evidence of a will to curb British consumption. The war provided it in the form of a dramatic interruption in world capitalism and world interconnectedness, a prolonged moment in which the channels of world trade were largely closed down and tropical commodities like tea, coffee, sugar, tobacco, and oil were suddenly in short supply. The effect was not to send Britain back to a nearly self-sufficient precapitalist state, but it was proof of sorts—and proof was exactly what Orwell needed—that the British could after all be something other than what they were. National identity was not fate, even in such visceral matters as habits of eating and drinking. Abolishing a part of yourself had become state policy—policy that was unpleasant and yet also, miraculously, popular.

The logic is never spelled out, but it is clear enough, and nothing else makes sense of Orwell's compulsive attention to a theme that was not obviously interesting to his Indian listeners while it also got him in trouble with the higher-ups at the BBC. If self-abolition had been British policy, the logic goes, then it could become policy again. It could not be legitimately assumed after all that British and Indian consumption were stuck forever at a ratio of 12 to 1. One day, collective asceticism might win another place on the political agenda, this time motivated by something other than the Nazi threat—by the desire for ecological survival, for a slower rate of immigration, and perhaps also (who knows?) for global justice. The wartime state prefigured the totalitarianism of *Nineteen Eighty-Four*, but it was also a genuine effort toward collective self-fashioning that prefigured other as yet unrealized possibilities, even if Orwell, who was already dying, never found the time or the occasion to look beyond the newborn Cold War and think them through.

This is not to suggest that British rationing ever did India any material good. During the period of Orwell's broadcasts, there was in fact a famine in India. But there was no rationing. As Lizzie Collingham notes in her book on food during World War II, "a considerable portion of the population was already living at a bare subsistence level. Rationing would have entitled the worst hit to at least a minimum of food."[28]

> If Britain were to meet India's request [for food], shipping and supplies would have to be withdrawn from either British soldiers fighting the Germans or British civilians making do on corned beef. . . . Churchill was not inclined to be generous with India at Britain's expense. He is said to have claimed that Indians had brought these problems on themselves by breeding like rabbits and must pay the price of their own improvidence.[29]

Nor is there any guarantee that collective asceticism, should it again become a real historical force, would further a cosmopolitan agenda. Some of the evidence seems to run in the opposite direction—toward a chauvinist agenda. I refer to the slew of books that have recently appeared, before as well as during the 2008 financial crisis, which mix ecological virtue—how to have less of an impact on the planet—with more or less undisguised xenophobia or anti-Chinese racism and a straightforward desire to be sure the United States gets the largest possible slice of the world economic pie. Examples include Sara Bongiorni's *A Year Without "Made in China"* (2007) and Roger Simmermaker's *How Americans Can Buy American: The Power of Consumer Patriotism* (2008), now in its third edition, and even Barbara Kingsolver's *Animal, Vegetable, Miracle: A Year of Food Life* (2007), which set about "to wring most of the petroleum out of our food chain, even if that meant giving up some things."[30]

Giving things up in order to eat local would obviously not raise the standard of living in places like China and as these titles suggest, it's not always meant to. The immediate result might well be the reverse. It seems impractical, therefore, to connect the ascetic impulse embodied in the locavore fashion with the utopian goal of a more equitable distribution of the world's resources. Perhaps the best way to take this episode is as a window briefly opening on certain still distant possibilities for a politics of global justice. It may be that a leveling in the world's resources will happen by means of violence. It may be that it will result from market forces, though neither the United States nor the Chinese government has ever allowed market forces to work unhindered. It may be that this leveling will not happen at all. None of these possible outcomes seems to me as desirable as a leveling that would happen by means of democratic decision making at a planetary scale—by a planetary equivalent to the once-equally-unimaginable process by which the United States decided democratically, against strong opposition, that it would have a graduated income tax. If we would like to equalize at least somewhat the life chances of the residents of planet earth, and if we would prefer to see that happen in a peaceful and democratic way, then we should surely value whatever evidence we can find, however skimpy and unsatisfying, that people who have more than their fair share are willing to imagine living on less, even when the evidence is as politically ambiguous as the American impulse to asceticism and self-sacrifice. As with rationing in World War II, proof that one can do without exotic commodities that had come to seem necessities is also proof that one can do without, full stop—proof that one can consume less, perhaps mainly herrings and potatoes, and be happy enough in doing so. This is precisely what would have to be demonstrated in order to make the case that global redistribution is more than a mere fantasy or an abstract ideal.

I want to conclude by acknowledging two objections to the argument I've just made. Objection #1: Sacrifice in the defense of a nation at war could plausibly be described as self-interested. My argument began with the embarrassment caused by George Kennan's statement of national self-interest, an embarrassment I take as evidence that self-interest is by no means an undisputed ideological norm. Still, my argument posits both an exceeding of self-interest and the emergence of a motive other than war. Is it possible to imagine a moral equivalent of war that could generate as much will to collective self-fashioning as the Nazi threat did while also extending its solidarity beyond the collectivity of wartime allies? I can't pretend to know. The recent adventures of finance capital in the United States, including the loss of many homes, jobs, and retirement funds along with considerable new experience of ontological insecurity, may be a step in this direction, a means of augmenting the capacity of Americans to empathize with victims of globalization elsewhere without actually eliminating the objective differences between globalization's victims and beneficiaries—that is, the degree to which others elsewhere suffer from the same forces and suffer more. If Americans as a nation are beneficiaries of global capitalism, as Orwell described his fellow Englishmen as beneficiaries of Empire, we are troubled and insecure beneficiaries. But for the moment the most obvious answer to the "moral equivalent of war" question is, of course, the threat of ecological catastrophe. That threat is the major nonracist impulse that the new ascetics are responding to. Whether you consider this self-interested or altruistic will depend on how far into the future you consider that your self extends. I would not like to think that it's only those of us with offspring who recognize ourselves in future collectivities, even if we can't know them, as well as in our present, delimited selves—which we don't know all that well either. Do I see striking evidence of people stretching themselves in time to anticipate severe ecological harm the way they anticipate coming to belong to the top 1 percent? Not for the moment. But I don't think the case is closed.

Objection #2: why the privileging of economic inequality? After all, inequality is not even the most peremptory of evils. I have not spoken here about absolute deprivation, only relative deprivation. Inequality can also seem too crudely utilitarian a target. Orwell's "herring and potatoes" line finds a tonal and philosophical echo in the philosopher Derek Parfit's argument against both egalitarianism and utilitarianism: "[E]ven if some change brings a great net benefit to those who are affected, it is a change for the worse if it involves the loss of one of the best things in life." The best things in life, for Parfit, are aesthetic. He therefore imagines (paraphrased by Malcolm Bull) that at first, "Mozart's music is lost, then Haydn's; then Venice is destroyed, then Verona, until eventually all that is left is a life of muzak and potatoes."[31] Either Parfit or Bull may be remembering Orwell's herring and potatoes, which would therefore count as an anticipation of what Parfit calls the "repugnant conclusion."

Bull's answer to Parfit concedes some of the repugnance but turns it around, making egalitarianism into something that is not merely utilitarian. What anti-utilitarians like Parfit mean by "leveling down," Bull suggests, is often something closer to "leveling out," that is, adding extra people from outside the given political community and treating them as if their standard of living mattered as much as that of those inside. Bull speaks of accommodating an "additional population of non-beneficiaries."[32] The threat of seemingly limitless additions, of a pressure to accommodate infinite and therefore seemingly impossible numbers of nonbeneficiaries, cannot be kept from infiltrating pious wishes for planetary democracy. In conceding this, Bull brings out an impulse in egalitarianism that is more philosophically interesting than a mere numbers game. He takes up a quote from Nietzsche in which Nietzsche seems to be attacking egalitarianism, in his most grandly antidemocratic manner, as "nihilistic." Yes, Bull says, egalitarianism is indeed nihilistic. But this should not be taken as a critique of it. Egalitarianism undercuts existing judgments of "value," like the superiority of Mozart to potatoes, by imagining

> the potential disappearance of what at the start of the process is the good being distributed. . . . [T]he revolutionary tradition has actually been inspired by the idea of advancing to that point where the absence of limits negates the existence of those things the limit seeks to preserve and distribute—property, class, law, or the state—and which equality serves to maintain precisely because it presupposes them. There is indeed a sense in which, as Nietzsche said, this is "the secret path to nothingness."[33]

Bull redefines equality, accordingly, as "a form of socially realized skepticism about value. Equality already functions like this in the case of positional goods, where sharing in, and diminishing the value of, are effected simultaneously."[34] This seems to me what Orwell means by abolishing a part of yourself, which is here presented not as therapy or self-flagellation but as a philosophical program worthy of and inviting us toward a collective cosmopolitics.

NOTES

1 George Orwell, *The Road to Wigan Pier* (London: Penguin, 1937/1962), 140; George Orwell, "Review of *Letters on India* by Mulk Raj Anand," *Tribune*, March 19, 1943, in *The Complete Works of George Orwell*, edited by Peter Davison, Vol. 15, "Two Wasted Years" (London: Secker and Warburg, 1998), 33. It was not simply courageous of Orwell to notice global inequality: in presenting all of Britain as dependent on a surplus drained from its colonies, he was perhaps also doing something to assuage the personal guilt of benefiting from class privileges within Britain.

2 Gavin Kendall, Ian Woodward, and Zlatko Skrbis, *The Sociology of Cosmopolitanism: Globalization, Identity, Culture and Government* (London: Palgrave Macmillan, 2009), 1.

3 Kwame Anthony Appiah, *Cosmopolitanism: Ethics in a World of Strangers* (New York: W. W. Norton, 2006), 164.

4 Pnina Werbner, ed., *Anthropology and the New Cosmopolitanism: Rooted, Feminist, and Vernacular Perspectives* (Oxford: Berg, 2008), 17.

5 James Seaton, *Weekly Standard*, October 9, 2006.

6 I discuss the recent development of the concept of cosmopolitanism in more detail in the introduction to my *Perpetual War: Cosmopolitanism from the Viewpoint of Violence* (Durham: Duke University Press, 2012).

7 James Clifford, "On Orientalism," In *The Predicament of Culture: Twentieth-Century Ethnography, Literature, and Art* (Cambridge: Harvard University Press, 1988), 255–276. The essay originally appeared in *History and Theory* 19 (1980), 204–223.

8 James Clifford, "Traveling Cultures," in *Cultural Studies*, edited by Lawrence Grossberg, Cary Nelson, and Paula Treichler (New York: Routledge, 1992), 106.

9 Ibid., 107.

10 David A. Hollinger, "Not Pluralists, Not Universalists, the New Cosmopolitans Find Their Own Way," *Constellations*, June 2001, 236–248.

11 This was a question that Paul Rabinow had posed explicitly in 1986, in a book Clifford coedited, when he spoke of a "critical cosmopolitanism." He described critical cosmopolitanism as "an oppositional position, one suspicious of sovereign powers, universal truths." Yet universalism has clearly not been banished from it, for it is also described as "suspicious [both] of its own imperial tendencies" and of "the tendency to essentialize difference" (258) it seems intended to lie in between "local identities" and "universal ones." In other words, the universal is not simply alien to it. Paul Rabinow, "Representations Are Social Facts: Modernity and Postmodernity in Anthropology," in *Writing Culture: The Poetics and Politics of Ethnography*, edited by James Clifford and George E. Marcus (Berkeley: University of California Press, 1986), 234–261.

12 See Gaëlle Krikorian, "A New Era of Access to Rights?" in *Nongovernmental Politics*, edited by Michel Feher with Gaëlle Krikorian and Yates McKee (New York: Zone Books, 2007), 247–259.

13 Christopher Hitchens, *Why Orwell Matters* (New York: Basic Books, 2002), 6.

14 Louis Menand, "Honest, Decent, Wrong: The Invention of George Orwell," *New Yorker*, January 27, 2003 (online).

15 Orwell, *The Road to Wigan Pier*, 140.

16 Ibid., 126.

17 Ibid., 141.

18 Ibid., 148.

19 Ibid., 142.

20 George Orwell, "Not Counting Niggers," in *The Collected Essays: Journalism and Letters*, edited by Sonia Orwell and Ian Angus, Vol. 1 (Harmondsworth: Penguin, 1970), 434–438.

21 Orwell, "Review of *Letters on India* by Mulk Raj Anand," 33.

22 *Orwell: The War Broadcasts*, edited by W. J. West (London: Duckworth/BBC, 1985), January 20, 1942, 72. West's theory is that his time as Talks producer in the Indian Section of the BBC's Eastern service was "the key to Orwell's evolution from the slightly pedantic and unpolished author of pre-war days" (p. 13). West opposes his theory to "the received view . . . that these were lost years for Orwell" (p. 13). "There were constraints and frustrations certainly," but he didn't stop writing, he wrote some of the talks himself, and saw what he said as "essentially truthful" (p. 13).

23 Ibid.

24 Ibid., 74.

25 Ibid., February 14, 1942, 53.

26 In his "London Letter" in *Partisan Review*, August 29, 1942, Orwell talks about the effects of the war on consumption. "The most sensational drop [under rationing] has been in the consumption of sugar and tea. . . . Two ounces of tea is a miserable ration by English standards . . . the endlessly stewing teapot was one of the bases of English life in the era of the dole, and though I shall miss the tea myself I have no doubt we are better off without it" (p. 519). "War and consequent abandonment of imports tend to reduce use to the natural diet of these islands, that is, oatmeal, herrings, milk, potatoes, green vegetables and apples, which is healthy if rather dull. . . . After the war Britain must necessarily become more of an agricultural country, because, however the war ends, many markets will have disappeared owing to industrialization in India, Australia, etc. In that case we shall have to return to a diet resembling that of our ancestors, and perhaps these war years are not a bad preparation" (p. 519). In much the same spirit, it can be said that Orwell's broadcasts are not a bad preparation today for a slow shift away from U.S. hegemony that is either in process now or a likely result of longer-term processes.

27 *Orwell: The War Broadcasts*, 64.

28 Lizzie Collingham, *The Taste of War: World War II and the Battle for Food* (New York: Penguin Books, 2013), 144.

29 Ibid., 145.

30 Barbara Kingsolver, *Animal, Vegetable, Miracle: A Year of Food Life* (New York: HarperCollins, 2007), 10.

31 Malcolm Bull, "Help Yourself," *London Review of Books*, February 21, 2013, 18.

32 Ibid., 15.

33 Ibid., 24.

34 Ibid.

3

Cosmopolitanism Goes to Class

WALTER BENN MICHAELS

I want to begin by briefly describing a scene in Kwame Anthony Appiah's book *Cosmopolitanism*. It takes place while Appiah is visiting his native country, Ghana, and waiting for an audience with the king of Asante, who will have just come from paying "his respects to the blackened stools of his ancestors" and who will later fly off to Washington (he tells Appiah) "to see Jim Wolfensohn."[1] Appiah's point in telling the story is partially, of course, to highlight the contrast between a world in which it makes sense to try to keep your ancestors happy by placing "food offerings on their stools" and the world in which you're traveling to the United States for a meeting with the president of the World Bank. At the same time, however, he wants to show that the contrast between these cultures, real as it is, doesn't require the king or even Appiah himself to choose between them. That is, even if you yourself do not feel the need to appease your ancestors, you also needn't experience any fundamental epistemic difficulties in understanding why some people do. Indeed, the fact that some people have beliefs and practices that are very different from our own is actually a commonplace of our everyday experience. Just to take a very obvious example, I don't believe the idea that Jesus Christ died for my sins is any more plausible than the idea that my dead ancestors have the power to intervene in my affairs, yet I have no problem living in a culture where many people do believe that Jesus did just that. One moral of Appiah's story (a moral I completely endorse) is that the very idea of cultural difference is vastly overrated—which is why the deflationist cosmopolitan account of it is a lot more convincing than the inflationist multicultural one.

More generally, insofar as cosmopolitanism and multiculturalism present us with a choice—between, say, the universalism of the cosmopolitan and the particularism of the multicultural, between cosmopolitanism's skepticism about the primacy of identity and multiculturalism's insistence on it, between cosmopolitanism's relaxed view of cultural changes and mixes and multiculturalism's preference for cultures which are preserved and kept separate—Appiah is entirely on the side of the cosmopolitan, and I am too. A multiculturalism that involves anything more than the usual liberal tolerance for beliefs that seem to you mistaken and practices that seem to you unattractive is hard to defend; indeed, the very idea of defending it seems problematic because you cannot make any judgments about its value without committing yourself to a real (albeit very thin) universalism. Even in cases where that universalism might be finessed—with respect, say, to cultural practices and differences that make no claim to truth, like linguistic difference—it makes no sense to want them to be preserved. I may care very much about my future descendants, but it's hard to see why I should care what language they speak, since whatever language it is, it will work fine for them. And why should they think that they somehow are obligated to speak the language I spoke? It is part of my cultural identity, not theirs. It would actually make more sense for them to pay their respects to my blackened stools, on the outside chance (very outside) that they might at least get something out of that.

But my real topic today has less to do with choosing cosmopolitanism over multiculturalism than with the choice we have already made in thinking of these two accounts of difference as the ones between which we should be choosing. We can begin to see what is at stake here by returning to the king of Asante and reconstructing for ourselves some sense of what he might have wanted to talk to James Wolfensohn about. The World Bank first got seriously involved in Ghana in 1983 when it supported the Economic Recovery Program under which the then-president of Ghana, Jerry Rawlings, got rid of subsidies and price controls and embarked on a project of privatization. Since then, Ghana has often been referred to as the World Bank's "star pupil" both during the period of what some call neoliberal fundamentalism in the 1980s and 1990s (with its model of the so-called minimal state) and more recently—since the significant debt reduction enacted in the early 2000s—during the shift from the "minimal state" to the "effective state" as a model for neoliberal reform. (What is supposed to make the "effective state" effective is its success in supporting private business.)

These, no doubt, are the kinds of things the king and Wolfensohn were discussing, and the good news about those discussions is that, at least until the collapse of 2008, they contributed to a real if moderate increase in the growth of Ghana's economy and a decrease in its poverty.

The bad news is that, even before the recent troubles, the economic growth disproportionately benefited the wealthy, producing what a 2007 article in the *African Journal of International Affairs* calls "extreme inequality in the distribution of wealth and income . . . a growing majority . . . becoming poorer while a small minority . . . becomes richer."[2] Thus, although poverty is down, the country is nevertheless experiencing what the most recent (2008) report of the Ghana Living Standard Survey calls "rising inequality, growing regional disparity and (continued) deep poverty."[3]

Of course, this bad news is not exactly unique to Ghana or other poor countries experiencing neoliberalization; the increase in inequality is also typical of rich ones, like the United States. From the 1950s through the late 1970s (what economists Levy and Temin refer to as the era of the Treaty of Detroit), the United States went through a period of relative economic equality. In 1970, for example, the highest quintile in income made 43.1 percent of all the money earned; the bottom three quintiles made 32.1 percent.[4] But in the 1980s (Levy and Temin call this the period of the Washington Consensus; we might more generally call it the period of neoliberalism and, for our purposes today, we might just think of it as the period in which the king of Asante began having urgent conversations with Wolfensohn), those numbers began to change. In 2000, the top quintile made 49.8 percent of money earned and the bottom three made 27.3 percent. In four of the past five years, the top quintile has made at least 50 percent; in 2008 (the most recent year for which we have figures), the top quintile made exactly 50 percent while the bottom three quintiles (that is, 60 percent of the country) made around 26.7 percent.

The stories we have told ourselves about this period, like the one Appiah tells about Ghana, are more concerned with the difference between cultures than the difference between quintiles. Indeed, if we think about praising the "beneficial effects" of multiculturalism while noting its limitations and suggesting the advantages of cosmopolitanism as "an alternative approach to difference," we can see that the functional significance of the discussion has nothing to do with choosing between cosmopolitanism and multiculturalism. Instead, it is about choosing the problems produced by cultural difference over the problems produced by economic difference. Even better, it is about urging us to stop thinking of difference as a problem and to start thinking of it as an "opportunity."

This is what every elite American university has committed itself to doing. Difference without inequality is called diversity, and "diversity," NYU President John Sexton has said, is "indispensable" to a university's "pursuit of excellence." Thus, every elite U.S. university trumpets its commitment to "racial and cultural diversity," "international diversity," "gender diversity," "spiritual diversity," and so on. If you look at NYU's extensive but entirely typical list of student clubs and organizations, you will find all these kinds of diversity plus several others well represented. You will find, for example, the Asian American Women's Alliance, the Biracial and Multiracial Students Association, the Women's Herstory Club, the Iranian Jewish club, and Outlaw for "lesbian, gay, bisexual, and transgender" law students. But you will not find the poor kids' club (you also won't find the rich kids' club—the whole place is the rich kids' club). The reason there is no poor kids' club is not just because there are so few poor kids: on the *U.S. News and World Report* economic diversity index, NYU gets 17 percent, worse than the University of Illinois at Chicago (37 percent) but better than Yale (10 percent). In any event, I bet there are more poor students on campus than there are Iranian Jews. The reason there is no poor kids' club is that poverty is not a cultural identity and the difference between the poor and the rich does not offer an opportunity, much less an occasion, to celebrate difference. African Americans and Asian Americans and Iranian Jews and transgendered lawyers are eager to celebrate their identity. They don't come to college to stop being who they are. But poor people do. No poor person goes to college in the hope of being able to hang on to her heritage of poverty and, if possible, transmit its distinctive features (say, bad teeth, ignorance, a commitment to living in dingy apartments in some particularly God-forsaken neighborhood in the Bronx, early onset diabetes) to her descendants. The opportunity colleges offer poor people is the elimination of difference.

As we have already begun to note, however, colleges don't offer this opportunity to very many poor people. As Richard Kahlenberg says, in the 146 elite colleges and universities, about three quarters of the students "come from the richest socioeconomic quarter of the population, and just 3 percent from the bottom quarter, a roughly 25:1 ratio."[5] The reason for this is not only the tuition and fees (which at American elite universities currently exceed the U.S. median household income); it is the fact that mainly students from relatively wealthy backgrounds have the kinds of education at the primary and secondary school levels that would enable them to be admitted to and do the work at an elite school. (Nothing says upper middle class like SAT scores in the low 700s.)

More important for our purposes, however, than the actual exclusion of the poor—which, after all, universities have always done (English majors, think *Jude the Obscure*)—is the multicultural/cosmopolitan innovation: the production of an image of the world in which the ability to calibrate respect for difference provides (from the standpoint of ethics) a model of social justice and (from the standpoint of epistemology) a model of managerial success. It is in this world— which on the website of a portal campus of his university President Sexton calls "a world of difference"—that "students from very different cultures" can learn to understand what one person on the site (she represents cultural difference by being the daughter not of an American but of an international banker) calls "the different aspects of culture" while at the same time, as another person says, being able to find "the stores you want" and get "the products" you need. The products she has in mind are appropriate clothes, but the product we are really selling (and she is really buying) is cultural difference. Whether we accessorize with multiculturalism or cosmopolitanism is in the end somewhat beside the point because either way we choose culture rather than class. Or perhaps, inasmuch as the investment in cultural difference already involves, as I have tried to suggest, a certain acquiescence in what has turned out to be the intensification of class difference, it would be better to say that choosing culture really is a way of choosing class—but maybe (at least from the standpoint of social justice) the wrong class.

NOTES
This chapter was originally a talk given at 19 Washington Square North, New York University, on January 25, 2010.

1 Kwame Anthony Appiah, *Cosmopolitanism* (New York: Norton, 2006).

2 K. A. Ninsin, "Markets and Liberal Democracy," quoted in Jasper Ayelazuno, "Democracy and Conflict Management in Africa: Is Ghana a Model or a Paradox?" *African Journal of International Affairs* 10, nos. 1 and 2 (2007): 29.

3 See www.ghanaweb.com.

4 Frank Levy and Peter Temin, *Inequality and Institutions in 20th Century America*, Massachusetts Institute of Technology Department of Economics Working Paper Series, May 1, 2007, abstract available at http://ssrn.com.

5 Richard Kahlenberg, "Is it Time for Class-Based Affirmative Action?" *Chronicle of Higher Education* (December 16, 2009), available online at http://chronicle.com.

4

Utonal Life

A Genealogy for Global Ethics

LEELA GANDHI

It has been obvious for many hundreds of years—to all those who have taken the trouble to listen and analyze—that utonality coexists with otonality in truly tuned "diatonic" scales; yet even now it is common to accord "major" with high honor, but to trifle with "minor," to doubt, frown upon, and reject it, and finally to relegate it to a dubious and bastard origin. Paul Hindemith, for example, calls it a "clouding" of "major, " and Hauptmann calls it "falsehood of the major."
—Harry Partch, *Genesis of a Music: An Account of Creative Work, Its Roots and Its Fulfillments* (1974)

I.

Since the 1990s many scholars, artists, and curators have been looking for alternative models to a dominant globalization paradigm that break with the narrative of mobility, circulation, and productivity linked to economic or diplomatic imperatives. Such autonomous models are not necessarily grand in scale. They can be intimate or based on subjective choice, poetics, or friendship.[1] These themes intersect closely with my work over the last two decades. I've been studying ethical enterprises— ethics in the sense of self-work or spiritual exercise rather than "morals" or "virtue"—which counter aggressive cultures of globalization (imperialism, fascism, totalitarianism) by seeking a connection between self and the world. This mutating ethics of connection is made up of myriad subjective, nonconformist, immature, inconsequential, heretical, and *minor* practices. It comes sharply into view in the context of modern imperialism through the nineteenth and twentieth centuries. I am convinced that it gives us a genealogy for the inner life of democracy, or a program for an inclusive and transnational quotidian ethics of the victim or underdog—but more of that later.

Of all the adjectives I've used so far, *minor* is perhaps the most salient for designating the unique style of anti-imperial ethical global democracy. In critical theory "minor" describes a debased position in relation to the "major" or nomothetic mode in any cultural situation; namely, whatever is currently dominant, conventional, normative, or institutional. The minor mode is low in the hierarchy. It is a scene of subjugation or underdevelopment—*deterritoralization* is the preferred term for the theorists Gilles Deleuze and Félix Guattari. As an (imposed) variation or deviancy from the norm, minorness is often dismissed as pathological. Sometimes minorness can evince a desire for normalization. It may incubate righteous ambition for a reversal of position. As Søren Kierkegaard might have it, it can also become the scene of *ressentiment* or the desire for a reactive reassignment of pain onto a perceived enemy who is considered responsible for one's reduced place in the world. But, treated differently as a resource—a cornucopia of heterodoxy—the minor can turn into a revolutionary practice akin to Gandhian passive resistance, which involves nonadversarial forms of protest aimed at widening the ambit of shared truth and justice rather than overthrowing an opponent. In this form a minor practice powerfully defies and protests the major mode. Yet it has no interest in becoming major either by recuperating some unadulterated and originary grandeur, or by instituting some new diktat. Nor does it crave requital/reprisal/avengement. Its sole interest is to make dissensual coexistence manifest whenever shared life is at risk of monopolization by a major mode, however apparently harmonious and harmonizing that might seem to be.

Our understanding of minor practice gains something from the lurking musical analogy of major (Otonal) and minor (Utonal) modes, and their phonological interaction. The minor mode, long derided for its cloudiness, messiness, and dysphoria, insists—through unforgiving acoustical interference—upon tonic coexistence with the major mode. Owing to its position earlier in the overtone series of any fundamental, the major mode is implicit and audible in most musical tones, unlike the (latecoming) minor. Thus, whenever we hear music in a minor mode we hear the minor and the major simultaneously, along with any other combinational, difference, and residual tones. The minor mode exposes the raw assembly and immiscible gathering of musical tones, and opens them out to a multiplicity of unfinished relationships. It breaches the exalted stability, consonance, and resolution of the major mode.[2] This is the crux of its work.

II.

In the context of colonial encounter, major/minor globalisms (otherwise, otonal/utonal; totalitalizing/democratic) play out in diachronic interactions between an imperial variant that presents as a model of *sovereignty*, and an anti-imperial variant that presents as a model of *relationality*. There are many disciplinary approaches to these models and their interface with each other (sociological, historical, economic). But they can also be parsed philosophically as an interlocked and internally antagonistic apparatus—namely, a set of discourses, institutions, crafts, designs, theories, practices, statements, and disciplines—against finitude.

What is meant by finitude? An apprehension, starkly presented in the opening proposition of Ludwig Wittgenstein's *Tractatus Logico-Philosophicus* (1922): "The world is everything that is the case."[3] The view that there is no more to existence than what is there, *tout court*, has been ubiquitous in the Western philosophical tradition from the time of early modernity, so called. René Descartes expresses it (theistically) as the instruction to refrain from entertaining any thought that is not manifestly certain. Immanuel Kant urges us (agnostically) to learn to live within the limits of reason alone. In his later gloss on the theme, Max Weber describes modernity (atheistically) as a state of progressive disenchantment in which we stoically accept the flight of the gods from everyday life. In return for this painful acquiescence to calculability and rationalization we can take away the petty consolation that we are no longer savages.

Two responses to this outlook or discourse on finitude emerge as pivotal to the philosophical problematic of colonial encounter between Europe and Asia/Africa from the mid-nineteenth to the mid-twentieth centuries. First, the totalitarian apparatus of major globalism (or sovereignty) protests finitude through enterprises of *infinite self-extension*.

G. W. F. Hegel's master-figure (from his canonical *Phenomenology of Spirit*) offers a good illustration of infinite self-extension. The master extends himself (as desired, compulsively) by erasing the alterity of the world and canceling out the foreignness of those he encounters on the way. Carl Schmitt (the controversial German jurist who held a very low view of parliamentary democracy and cosmopolitanism, and became a significant political theorist for National Socialism) provides a kin paradigm in his hypothesis of the relationship between sovereignty and exception. The sovereign, Schmitt maintains, is the one with sole access to exception or exemption from the limits of law and nature. Only the sovereign has the potential to escape from and to alter the limit. By contrast, those under her jurisdiction are standardized and condemned to normativity. By dint of these examples we could describe infinite self-extension, almost sympathetically, as a violent will to life. In *The Greek Alexander Romance* the Macedonian emperor Alexander ventriloquizes an interesting defense of imperial sovereignty, thus, as a perverse prompt to generation. Without aggressors, he argues, there would no activity in the world: no traffic in the seas, no farming of land, no consummation of marriages, no begetting of children. Without war, Pierre-Joseph Proudhon echoes closer to our time, mankind would be in a state of permanent siesta.

But there's a second response to the crisis of finitude (favorable to the joys of siesta and *mañana*) that comes out of the field of minor globalism. It shares a preliminary family resemblance and taxonomy with major globalism, and protests finitude in a strictly phenomenological register. However, it is expressed as an enterprise of *horizontal infinitude*, based on laws of interconnection and self-widening that refuse boundaries or limits between one self and another or, indeed, between discrepant substances.

There are many models for this latter project. It is present in Alexandre Kojève's recuperation, in his 1947 *Lectures on the Phenomenology of Spirit*, of Hegel's slave figure as a sort of sage who keenly understands the reciprocal and relational nature of coexistent life. The slave binds herself both to the master and to the raw materiality of the given world through labor. We can also look to William James's philosophy of radical empiricism whose ethical hero is a "conjunctive" subject for whom being in the world meaningfully or well is a function of being in relation to others:

"with, near, next, like, from, toward, against, because, for, through."[4] And then comes a luminous example from the British writer and spiritualist, Arthur Koestler, for whom the answer to twentieth-century totalitarianism belongs to the path of the yogi. Koestler's yogi is convinced that every individual is at the same time alone and attached to all by a secret cord. He understands that his only task in earthly life is to avoid any action, emotion, or thought which might break this cord. He knows that such avoidance-of-breaking-connection is a complex and difficult *technē*; that is, a craft or art or practice that must be carefully cultivated throughout one's life.

The way in which minor globalism protests finitude through enterprises of horizontal infinitude or relationality—its materialist *metaphysics* as it were—yields its signatory ethical content as well. The same applies to major globalism. Minor globalism is our main theme, however, and the question is: what can we adduce about its particular *askesis*? What are its general principles? How does it actually engage and act upon the world? Three key features can be enumerated directly: 1. This project involves a dissonant and sometimes counterintuitive ethics. We tend to understand ethics in the strict Kantian sense as a sphere of autonomy in us through which we can resist the way an external world or law tries to regulate us. But in the case of horizontal infinitude/relationality we are in the presence of an obverse practice: of binding the self more and more closely to the world, without apparent care for questions of autonomy or authenticity. 2. Very often the *technē* of binding/connection is expressed as a system of intimate correspondences whereby the most miniscule form of self-discipline is thought to interfere with, or to influence, or to participate reparatively in everything out there, seemingly beyond the self. 3. In this way—and here's a trickier point—minor globalism also rehabilitates a form of postsecular magical thinking; namely, the belief that there are causal relationships between anomalous actions and events that cannot be justified by reason and observation alone.

Many variants obtain within this set, but two in particular have especially engaged my interest and seem to spell out the chief characteristics of minor globalism as an ethical practice. Keeping the resonance of (postsecular) magical thinking in mind, let me call these *conjuring* and *disapparation* or *dematerialization*, respectively. The ethics of *conjuring* is about practicing relationships that make the diversity of the world manifest, often inappropriately or ektopically upon the undifferentiated, totalitarian terrain of global sovereignty. (Note that in entertainment magic "conjuring" is often about producing things/entities that do not belong or are not proper to a given setting: flowers in a top hat, a pigeon in a handbag.) A clear example is the Epicurean ideal of *xenophilia* or friendship toward guests and foreigners that quite literally conjures strangers and others within the racial/homophilic boundaries of the *polis*. Remember, in his *Nichomachean Ethics* Aristotle famously describes the *polis* as a community of similars or familiars in which, we might add, the good life of a select few is founded on a principle of exception (e.g., *only* the man, *only* the free man, *only* the virtuous free man, *only* the native, is entitled to the *eudaimonia* of democracy). The conjurations of friendship defy this embargo. Other forms of conjuring could involve summoning the dead among the self-satisfied community of the living; or animals within the species-boundaries of the human; or queerness within the boundaries of gender; or divine beings within the boundaries of disenchantment; or things within the bounds of sentience, and so on.

The second subspecies of minor globalism, *disapparation* or *dematerialization*, involves an ethics of making things disappear—often to the same end as conjuration. It works outwardly to unsettle institutional structures, say of the imperium through classic anticolonial struggle. And it works inwardly, as a style of botching our own capacity to reproduce or instantiate sovereign imperial globalism effectively (so that it can disappear even as it appears in our consciousness, like a sand mandala). These ventures belong to the field of motivated *moral imperfectionism*, whereby the subject of ethics seeks a way out from the status quo and its ample rewards, and dissolves it in the process—within herself. The sense of imperfection, as I'm using it here, is clarified further in the grammatical denotation of the imperfect verb form. Unlike the preterit form, which implies an already completed past action, the imperfective aspect renders an apparently concluded (perfected) action unfinished and suddenly infinitive. In this way the imperfectionism at the core of disapparation makes the subject of ethics into a perpetual—restless—work in progress.

How do these ethical practices of minor globalism (conjuring and disapparation, friendship and imperfection) advance ameliorative political life or social justice? How does self-work achieve a collective value or *agencement* (to borrow some more terms from Deleuze and Guattari— for whom, by the by, everything in the minor is political). There is no easy answer to these questions as there are in fact significant tensions in the relation between the realm of the political, *eo ipso*, and the sort of ethics that pertains to horizontal infinitude. Many of the characters and groups who have populated the histories I've been looking at were excluded both from established public spheres and the orthodox revolutionary politics of their own time. The ethico-political aspirations of late-Victorian anti-imperial utopian socialists were dismissed as immature or nonrealistic by their more institutionally oriented and programmatic socialist peers. In the twentieth century, the ethical radicalism of colonized populations who did not have access to a free public sphere was likewise dismissed by colonial political thinkers as merely prepolitical or even nonpolitical. As it happens all these groups—utopian and anticolonial—were themselves fairly critical of the available forms of mainstream or institutional politics. In an essay written in 1920, entitled "Neither a Saint nor a Politician," M. K. Gandhi speaks for many likeminded radicals of the age when he declares that systemic politics is at best a necessary evil. He writes, somewhat histrionically, "[I]f I seem to take part in politics it is only because politics encircle us today like the coil of a snake from which one cannot get out, no matter how much one tries. I wish therefore to wrestle with the snake."[5]

The ethics of minor globalism, then, is not synonymous with the political, yet—exactly for this reason—it has a powerful and transformative effect upon political culture. Let's turn for a moment to Michel Foucault's lectures of 1975–76 at the Collège de France, posthumously gathered in the volume *Society Must Be Defended* (2003). Introducing these lectures Foucault famously inverts Carl von Clausewitz's saying, "war is the continuation of politics by other means," to give us the aphorism, "politics is the continuation of war by other means."[6] He implies, pessimistically, that civil society or civil peace is not so great after all. It just internalizes the affect of war and reinscribes this in the prevailing institutions and attitudes—even in the bodies of participating subjects. *But practices of horizontal infinitude actively stall/deflect/interrupt such reinscription.* This is the burden of their political effect. Acting in minor or utonal register (to recall an earlier moment in this discussion) they reintroduce foreign elements and a tonal/relational medley that cannot be resolved into consensus and consonance; gatherings and collectivities that cannot be conclusively collectivized. They disturb the peace of established harmonies so as to prevent politics from closing itself off as a system of adversariality, or war by other means, or violence. In other words, they keep the field of politics open and potential—based on the belief that true democracy is nothing without the supplement of ever widening interconnection, which we have to discover for ourselves. And this is something involving spiritual work on selves.

In what follows I want to weave these hypotheses more closely into their diverse historical coordinates.

III.

Some time ago when researching the colonized experience of intercultural contact in the context of late-nineteenth-century industrial imperialisms I came across the incredibly powerful scene of *fin de siècle* utopian socialisms. Nowadays, following the "scientific" and "programmatic" and "parliamentary" socialisms of the twentieth century (good, bad, and ugly), we think of utopian socialisms—when we do at all—as incidental and marginal phenomena. This was certainly the opinion of many late-nineteenth-century political and social thinkers and leaders. H. M. Hyndman, the founder of the Social Democratic Federation, reputedly described utopian socialism as a "depository of old cranks, humanitarians, vegetarians, anti-vivisectionists . . . anti-vaccinationists, arty-crafties."[7] Yet utopian socialism was very influential and life-transforming in Britain, and also on the continent. Enough for Friedrich Engels to single it out in his 1892 *Socialism, from Utopia to Science* (however dismissively), as *the* competing radicalism for Marxism. Let me describe this scene briefly.

Utopian socialism was a creature of the 1880s born of the growing discontent with Gladstone's Liberal government, which was seen as oppressive both to the domestic working classes (who were suffering from a severe depression and unemployment at home), and to overseas native races (who were suffering from a newly aggressive British foreign policy with military interventions in South Africa, Afghanistan, and Egypt, not to mention increasing police terror in Ireland). Though the jury is out

on whether Gladstonian foreign policy was driven by authentic ideological imperialism or mere parliamentary tactics (whatever the difference), the liberal leader reentered the political arena with a self-styled
manifesto for "Inequalitarianism"—taking his cue from John Stuart
Mill's philosophical derision for unpropertied and ungraded social life,
and from the great contradiction of democracy and empire in the latter's
thinking. Radicals of the time reacted strongly to the new dispensation.
An angry cartoon by an anonymous undergraduate protesting the ex-
ponential jingoism of British foreign policy is still etched on the outer
wall of the Junior Common Rooms in the garden quadrangle at Balliol
College, Oxford. It outlines Gladstone in profile with the legend, "No
More Jabuba" scored next to the image—hinting darkly, albeit obscurely,
at liberalism's misdemeanors in faraway places.

In this milieu, utopian socialism emerged as an early alliance of race
and class politics, domestic and overseas causes, based on the perception
that there is a symbiosis (or homeostasis) between inequities of class,
caste, gender, sexuality, race, species, and so on. Its multifaceted and
cosmopolitan mode was not entirely *sui generis*, however, but was built
on radical pathways opened up in the very early decades of the nineteenth century by the London Chartists and their metropolitan offshoot,
the Fraternal Democrats.

These earlier groups engaged in a unique if inchoate blend of democratic internationalism and opposed despotism in all its forms, including imperialism and territorial war mongering. The Chartists are well
known for galvanizing British workers in the cause of the countless Pol-
ish revolutionaries and exiles who poured into the Continent in wake
of the baulked November Uprising of 1830–31 against the expansionist
Russian Empire. Chartist sympathies extended even farther afield. In
1847 the colorful Chartist leader George Julian Harney took a public
stand against British foreign policy in the Near East, reserving particular spleen for Britain's part in the first Opium War and commending all
acts of Chinese retaliation. Such objections, Harney averred on many
occasions, were *pari passu* with Chartism's loathing for nationalism and
jingoism. "We repudiate the word 'foreigner,' " he thundered to great
applause at a Chartist meeting at the Highbury Barn Tavern, "it shall
not exist in our Democratic vocabulary."[8] Chartism earned the private disdain of the then very young and already very opinionated Karl Marx and

Friedrich Engels for its diffuse emphasis on interpersonal connection rather than class war, and its even more suspect emphasis on self-work rather than the historical playing out of the objective laws of revolution. But in fact, one key reason for London Chartism's idiosyncratic umbrella politics—important to the genealogy of minor globalism that we are trying to plot out here—was *precisely* its disorganized and heterogeneous organization. Its home base, the great Port of London, was not dominated by the new factory manufacturing industries of the North. An enduring network of ancient workshops for specialized trades and so-called handicrafts, such as silk weaving, watch making, and millinery made for diversity in wages, working hours, and vocational styles. There was little prompt here for the fomentation of a monolithic (major) mass movement, and random sympathies could be forged just as easily with exiles and foreigners as with fellow workers. Chartism's detractors tend to slight the movement on such counts as a nonrevolution that neither knew where it was headed nor added up to an exemplary event. This may well be the heft of its legacy.

The utopian socialists of the late nineteenth century gathered up the signatory disorganization, ethical accent, and patchwork democratic internationalism of their near predecessors, and put them together into one of the most curious and creative potions in the history of European socialism. Their belief that empire and capital are bound together in an unholy dyad was supplemented by the rather more surprising surmise that this dyad was best opposed not through a coherent ideology or a revolutionary party or program, but rather by certain kinds of very intimate, small-scale lifestyles or "ways of life," or practices of self: vegetarianism, homosexuality, antivivisectionism, dress reform, and spiritualism, among others. An intriguing comment in 1897 by the labor leader Robert Blatchford conveys the texture of the movement: "We have the right to refuse the name socialist to those who have not grasped the economic truth. But . . . you must widen your definition of socialism. You must draw out all the ethical and spiritual implications of these efforts and desires for a juster social order. . . . A new conception of life is taking shape."[9]

This emphasis on the inner life of egalitarian politics was ubiquitous at the time. The homosexual, socialist, radical Edward Carpenter described democracy itself as "a thing of the heart rather than a political creed."[10] Oscar Wilde famously spoke about the singular importance of the soul of socialism. By degrees, *fin de siècle* utopianism's core belief in the political effects of spiritual/ethical praxis translated into arguments about revolutionary *occult correspondence* or sympathetic magic: namely, that the making and wearing of a certain kind of handcrafted sandals, or the saving of a rabbit from vivisection, or a careful self-exemption from gender fixity simultaneously advances the cause of Irish independence and diminishes the potency of industrial capitalism and produces incalculable anti-imperial effects.

Now the view that every individual's way of life is politically or socially contagious was strongly informed by the revolutionary and popular Darwinism of the time, with its hypothesis of the entangled web of life and argument that highly specific or localized actions—say, a woodpecker's pecking of a troublesome bark protecting a forward thinking carpenter ant—has evolutionary consequences for species-life itself. That is to say, all ontogenesis is phylogenetic, or, that my personal gestation is somehow inextricable from world consciousness. Such knowledge, Edward Carpenter believed, is *the* secret of spiritual (democratic) socialism; namely, what we think of as the self is not a private property but rather the one good that we truly share and hold in common with all (with what is and perhaps even that which is not). Carpenter wrote, "I also immediately saw, or rather *felt*, that this region of Self existing in me existed equally (though not always equally *consciously*) in others. In regard to it the mere diversities of temperament which ordinarily distinguish and divide people dropped away and became indifferent, and a field was opened in which all might meet, in which all were truly Equal. Thus I found the common ground which I wanted; and the two words, Freedom and Equality came for the time being to control all my thought and expression."[11] In this same period the Indian physicist-turned-botanist J. C. Bose considered his main scientific mission to be the demonstration of shared life energy even amongst the most apparently inanimate substances. He conducted a series of public experiments—some before a jam-packed audience of famous scientists at the Royal Society in London (on May 10, 1901)—during which he showed himself catching the mood of the laboratory apparatus or influencing, by his own psychic state, the disposition of the plant (or other substance) under observation.

Countless such cases attest to the transmission and transmutation of minor globalism through the dense years of the *fin de siècle*. Then it reappears, flickeringly and in altered form through the early part of the twentieth century. The Guild and syndicalist socialisms of this era—guided in Britain by figures such as R. H. Tawney and G. D. H. Cole (many harking back to the artsy-crafty genius of William Morris), and on the Continent by more complicated mentors like Georges Eugène Sorel—explicitly named themselves "ethical socialists." Not everything in this phase is useable for our purposes. European syndicalists, for example, headed in an explicitly fascist direction by declaring ethical-politics to be the talismanic style of the elite few in the common mass. Yet two features merit closer attention and recapitulation. First, twentieth-century minor globalism just gets that much more global. It extends beyond the geographical ambit of European socialism to include many more participant worlds—keeping pace with the enormous spread of empires (Western and non-Western) in this era. An example is the cosmopolitan interfaith group around M. K. Gandhi's South African periodical, *Indian Opinion*, which was involved, as Isabel Hofmeyr has shown us in her beautiful book, *Gandhi's Printing Press* (2013), in practices of slow reading so as to counteract the violent speed and communicational tempo of new imperialism. Second, there's a climacteric change in the direction or flow of minor globalism. The horizontal infinitude or relational aspect of *fin de siècle* utopian socialism is fundamentally directed at the well-being of victims, and this makes it self-reforming and upbeat and even joyful—in the way we all feel when we say goodbye to our worst selves. By the early twentieth century, however, there's a strange new emphasis on healing and curing oppressors. With this shift toward cultivating care and regard for those who cause harm and pain in the world there comes a significant change of mood and style. A timbre of edgy realism or antiromanticism enters the world of ethical-politics.

To fathom these mutations—indeed, to make them legible—we need to review (very summarily) the influence of some contemporary Western moral and political philosophy on our current critical thinking.

IV.

Any inquiry into global ethics benefits hugely from the so-called "ethical turn" in critical theory. By ethical turn I mean the rich tradition of other-directed or alterity-based thought in continental philosophy provoked by Hegel's influential master-slave dialectic, and including the findings of transcendental phenomenology, existenz-ontology, and existentialism. This philosophical revolution is concatenated around the profound other-regard that marks the thought of Martin Buber, Emmanuel Levinas, and Jacques Derrida (his later work). All the above thinkers are exquisitely reanimated in Judith Butler's recent meditations on precarious and grievable life. This core curriculum on alterity ethics was really helpful to me when working at the scene of utopian socialism on the colonizer morality of *xenophilia* (or friendship toward subjugated foreigners, strangers, and insignificant others). But it was strikingly less helpful when mapping the multicultural turn (and reversed directionality) of twentieth-century global ethical consciousness. Why?

Let me consider the question under the headings *passivity, reciprocity*, and *comparatism*. First, ethical programs of other-regard, along with the kin concepts of hospitality and cosmopolitanism, convey—perhaps quite unintentionally—the ethical passivity of those at the receiving end of violence in all its historical variety. The other of alterity theory, the guest of hospitality theory, or the stranger of neo-cosmopolitan theory may well inspire the ethical action—indeed, the ethical heroism—of reformed host/cosmopolitan/subjects. Yet s/he herself seems to be ethically inert as an unreciprocating recipient of onerous moral gifts.

Second, thus, though ethical programs of other-regard are nothing if not victim oriented (e.g., always asking, how can we protect those who are vulnerable to us?) they do not quite engage the resources and reversals of victim consciousness. This ethical condition morphs around the very different question: how can we protect those to whom we are vulnerable? Other variations follow. For instance, what is involved in disposing ourselves ethically in relation to oppressors/perpetrators/masters/sovereigns? How can we produce an ethics of suffering in which solidarities have to be formed (nauseatingly enough) with perpetrators? What are the techniques that might help the (minor) moral subject to interject an ethical synapse between her experience of powerlessness and her desire for revenge and reversal? Such ethical conundrums (or rather these desires for ethical agency for everybody: colonizer *and* colonized, as Albert Memmi puts it) were at the heart of early twentieth-century anticolonial thought and politics. And they were often formalized as the following plea for intercivilizational coadjuvancy and planetary entente: *How can we—all of us together, Western and non-Western, plaintiff and perpetrator—save Europe from its worst self?* The query haunts the work of M. K. Gandhi, Frantz Fanon, and Aimé Césaire, among many others. At its heart is an attitude that I find most clearly expressed by Edward Maitland, a *fin de siècle* mystic, vegetarian lobbyist, antivivisectionist, and close interlocutor of M. K. Gandhi's. Maitland says, "Terrible as is the lot of the subjects of cruelty and injustice, that of the perpetrators is even worse, by reason of the debasement and degradation of character implied and incurred."[12]

Third, though directed toward putative others our thinking on alterity is as yet markedly non-comparatist. Consider, for example, the precedent of Asian nondualisms. This concerns a set of overlapping heterodox-orthodox philosophies (post-Vedic, Buddhist, even Sufi) that call simultaneously for practices of "unselfing" (*anatta*) and "unothering" (*ananya*) as the formula for enlightened global consciousness: upon the assumption that we are never merely ourselves, yet there are no others. Why should thinking of this order be excluded from the ethical syllabus: that place of rare disciplinary interstitiality between secular and religious fundamentalisms, *theologia* and *atheologia*?

I am not making a case for the revival of some nativist moral philosophy (though I am doubtless guilty of the desire to treat so-called non-Western "religious cultures" as epistemological; that is, as philosophical, ethical, and as a common resource, to boot). As it happens, the bid to introduce greater flexibility within alterity ethics, so as to bring certain micrological *asketic* histories into view, is hugely enabled from well within critical theory by Michel Foucault's ethical work. His mature hypotheses on cynicism and last lectures on Diogenes of Sinope, chiefly, radicalize the sphere of Western ethics and make it more readily amenable to wider historical application. Consider, first, the almost inadvertent yet irresistible transnationalism in Foucault's hypothesis of modern cynicism. For this otherwise most Eurocentric of thinkers it is the rare occasion on which he admits to the reforming if not quite civilizing effects of intercultural contact for Europe. In his Berkeley lectures of October–November 1983 he discredits the traditional explanation given for the rise of the Cynic Sects as a negative form of aggressive individualism, which arose with the collapse of the political structures of the ancient world. There's a far more interesting account, he argues, that explains the appearance of the Cynics on the Greek philosophical scene as a consequence of the expanding Macedonian Empire. With Alexander's conquests various South Asian philosophies—in particular, the monastic and ascetic teaching of Indian sects like the Gymnosophists—became more familiar to the Greeks. (There are various speculations by South Asia historians about who these "gymnosophists" might actually have been—Ajivikas, Charvakas, Lokayatas, maybe even Jains or Buddhists? But these don't concern us here. Either way, the so-called gymnosophists are a wonderful idea.)

Second, besides this closeted gesture at East-West comparatism, there's another more general way in which Foucault's later ethical postulates are truly inclusive. As a type of embodied theory or a philosophical way of life Foucauldian cynicism opens up a democratic field of analysis, which incorporates a wide range of nonexpert, everyday, maverick behaviors and practices within moral philosophy. Foucault says, "The high value which the Cynics attributed to a person's way of life does not mean that they had no interest in theoretical philosophy, but reflects their view that the manner in which a person lived was a touchstone of his or her relation to truth."[13] Which is to suggest that under this dispensation almost everybody and every kind of way of living or set of practices can stake a claim to ethical life.

Finally, in view of the problem of the reversed directionality of twentieth-century radical ethics, it is a great help that Foucauldian cynicism posits an ethics of fallen figures—the victim/the underdog/the injured party. Cynicism comes from below and is directed above, and its bearer, Foucault writes, "is the man with the staff, the cloak, the man in sandals or bare feet, the man with the long beard, the dirty man. He is also the man who roams, who is not integrated into society, has no household, family, hearth or country . . . and he is also a beggar."[14] Notably, this ethics of fallen figures/the debased/the subjugated subtly undercuts the presuppositions of normative ethics—which is all about how privileged (uncommon) subjects can care for the self and achieve the good life. Cynic *askesis*, *à la* Foucault, tends in the opposite direction as an affirmative *via negativa*: a therapeutic *anticare of the self* for the commoner. It demands a wandering away from the self, releasing oneself from oneself, *égarement* or straying afield from or deserting oneself— moving toward interconnection, yes, though not necessarily directed toward a reified other.

This program for an inclusive and transnational quotidian ethics of the victim or underdog, which (furthermore) consists of informing oppositions between self-care and an anticare of the self, or between the good life and the scandalous/eccentric life, is pivotal, I've been saying, to understanding the altered history of minor globalism in the early twentieth century. It is also key to understanding it as a story about the pandemic inner life of democracy.

V.

Even in the blink of the eyelid that separates *fin de siècle* utopian socialisms from *belle époque* ethical socialisms, the conditions of modern empire changed dramatically and drastically. The 1900 Khaki election in Britain—declared right in the middle of the Boer war—resulted in a landslide victory for the incumbent conservatives against the Liberal Party, the latter already dominated by liberal imperialists and redefining its values following the retirement of William Gladstone. From this time on the evolution of global democracy also came severely under threat through an invidious conjunction between imperial interests and protofascism, marking (Hannah Arendt has famously argued) the origin of totalitarianism.

A fresh scramble for overseas territories during the late *fin de siècle* resulted in the new imperialisms of the twentieth century. Most gains went to Britain, France, and Portugal, but newcomers such as Germany, Belgium, Italy, Japan, the United States, and Russia secured significant territories and interests. By the start of the twentieth century, we learn from the English New Liberal economist, J. A. Hobson, that nearly 23 million square miles of the earth's surface were under imperial dominion, and some 522 million of the world's people had been placed under foreign rule. As in the Gladstonian 1880s, such expansionism abroad combined inexorably with a reaction against the progress of reform movements within Europe, bringing the specter of democracy closer to home as a nightmare of representation from the domestic public sphere.

New Imperialist ideologues strongly believed that the threat of democracy was best answered through totalitarian self-development (also an *askesis*) based upon the cultivation of rank, purity, excellence, strength, heroism, exceptionality, and so forth. The key therapeutic questions for many totalitarian ideologues were: how do we free the rare individual from the constraints of rationalization/bureaucratization/utility that democracy was ushering in? How can we achieve verticality (or infinite self-extension) in the context of secular democracy? How to distinguish the rare individual from the common lot? The upshot, well-diagnosed by William James in the Gifford lectures that became the basis for his *The Varieties of Religious Experience* (1902), was a resumption of the heroic standard of life, fetishizing leadership and glorifying "the chief . . . the actual tyrant, the masterful, overpowering man of prey."[15]

But in this context there also emerges, in diverse anticolonial and antifascist quarters, a refashioning of democracy itself as a counter-*askesis*, or spiritual regimen of imperfectionism, comprising defiant and aberrant practices of self-ruination, ordinariness, and inconsequence—all endeavors to make oneself small, to ruin or botch one's own perfection *in order to enter into sympathetic connections and relationships, withal*. The enterprise can be clarified with reference to the Bodhisattva ideal—a powerful trope in twentieth-century global neo-Buddhism, and reactivated through the great movements of caste reform in contemporary South Asia that were galvanized by the path-breaking reformer B. R. Ambedkar. (N.B., much to his chagrin, Ambedkar was sometimes regarded among Dalit neo-Buddhists as a Bodhisattva: an enlightened and compassionate being that responds without discrimination to all cries for help.) In the orthodox Hīnayāna tradition, enlightenment (*bodhicitta*) is the preserve of the *arhat*: the rare and perfected one, he who is worthy, the exceptional spiritual adept. By contrast, in the Mahāyāna tradition everyone is invited to attempt *bodhicitta*. Yet the figure of the Bodhisattva is in a way the sole and strange exception to the case (and, thence, an inversion of the *arhat* ideal). She alone must put off her enlightenment and deliverance from the mundane world so as to help others achieve liberation. She is the last to go, the one who lingers on, unfinished and imperfective, so that she may accompany all others in the passage of mortality. In exchange for this practice of autoimmune luminosity—her lightless light—she can claim the gift of horizontal infinitude.[16]

In strictly archival terms, though, moral imperfectionism (and its corollary, modern cynicism) is much harder to track and schematize owing to its diffuse and wide network. Nonetheless, the multifaceted texture of the project is conveyed in a glance at three important transnational nodes. The first is the truly cosmopolitan event of the Chicago Parliament of Religions, which was convened in 1893 in an effort to set up a global dialogue between discrepant spiritual practices and present a crucial charter for nonviolent collectivity. Its declared aim was "to show . . . how many . . . truths the various Religions hold . . . in common . . . [and] to bring the nations of the earth into a more friendly fellowship, in the hope of securing permanent international peace."[17] A notable speaker at this convention, the Indian monk Swami Vivekananda put out an urgent and visionary appeal (given what would happen in the next few decades) for global amnesty toward "the persecuted and the refugees of all religions and all the nations of the earth."[18] A second confluence obtains from the international interwar multicultures of pacifism (born of perpetual world war). Participants at this ecumenical scene—including the religious minded, atheists, socialists, antiracists, anti-imperialists, prison reformers, refugee-relief workers, and activists in mental health institutions, all from around the world—launched a like appeal for collective coexistence on an even plane. Taken together, they stipulated a division between parochial political interest and the catholicity of conscience. We hear from Roy Kepler of the American War Resister's League (WRL) that a coup is most like itself without itself; in his words, "power comes in giving up power."[19] Third, we can register the mid-twentieth-century protomovements of civil rights and liberties in America, which also defended similar core values. Assorted activists at the scene searched for a shared, dynamic global public sphere in which it was possible to give merit to the opponent. An illustrated training manual from this time conveys the message clearly: "This is the unusual thing about nonviolence—*nobody* is defeated, everybody shares in the victory."[20]

There were significant convergences across these elements, most notably in the life and work of the anti-imperial leader Mohandas Karamchand Gandhi. Though he has been haunting this essay, the point is not that Gandhi was the hero or even muse for the movements that I've itemized above. Rather, his itinerant and sociable life (his porous susceptibility to countless influences) had made him into something of a *gesamtkunstwerk*—a synthesis or total artwork—for the heterogeneous/dissonant ensemble of moral imperfectionism. He participated avidly in the world of *fin de siècle* lifestyle-based socialisms. In the early twentieth century he haunted the ethical societies favored by *belle époque* socialists and new liberals. In this period he was in ardent conversation with William Salter, the American author of *Ethical Religion* and lecturer for the Ethical Culture Society in Chicago. By the 1920s he was fully immersed in international pacifist ethics: in America through the labors of the Harvard Divinity School graduate John Haynes Holmes, and on the Continent through the efforts of the French thinker and activist Romain Rolland. In the 1940s his techniques were extended by the African American pacifist, civil rights (and later, gay rights) activist, Bayard Rustin, and put to exemplary use in the Journey of Reconciliation—to contest segregation on interstate buses in the South. This evolving worldview of early and mid-twentieth-century nonviolence was further developed by Gandhi's close associate, Bāchā Khān: a Pashtun independence activist and devout Muslim, who started a popular movement of nonviolent Islam in the Peshawar valley that went by the name *Khudai Khidmatgar*, or "servants of god." Members were committed to live by nonviolent principles and forswore any rewards for their service, either in this life or in the hereafter.

All such nodes show up (often at the same time) in the utonality of the Gandhian *oeuvre*. Thus, as early as 1925 or 1926 the Portuguese poet Fernando Pessoa attests, in some fragmentary notes, to Gandhi's curious status as a potent assemblage of ethical nonachievement in the twentieth century. In one passage he scorns the so-called noteworthy eminences of the time, among them the American automobile industrialist Henry Ford and the politician Georges Clemenceau. In another passage he praises Gandhi because prevailing standards of greatness are as nothing to him: "an unarmed hero, he puts rust on our countless swords, rifles and cannons. With his single, firm will, he hovers above our political intrigue . . . our accidental firmness, our drunken bouts of achievement."[21]

Besides the Gandhian *gesamtkunstwerk*, which gathers in diverse material practices on the ground, clear strains of imperfectionism can also be heard in various coeval versions of twentieth-century material-ist philosophy (responding *epistemologically* to the totalitarianisms of the era)—global phenomenology, existentialism, and neo-Marxism in-cluded. In European iterations, we hear its timbre whenever the philoso-pher Edmund Husserl says that we can only resist the prevailing culture of profit and conquest by somehow amputating our own consciousness through the laborious exercise of self-reduction. It is equally on view when Henri Bergson urges us to give up on the myth of humanist sover-eignty and enter into productive fellowship with inanimate things. And we hear it again, much later, when Theodor Adorno puts out his pro-gram for a lesser ethics or *minima moralia*, arguing that in the wake of Europe's multiple catastrophes all that remains is damaged life and the courage of fidelity to the crisis at hand in all its shattered variety.

VI.

The genealogy of minor globalism involves histories of revolution-ary and ameliorative inner life, which lies in the shadow of political structures and movements—whether this is the inner life of anticolo-nialism or democracy or socialism or welfare. In order to show such "affective and relational virtualities," however, concerning events and entities that are almost real or nearly visible, we need a minor method-ology.[22] There's help along the way. Raymond Williams's notion of the *subjunctive mode* offers a way of approaching history not through "it so happened" assertions but rather through "what if," "would that," "if only," or "let us suppose that," questions. The theorist and curator Ari-ella Azoulay has written eloquently about *potential histories* in honor of which we can always claim the right to intervene in the constituent vio-lence of any given past and claim its transformation.[23] The term I like to use is *ahimsaic* (or nonviolent) *historiography*. This elicits an approach that is epistemologically nonviolent (toward its objects, its public), and stringently in pursuit of the nonevent of nonviolence: the apparently anodyne stuff of coexistence that is not newsworthy or noteworthy. And here our procedural stakes become sharper.

In his famous essay on the *longue durée*—part of a crucial intel-lectual effort to deprovincialize history and make it substantively transnational—the French Annales School historian and philosopher

Fernand Braudel insists that all cultures, modern and premodern, Western and non-Western, partake equally of world-time. But, he adds, only some kinds of temporalities actually meet the stylistic requirements of world-time, which is the time of those extraordinary and powerful events that can change a whole era: wars, scientific discoveries, and so on. This sort of temporality (always momentous and imperious) wins out in the annals over the ordinary time of the conjuncture and the event. *Ahimsaic historiography reverses Braudel's hierarchy of temporalities*. It reaches precisely for those everyday events and conjunctures— e.g., civility among strangers and friends—that transform the existential texture of life and make it miraculously livable.

We can take a cue from M. K. Gandhi's complaint about grand historical narrative in his *Hind Swaraj*. He writes, "[H]undreds of nations live in peace. History does not, and cannot take note of this fact. History is really the record of every interruption of the even working of the force of love. . . . Two brothers quarrel; one of them repents . . . the two again begin to live in peace; nobody takes note of this."[24] For Gandhi, momentous or imperious history hinders the creative leap of faith that is needed to apprehend the extraordinary in the ordinary. Thus, *ahimsaic historiography* provides a vital imaginative supplement for the task. It incorporates three (provisional) conditions of possibility for the emergence—in the record—of utonal life. *Nonexpertise, accord,* and *counterfactuality*. We must be willing to sacrifice credited disciplinary proficiency in exchange for the knowledge of unimportant/insignificant/minor things. We must enter into affiliative relationships with the objects of analysis so as to liberate or potentiate their best meanings and aspirational content. We must practice a nonveridical critical idealism, which concedes that the object's unexpressed content may sometimes call for imaginative elaboration and collaboration more than scrupulous description and documentation. Can we?

NOTES

1 This essay grew out of a long collaboration with the Practice International research project, an initiative of Casco—Office for Art, Design and Theory (Utrecht), Iaspis (Stockholm), and Iniva—the Institute of International Visual Arts (London); three European arts organizations that are concerned with internationalism, collaborating with non-European institutions such as the Raw Material Company (Dakar). For more information visit http://practiceinternational

.org. Another version of the essay will appear in a catalogue volume arising from this work (Valiz, Amsterdam, forthcoming 2017). I am grateful to the Practice International Collective, and to the editors of the present volume, Bruce Robbins and Paulo Horta, for this opportunity to prepare a statement on my research, especially including *Postcolonial Theory: A Critical Introduction* (New York: Columbia University Press, 1998), *Affective Communities: Anticolonial Thought, Fin-de-Siècle Radicalism, and the Politics of Friendship* (Durham: Duke University Press, 2006), and *The Common Cause: Postcolonial Ethics and the Practice of Democracy, 1900–1955* (Chicago: University of Chicago Press, 2014).

I have gained enormously from feedback and conversations with Binna Choi, Kodwo Eshun, Christian Nyampeta, Lisa Rosendahl, Anjalika Sagar, and Grant Watson. While I was working on this essay, my colleague Kevin McLaughlin helped me to understand that imperfection is not merely the opposite of perfection, but something far more interesting. Rustom Barucha and Lucia King of the VisionMix network prompted more work on the "minor." Thanks are also due to my graduate students at Brown University for their lucid and stimulating conversation, especially the participants in the "Human Sciences" and "Postcolonial Theory" seminars in 2014–15.

2 The attribution of "otonality" and "utonality" to the "major" and "minor" musical modes, respectively, is credited to Harry Partch—an American musicologist, composer, and instrument maker with a deep interest in reaccomodating the transnational musical tonalities that he believed were excluded from Western music with the spread of equal tempering as a normative tuning practice. Partch (who was also gay and styled himself as an anti-institutional autodidact and hobo) deployed otonal/utonal to indicate chords that occurred in the overtone/ undertone series, and felt that this terminology did away with the implicit bias of the major/minor binary. Musical theorists otherwise averse to the utonal-minor mode have argued that only the overtone series is musically substantive while the undertone is derivative and lacks independent existence. In this debate, some writers (admittedly at the occultist end of musical thinking) make a case for otonality-major as the sound of sentient existence and of utonality-minor as the unsettling sound of spiritual life. The theosophist Rudolf Steiner was amongst those who argued that the minor mode represents the triumph of an "ether body" over a "sentient"—producing what we could describe as a temporary sensation of groundlessness (temporary because, for Steiner at any rate, the ethereal realm was the true resting place of the soul). This conceit of groundlessness as an effect of the minor can be further semantically amplified if we allow ourselves to riff on the multiple resources of the prefix "ou"—as it is used in "u-topia," for instance, to designate a place (a ground) that does not-yet-exist or whose existence is indefinitely deferred and unrealized. U-tonality, no less, also incorporates a not-yet or yet-to-come dimension. But after Partch (who emphasizes the veracity and corporeality of the minor), we can conjecture that the tonal groundlessness or inconclusivity in utonality is not an effect of its nonexistence (or ethereality) as

of its aurally disorienting but insistent *coexistence* with otonality in any mono-phonic system of just notation.

3 Ludwig Wittgenstein, *Tractatus Logico-Philosophicus* (New York: Cosimo, 2007 [1922]), 29.

4 William James, *Essays in Radical Empiricism* (Lincoln: University of Nebraska Press, 1996), 45.

5 M. K. Gandhi, *Non-Violent Resistance* (New York: Schocken Books, 1961), 111.

6 Michel Foucault, *"Society Must Be Defended": Lectures at the Collège de France, 1975–76*, eds. Mauro Bertani and Alessandro Fontana, trans. David Macey (Harmondsworth: Penguin, 2003), 15.

7 As reported in Stephen Winsten, *Salt and His Circle* (London: Hutchinson, 1951), 64.

8 *Northern Star*, September 27, 1845, 5.

9 *Labour Prophet*, April 1897, n.p.

10 Gilbert Beith, "Foreword," in Edward Carpenter, *Toward Democracy* (London: GMP Publishers, 1985), 12.

11 *Labour Prophet*, May 1894, n.p.

12 Cited in Henry Salt, *Animal Rights: Considered in Relation to Social Progress* (New York: Macmillan and Co, 1894), 35.

13 Michel Foucault, "The Practice of Parrhesia," in *Discourse and Truth: The Problematization of Parrhesia, 6 Lectures Given by Michel Foucault at the University of California at Berkeley, October–November, 1983*, ed. Joseph Pearson. Digital Archive: Foucault.info, 1999.

14 Michel Foucault, *The Courage of Truth*, vol. 2 of *The Government of Self and Others, Lectures at the Collège de France, 1983–1984*, ed. Fredric Gros, trans. Graham Burchell (Basingstoke, U.K.: Palgrave Macmillan, 2011), 170.

15 William James, *The Varieties of Religious Experience* (New York: Simon & Schuster, 1997), 229, 296.

16 For an inspired discussion of the Bodhisattava idea in the pan-Asian Mahāyāna tradition, see Chung-Fang Yu, *Kuan-Yin: The Chinese Transformation of Avalokitesvara* (New York: Columbia University Press, 2001).

17 John Henry Barrows, *The Parliament of Religions*, 2 vols. (Chicago, 1893), vol. 1, 18.

18 Swami Vivekananda, *The Complete Works of Swami Vivekananda*, ed. Swami Mumukshananda, Mayavati Memorial Edition, 9 vols. (Calcutta: Advaita Ashram, 2000), vol. 1, 3–4.

19 Cited in Marian Mollin, *Radical Pacifism in Modern America: Egalitarianism and Protest* (Philadelphia: University of Pennsylvania Press, 2006), 62.

20 Fellowship of Reconciliation, *Martin Luther King and the Montgomery Story* (New York: Fellowship of Reconciliation, 1956), 13.

21 These passages are as yet unpublished and have been taken from Richard Zenith's forthcoming biography of Fernando Pessoa. I am immeasurably grateful to Richard Zenith and Anna M. Klobucka for transcribing this material and sharing it with me. The discussion on Pessoa above draws upon my essay, "Pessoa's Gandhi: Meditations on a Lost Heteronym," in Hilary Owen and Anna M. Klobucka, eds.,

Gender, Empire, and Postcolony: Luso-Afro-Brazilian Intersections (Basingstoke, U.K.: Palgrave Macmillan, 2014), 19–32.

22 The invaluable phrase is from Michel Foucault, "Friendship as a Way of Life," in *The Essential Works of Michel Foucault, vol. 1, Ethics: Subjectivity and Truth*, ed. Paul Rabinow (New York: New Press, 1997), 138.

23 See Raymond Williams, "Forms of English Fiction in 1848," in his *Writing and Society* (London: Verso, 1983), 150–65; and Ariella Azoulay, "Potential History: Thinking through Violence," *Critical Inquiry*, vol. 39, no. 3 (Spring 2013), 548–574.

24 M. K. Gandhi, *Hind Swaraj and Other Writings*, ed. Anthony J. Parel (Cambridge: Cambridge University Press, 1997), 90.

PART II

Solidarity

5

Cosmopolitanism and the Problem of Solidarity

DAVID A. HOLLINGER

W. E. B. Du Bois was surely right to declare that "the problem of the color line" was "the problem of the 20th century."[1] If Du Bois were alive today, I believe he would join those of us who are now saying that the problem of the twenty-first century is that of solidarity. Thanks to the struggles led by Du Bois and other men and women who shared his antiracist commitments, the color line is now more contested than at any other time in modern history. As late as 1963, when Du Bois died, Americans had yet to enact the Civil Rights Act or the Voting Rights Act, and the U.S. Supreme Court had yet to invalidate state laws prohibiting marriages across the color line. One does not have to exaggerate the significance of the election of a black man as president of the United States to observe that the color line today does not control as much of American life as it did during most of the twentieth century. And one does not have to exaggerate the significance of the global migrations of recent decades to observe that long-standing links between ethnoracial groups and political authority have weakened considerably.

Solidarity is an experience of willed affiliation. Just who belongs together with whom, for what purposes, and on what authority? Where and why do the claims of descent, religion, nationality, economic position, ideology, gender, and "civilization" trump one another in the competition for the loyalties of individuals in an epoch of increased global integration? How much do we owe "to our own kind"—whatever that may mean—and how much to "strangers," the rest of humankind? To confront these questions is to engage the problem of solidarity. The problem of solidarity thus emerges when there is at least some opportunity for choice, when people can exercise some influence over what "we" they help constitute.[2]

Ascribed and taken-for-granted identities are being disrupted by a multitude of social transformations throughout the world, especially in the United States. The question of who "we" are is not new, but it now arises with some urgency. The "we" question does not press itself on individuals who are supremely confident about the groups to which they belong and to which they are the most deeply committed. Such people know their basic "identity," even if only because they have been told repeatedly what it is. They may never have had cause to question it and may never have been allowed any choice in the matter. Uncontested ascription has always been a powerful adhesive, and still is. If Du Bois were alive now, he would surely be among those who would remind us the most vigorously that even today, the darker one's skin, the less choice one has about with whom one can affiliate. But all this is a matter of degree. For millions in many parts of the globe today, a multitude of events, some of which are world-historical in scope, have destabilized old identities. Our most discerning social observers often conclude that "the boundaries of responsibility are increasingly contested."[3]

How should one respond to the problem of solidarity? No single formula will apply in every situation where the allocation of energies amid a variety of overlapping and sometimes competing affiliations is at issue. The problem of solidarity has to be addressed differently depending on the specific constitutional and cultural circumstances in which it arises. Wide solidarities are obviously demanded by our historical situation, but universalist projects neglect at their peril the demands for belonging and intimacy that fuel particularist movements. A determination to balance the wide and the narrow lies behind the prodigious flowering of programs and proposals recently advanced as "cosmopolitan," all of which can be construed as a family of responses to the problem of solidarity.[4]

The cosmopolitan family of responses to the problem of solidarity recognizes that there are fewer places to hide from forces that operate in a global arena. "There's no hiding place down there," warned an old gospel song. Nor is there a hiding place "up here." If we do not take on as much of the world as we can, the world will come to us, and on terms over which we will have even less control than we do now. Cosmopolitanism, rightly understood, at least recognizes this challenge.

Cosmopolitanism has a great deal of work ahead of it, including in the United States, which inherits an elaborate, deeply entrenched, but increasingly anachronistic intellectual and institutional apparatus for dealing with diversity. This apparatus conflates the circumstances of the various minority groups while homogenizing each of them. One might compare this apparatus to a Mercator projection map of the world, in which Greenland, Patagonia, and Spitsbergen are huge, while Nigeria, Indonesia, and Ecuador are tiny. Just as a Mercator projection of the globe served the specific and valuable purpose of enabling a flat wall hanging, so too did the multiculturalist programs organized around the color-coded ethnoracial pentagon—everybody is either white, black, yellow, brown, or red—serve the specific and valuable purpose of supporting affirmative action as put into effect in the United States in the late 1960s and early 1970s. But for some purposes, we want maps of the world other than the Mercator projection: maps that give us the actual geographical proportions of various parts of the globe. For some purposes, we want an intellectual and institutional apparatus for dealing with cultural diversity that is not written onto the top of affirmative action as understood at the time of its first institutionalization, but one that is based on the deepest and most comprehensive analysis we can develop of actual diversity and its dynamics today.

Such an analysis is one of the things people are looking for when the ideal of cosmopolitanism is invoked. Indeed, this ideal has become more current in the context of a quarrel within multiculturalism, broadly construed, between the people I call pluralist multiculturalists on the one hand, and those I call cosmopolitan multiculturalists on the other hand. In this way of framing the debate, the pluralists are more concerned to protect and perpetuate the cultures of groups already well established, whereas cosmopolitans are more inclined to encourage the voluntary formation of new communities of wider scope. Cosmopolitanism is, after all, more liberal in style, appreciating that individuals can be simultaneously affiliated with many groups, whereas pluralism is more conservative, oriented to preexisting groups and likely to ascribe identity to a single community of descent. Cosmopolitans are specialists in the creating of the new, while cautious about destroying the old; pluralists are specialists in the conservation of the old and are cautious about developing the new. By and large, the pluralists won the argument over what multiculturalism should be, so when reference is made to standardized or orthodox multiculturalism, it is decidedly the pluralist version—the version associated with "identity politics"—that takes

center stage. Hence people like me who were pushing for the cosmopolitan side of the argument began about 1995 to talk about getting "beyond
multiculturalism," meaning beyond the pluralist kind.[5]

The situation in the United States, including the historic victory of
the pluralists in the 1990s and the increasing credibility of the cosmopolitans in the new century, is worthy of attention simply because the
United States is one of the most conspicuous of world-historical arenas
for the interaction of different communities of descent in relation to a
single, overarching state with democratic aspirations formally committed to equality of opportunity regardless of ethnoracial classification and
burdened with a history of racism. Hence, what happens in the United
States is important not only to those like me who are personally invested
in the American project and eager to see it critically revised, but to the
larger community of people who—with their eyes on Germany or India
or Brazil or the Netherlands or wherever—are eager to discover the
promises and pitfalls of various egalitarian policies and practices and
strategies. The history, current state, and possible future of the American experience with diversity is potentially relevant even to decidedly
global ventures like portal campuses of American universities abroad,
designed to encourage cross-cultural understanding. I try to address the
American case, then, with this larger panorama in mind.

The efforts now being made to get beyond the cultural equivalent of
the Mercator projection were dramatized for me by a conversation I had
on the floor of the convention of the National Conference on Race and
Ethnicity in American Higher Education.[6] After I had delivered my address, a young African American woman whose job at a leading university is to organize and operate a "multicultural office, African American
section," rose from the audience. A dilemma she faces in carrying out
her work, she explained to me at this conference of multicultural program officers and staff, is as follows. The senior administrators to whom
she reports expect her to design and implement a program that would
enable black students to feel more at home on campus and enable non-
black students and faculty to come to a greater appreciation of the special circumstances of black students. But the black students she works
with are strikingly different from one another in cultural orientation,
social experience, and campus-related needs, especially along two ances-
tral lines. The immigrants and children of immigrants from Caribbean

countries and those from African countries, she observed, have very little in common with the students whose families experienced Jim Crow segregation and other forms of institutionalized debasement within the United States over many generations. The immigrant-based black populations of students she works with are also different from one another, those from Kenya and Nigeria having relatively little in common with those from Jamaica and Barbados, although the traditions of the British education system strikingly distinguish all of them from the students with a multigeneration ancestry in the United States. Yet this woman finds that when she takes this dilemma to her administrative superiors for counsel—what makes you think all black people are alike? she asks them—they are reluctant to listen because they have so much invested in multicultural approaches generated many years ago, emphasizing the centrality of color, the sharpness of color lines, and the close connection between color and culture. They are still using the Mercator projection.

A second example of efforts to get beyond the cultural equivalent of the Mercator projection is the increasing pressure for diversity programs to pay attention to Arab Americans, Jewish Americans, religiously defined rather than color-defined cultures, and specific European-derived ethnic groups erased by orthodox multiculturalism. I illustrate this with the case of Jewish Americans.

Jews had long been prominent in discussions of American pluralism, as in Will Herberg's famous book of 1955, *Protestant Catholic Jew.*[7] But Jews were almost never counted as relevant to standard multiculturalism. Jews eager to be part of the multicultural conversation right down through the 1990s were surrounded by a discourse of group identity that systematically deemphasized religion, yet the religious component in Jewish history was vitally important. This pervasive discourse of identity privileged color, yet color did not distinguish most Jews from white people in general. This discourse downplayed the linguistic and historical particularity of the different descent communities within each of the color-coded segments of the ethnoracial pentagon, yet for Jews, linguistic and historical particularity was basic to group identity. This discourse nested issues of identity and culture in a matrix of unequally distributed power and often aspired to allocate social benefits on the basis of demographically proportional representation, yet Jews were the richest and most empowered of any of society's prominently recognized ethnoracial groups. This discourse placed great emphasis on the barriers that minorities faced in the United States, yet the Jewish case constituted the most dramatic instance in all American history of a stigmatized descent group that had been discriminated against under the protection of law suddenly becoming overrepresented many times over in social spaces where its members' progress had previously been seriously inhibited. A younger generation of specialists in Jewish history and Jewish studies more generally are now working to integrate the Jewish story into the larger story of cultural diversity.[8]

These cases exemplify something we are seeing more of today in the United States: an escalating tension between, on the one hand, a greater sensitivity to the particularity of the historical circumstances, economic condition, and cultural orientation of the various natal communities and, on the other hand, a conceptual and institutional apparatus inherited from the late 1960s and 1970s that assumed the ethnoracial groups relevant to antiracist initiatives to be clearly bounded, enduring, color-coded, analogically structured entities, each with its own culture and its own myth of diaspora.

This tension is not new. Throughout the 1990s and in the first decade of the twenty-first century a number of antiracist voices criticized the Old Religion inherited from the civil rights era. As late as 1998, President Bill Clinton's initiative on race, *One America in the 21st Century* (the only presidential commission to deal with race since the Kerner Commission of thirty years before), resoundingly reinforced the inherited apparatus; systematically denied that there were salient differences between African Americans, Asian Americans, and Hispanic Americans; and offered fifty-three specific recommendations for multicultural programs and antidiscrimination remedies, not a single one of which dealt with the historically unique situation of the black Americans whose lives had been affected by centuries of legally sanctioned slavery, violently enforced discrimination, and cataclysmically inadequate educational opportunities.[9] During the years following 1998, the tension has increased between those who still think in terms of the Old Religion and those who are trying to find approaches to structural inequality that take account of the shifting conditions under which the struggle against inequality is now carried out.

Central to these shifting conditions are the character and extent of immigration, which was almost never discussed when the Old Religion was young. The latest census figures show that immigrants respond to identity questions very differently than nonimmigrants, and both the numbers of immigrants and their different ways of identifying themselves are playing havoc with the Census Bureau's inherited categories.[10] Kenneth Prewitt, a former director of the Census Bureau, has recently proposed a radically changed "race question" for the 2020 census that reflects the reality so long denied.[11] More than a quarter of all children under the age of six in this country are being raised by at least one foreign-born parent. I can report from my own university that 67 percent of our freshmen at Berkeley have at least one foreign-born parent.

One such immigration-related change has already been mentioned here. This is the appearance in the United States of dramatically increasing numbers of black-skinned people who came voluntarily from Africa and the Caribbean. By the 1990s, and especially since 2005, our social scientists and investigative journalists produced study after study showing that these immigrants and their children managed to overcome the barriers created by antiblack racism to a greater extent than nonimmigrant blacks.[12] These studies imply that blackness itself is not enough to explain the enduringly weak class position of the bulk of American black people. Perhaps the educational and economic circumstances of the immigrants from Africa and the Caribbean make a difference? President Barack Obama himself is relevant here, because his blackness derives from a Kenyan immigrant and he has candidly suggested that his own daughters might not be appropriate targets for affirmative action.

If we are going to go down the road of distinguishing between various kinds of black people, we will have to revise a system that is based on treating all blacks who get jobs or get admitted to college as displaying the same statistical meaning. If immigrants and the children of immigrants are overrepresented by hundreds of percentage points among the blacks who get into Ivy League colleges, where does that leave us? If facts of that order do not mean that blackness is less relevant than historically different social circumstances, what do such facts mean?

What would be the implications for Hispanic Americans if officials suddenly decided that not all black people are equally eligible for diversity programs? This question about Hispanics is a crucial question because the overwhelming majority of the Hispanic population in the United States is an immigrant-derived population. Are we going to say that brown immigrants are more eligible for special attention than black immigrants are? If so, on the basis of what theory? The Old Religion was based on the idea that Hispanic Americans, Asian Americans, and American Indians were all "like blacks" in their relation to U.S. society and were thus covered by the same theory. But if we are now going to say that even some blacks are not "like blacks," how can Hispanics be? Or Cambodians? Or Filipinos? The Old Religion and its various interpreters have almost never discussed the issue of immigrant eligibility for the programs developed in the late 1960s and 1970s; even today, mere mention of it makes many people nervous. I raised it at a meeting of the diversity committee on my own campus, and got the impression that everyone wanted to run from the room.

The presence of immigrants from Africa and the Caribbean is not the only pertinent aspect of this new immigration since the 1970s. Another is the presence of people from China, Japan, Korea, India, and other countries in Asia, who have done well by conventional economic and educational indicators. The historic experience of Asian Americans is too often put aside rather than analyzed in relation to the dynamics of racism, inequality, and incorporation into a society of predominantly European origins. The great majority of the adult immigrants from Korea are college graduates, and a substantial segment of the immigrants from several other Asian countries are highly skilled and literate in English when they arrive, which is not the case with most immigrants from Mexico, Guatemala, and the other Latin American countries that provide so much of the low-skilled labor force in the United States.

The juxtaposition of the pre-immigration social circumstances of migrants from Latin America with the pre-immigration social circumstances of migrants from several East and South Asian countries can remind us that attention to particular histories, especially to the educational and economic background of immigrants, presents us with a radically different picture of diversity than the picture inherited from the civil rights era. Do Hispanic Americans have a claim on special treatment? Perhaps they do, but the most plausible theory that would justify such special treatment would surely be economic, pivoting on the fact that the United States persistently encourages (indeed, demands) an underclass of workers who will do low-skilled work for relatively low wages and are not likely to join labor unions. Our system, however, deals with the Hispanic population in its capacity as an ethnoracial group. We use ethnorace as a proxy for economic inequality, designing programs targeted at an ethnoracially defined population, when the most salient property of that population is instead its economic status.[13]

Discrimination against Hispanic Americans as Hispanics does have a real history, including school segregation and exclusion from juries in several states until the 1950s, but unlike the immigrants from Mexico, those from East Asia and South Asia were not even able to achieve naturalized citizenship in 1952. We cannot remind ourselves often enough that Asian Americans were taken from their homes and thrown into internment camps in my own lifetime and within a few miles of where I now live in California. The different trajectories of Mexican Americans, on the one hand, and the several varieties of Asian Americans, on the other hand, should turn us away from the idea that the operative force is racism in the eye of the empowered white beholder. We do not have to claim that empowered whites have fully renounced racism to confront the fact that the power of this racism to damage its victims now varies enormously according to the economic and educational circumstances of the victims.

Another big change, beyond those centering around immigration, is the increase of mixture, that is, the greater frequency of marriage and cohabitation and reproduction across the lines of the standardized groups. Black-white marriages are still rare in comparison with the statistics for out-marriage among Hispanic Americans, American Indians, and the various groups of Asian Americans, but the black-white case demands more attention because of the long and deep opposition to black-white marriages, lasting well beyond 1967, when the laws prohibiting such marriages still in effect in a dozen states were finally eliminated by the U.S. Supreme Court. Our demographers use a number of different statistical methods to determine the rate of black-white mixing, with slightly different results, but all agree on the reality of a steady increase over the past forty years. One of the most interesting studies was carried out by demographer Joshua Goldstein. The Goldstein study, as reported in the *New York Times*,[14] calculates the percentage of families who had a mixed-race marriage within their extended kinship network. Goldstein found that among census-identified whites, by 2000 about 30 percent of white Americans had within their kinship network of ten marriages over three generations at least one white-nonwhite marriage, and in that same year, nearly two thirds of census-identified black Americans did. The percentage for Asian Americans with such families was 92 percent. These figures were up dramatically from 1990, and of course from earlier censuses. In 1960, only about 2 percent of census-identified whites had in their kinship network a single white-nonwhite marriage. In forty years, then, the number of white families with a black relative increased to fifteen times what it had been.

The significance of the increase in cross-group marriage has been exaggerated, I believe, especially by those who predict the end of standardized communities of descent within the next two or three generations. What is significant are not only the increases as measured statistically but the shift in cultural attitudes as measured by opinion polls and visible in popular culture. That is one reason I focus here on the Goldstein study rather than those by Mary Walters and Joel Perlmann and others:[15] our social psychologists tell us that acceptance for mixed-race marriage, like acceptance of same-sex relationships, increases with intimate familiarity. That is, opposition to gay relationships, like opposition to mixed-race marriage, cohabitation, and reproduction, diminishes when someone in your own family is in one of these traditionally stigmatized relationships. The way this plays into the tension I have been discussing between the Old Religion and the struggles for a new dispensation is that group boundaries are simply less sharp than they were when our categories and their prescribed meaning were consolidated in the 1960s and 1970s.

A new dispensation? The cosmopolitan struggle for it continues, but we will not make much progress as long as we continue to believe that the basic problem is simply that of the color line. Cosmopolitans understand that we must now confront that problem in the context of the broader and deeper problem of solidarity.

NOTES

1 W. E. B. Du Bois, *The Souls of Black Folk* (Chicago: A. C. McClurg & Co., 1903), p. 1.
2 This paragraph and several others in this essay draw on my "From Identity to Solidarity," *Daedalus* (Fall 2006): 23–31, in which I offer a more detailed account of the problem of solidarity.

3 Samuel Scheffler, *Boundaries and Allegiances: Problems of Justice and Responsibility in Liberal Thought* (New York: Oxford University Press, 2001), p. 65.

4 Of the many recent collections of essays clarifying the varieties of cosmopolitanism, two are especially helpful: Steve Vertovec and Robin Cohen, eds., *Conceiving Cosmopolitanism: Theory, Context, and Practice* (Oxford: Oxford University Press, 2002), and the special issue of *Daedalus*, "On Cosmopolitanism," summer 2008. See also the vigorous manifestos by Kwame Anthony Appiah, *Cosmopolitanism: Ethics in a World of Strangers* (New York: W. W. Norton, 2006), and Bruce Robbins, *Perpetual War: Cosmopolitanism from the Viewpoint of Violence* (Durham: Duke University Press, 2012).

5 For an extended, critical account in these terms of the multiculturalist movement of the United States, see my *Postethnic America: Beyond Multiculturalism*, 3rd ed. (New York: Basic Books, 2006).

6 National Conference on Race and Ethnicity in American Higher Education (NCORE), San Diego, California.

7 Will Herberg, *Protestant Catholic Jew* (New York: Doubleday, 1955).

8 See the contributions by Hasia Diner, Paula Hyman, Alan Kraut, and Tony Michels in the symposium "American Jewish History and American Historical Writing," *American Jewish History* (March 2009): 1–78.

9 *One American in the 21st Century: The President's Initiative on Race* (Washington, D.C.: President's Initiative on Race, 1998).

10 *New York Times*, January 22, 2010.

11 Kenneth Prewitt, *What Is Your Race? The Census and Our Flawed Efforts to Classify Americans* (Princeton: Princeton University Press, 2013).

12 One of the most widely publicized of these studies showed that among black students at Ivy League colleges, immigrants and the children of immigrants were greatly overrepresented. See Douglas Massey et al., *American Journal of Education* (February 2007).

13 This paragraph and several others draw upon my "Obama, the Instability of Color Lines, and the Promise of a Postethnic Future," *Callaloo* 31, no. 4 (2008): 1033–1037.

14 "Nation's Many Faces in Extended First Family," *New York Times*, January 20, 2009. See also J. R. Goldstein, "Kinship Networks that Cross Racial Lines: The Exception or the Rule?" *Demography* 36 (1999): 399–407.

15 For example, Joel Perlmann and Mary C. Waters, "Intermarriage Then and Now: Race, Generation, and the Changing Meaning of Marriage," in *Not Just Black and White: Historical and Contemporary Perspectives on Immigration, Race, and Ethnicity in the United States*, ed. Nancy Foner and George Fredrickson (Washington, D.C.: Russell Sage Foundation, 2004), p. 275.

6

Afropolitanism

ACHILLE MBEMBE

Translated by Paulo Lemos Horta

For almost a century, African discourse, whether of literature, philosophy, or the arts, has been dominated by three intellectual and political paradigms which, as it happens, are not mutually exclusive.

First, there are several variations of anticolonial nationalism, which have had a deep influence on culture, politics, economics, and even religion. Second, there are various reinterpretations of Marxism from which many forms of "African socialism" have developed. Finally, there is a pan-African sphere of influence that has privileged two types of solidarity—a racial and transnational solidarity, and an anti-imperialist and international solidarity.

At the beginning of the twenty-first century, this intellectual trend has not changed fundamentally, even if behind the scenes important social and cultural transformations are taking place. The gap between the real life of a society on the one hand and the intellectual tools a society uses to understand its future on the other can pose risks to thought and culture. Indeed, the three intellectual and political paradigms have grown so institutionalized and ossified that today they can no longer be used to analyze ongoing transitions with the slightest bit of credibility. Almost without exception, the institutions embodying these paradigms function as "guaranteed incomes." Moreover, they hinder the renewal of cultural criticism, stifle artistic and philosophical creativity, and reduce our ability to contribute to contemporary thought on culture and democracy.

Worlds in Movement

Of all the transformations taking place, two in particular could weigh heavily on cultural life as well as artistic and political creativity in the coming years. First of all, answers to the question "Who is African and who is not?" are being reconfigured.

For many, to be "African" is to be "black" and therefore "not white," the degree of authenticity measured on a scale of raw racial difference. Thus, many kinds of people have a link to or some connection with Africa—something that gives them the right ipso facto to claim "African citizenship." Naturally, there are black Africans. They were born and live in African states as nationals. Yet if black Africans form the majority population of the continent, they are neither its sole inhabitants nor the sole producers of its art and culture.

From Asia, the Middle East, and Europe, other populations have settled in various parts of the continent, during various periods of history, and for various reasons. Some, like the Arabs and Europeans, came as conquerors, traders, or missionaries. Fleeing persecution or misfortune, filled with hope of a peaceful life, or driven by thirst for wealth, others, like the Jews and Afrikaners, settled under more or less tragic historical circumstances. Still others, like the Malays, Indians, and Chinese in South Africa, came essentially as migrant laborers, settling down and starting families. More recently, Lebanese, Syrian, Indo-Pakistani, and hundreds of thousands of Chinese migrants have come onto the scene. They all arrived with different languages, customs, cuisines, fashions, prayers—in other words, their own ways of being and doing. Today, the relationship between these diasporas and their societies of origin is complex. Though their members may also belong somewhere else, many of them see themselves as full-fledged Africans.

While Africa has long been the destination of many different population movements and cultural flows, the continent has also been a point of departure to other regions of the world for centuries. This ancient process took place throughout what is usually referred to as modern times, and followed the three routes of the Sahara, the Atlantic Ocean, and the Indian Ocean. The creation of black African diasporas in the New World is the result of such a dispersal. Slavery, which involved not only the European-American world but also the Arab-Asian world, played a decisive role in this process. As a consequence, traces of Africans are spread across the capitalist and Islamic worlds from one end to the other. In addition to the forced migrations of previous centuries, colonialism has also driven migrations. Today, millions of people of African origin are citizens of countries around the world.

Even with a definition of who and what is "Africa[n]," when discussions arise about aesthetic creativity in contemporary Africa, political and cultural critics tend to pass over in silence this historical phenomenon of worlds in movement. From an African point of view, the worlds-in-movement phenomenon has at least two facets: dispersion and immersion. Historically, the dispersal of African populations and cultures was not only a matter of foreigners coming to settle in our backyard. In fact, the precolonial history of African societies is one of peoples in perpetual movement over the continent. It is a history of colliding cultures, caught in a maelstrom of war, invasion, migration, intermarriage. It is a history of the various religions we make our own, of the technologies we exchange, and of the goods we trade. The cultural history of the continent can hardly be understood outside a paradigm of itinerancy, mobility, and displacement.

Colonialism once threatened to freeze this culture of mobility through the modern institution of borders. Recalling the history of itinerancy requires discussion of mixing, blending, and superimposing. In opposition to the fundamentalists preaching "custom" and "autochthony," we can go so far as to assert that what we call "tradition" does not in fact exist. Whether one is speaking of Islam or Christianity, trade or speech, ways of dressing or even of eating, no institution or cultural practice has survived the bulldozer of miscegenation and vernacularization. This was the case well before the colonization of Africa. Indeed, there is a precolonial African modernity that has not yet been taken into account in contemporary creativity.

The other aspect of the worlds-in-movement is immersion, which affected the minorities that came from afar to ultimately settle and start families on the continent. Over time, links with their countries of origin, whether European or Asian, became remarkably complex. These minorities became cultural hybrids through contact with a new geography, climate, and people. Yet due to the history of colonialism, Euro-Africans in particular continued to aspire to racial supremacy and to mark their difference from, even contempt for, anything "African" or "indigenous." This is especially true in the case of the Afrikaners, whose very name means "Africans." There is the same ambivalence among

Indians, Lebanese, and Syrians. Most of these immigrant populations express themselves in the local languages and participate in certain national customs; nevertheless, they live in relatively closed communities and do not marry outside them.

Thus, a part of African history lies elsewhere, outside the continent, but a part of the history of the rest of the world, of which we are inevitably the actors and guardians, also lies inside Africa. Our way of belonging to the world, of being in the world, and of inhabiting the world, has always been marked if not by cultural mixing, then at least by the interweaving of worlds. That interweaving is a slow and sometimes incoherent dance with forms and signs which we have not been able to choose freely, but which we have succeeded as best we can in domesticating and putting at our disposal.

It is this cultural, historical, and aesthetic sensitivity that underlies the term "Afropolitanism"—awareness of the interweaving of the here and there, the presence of the elsewhere in the here and vice versa, the relativization of primary roots and memberships and the way of embracing, with full knowledge of the facts, strangeness, foreignness, and remoteness, the ability to recognize one's face in that of a foreigner and make the most of the traces of remoteness in closeness, to domesticate the unfamiliar to work with what seem to be opposites.

The Nativistic Reflex

The second ongoing transformation pertains to the rise in power of the nativistic reflex. In its mild form, nativism manifests as an ideology glorifying differences and diversity, while fighting to safeguard customs and identities perceived as threatened. According to nativistic logic, identity and political struggle are founded on a distinction between "those who are from here"—autochthons—and "those who came from outside"—nonnatives. Nativists forget, however, that in their stereotyped form the customs and traditions which they profess to follow were often created not by actual autochthons, but by missionaries and settlers.

Thus, during the second half of the twentieth century, a form of bioracism—autochthons versus nonnatives—appeared almost everywhere on the continent, cultivated in politics by a particular idea of victimization and resentment. Violence stemming from such ideologies is seldom directed toward the victim's actual torturer. The victim almost always turns against an imagined torturer who, coincidentally, is weaker—that is, another victim who has nothing to do with the original violence. A genocidal impulse inhabits victimization ideologies, as demonstrated in many countries, and not only in Africa. Such ideologies create a culture of hatred with an incredible power of destruction, as we have seen in Rwanda and elsewhere.

Afropolitanism is not the same as Pan-Africanism or negritude, but rather an aesthetic and a particular poetics of the world. It is a way of being in the world, rejecting on principle any identity based on victimhood—which does not mean that it is blind to the injustice and violence inflicted on the continent and its people by the law of the world. It is also a political and cultural stance toward the nation, to race, and to difference in general. Insofar as African states are total inventions, and recent ones at that, strictly speaking there is nothing in their essential nature that can force us to worship them—which is not to say that we are indifferent to their fate.

As for African nationalism, it originally stood for a powerful utopia with an unlimited insurrectionary potential—an enticement toward self-recognition, toward facing the world with dignity as beings endowed with a human face. But as soon as nationalism turned into the official ideology of a predatory state, it lost any ethical heart, becoming a demon "who roams at night and flees the light of day." Nationalism and nativism both continue to come up against the human countenance and dignity. Racial solidarity as advocated by Pan-Africanism does not evade these dilemmas. Once contemporary Africa awakens to the notions of multiplicity, including racial multiplicity, that are integral to its identity, it will become untenable to reject the continent solely on the basis of a form of African solidarity. Moreover, how can we not see that this so-called solidarity is deeply harmed by the violence of brothers against brothers, the violence of brothers against mothers and sisters, that has occurred since the end of direct colonialism?

Broad-Mindedness

Thus, we must move forward to something else if we are to revive the intellectual life of Africa and at the same time the possibilities of an art, a philosophy, and an aesthetics that can say something new and meaningful to the world in general. Today, many Africans live outside Africa. Others have chosen of their own accord to live on the continent but not necessarily in their countries of birth. Many of them have had the opportunity to experience several worlds in their ceaseless comings and goings, developing an invaluable wealth of perceptivity and sensitivity in the course of movement. These people can usually express themselves in more than one language. They are developing, sometimes unknowingly, a transnational culture which I call "Afropolitan" culture.

Among them, there are many professionals who go about their daily business continually measuring themselves not against the village next door, but against the world at large. A great number of artists, musicians, composers, writers, poets, and painters have exhibited a deep sense of such "broad-mindedness" since the beginning of the postcolonial era. On another level, a small number of metropolises can be counted as "Afropolitan." In the latter half of the twentieth century, Dakar and Abidjan fulfilled this purpose in West Africa. Dakar represented the cultural counterpart of Abidjan, the business center of the subregion. Unfortunately, today Abidjan has been undermined by the cancer of nativism. In East Africa, Nairobi once occupied the role of the region's business center and seat of several international institutions.

But today the preeminent center of Afropolitanism is Johannesburg, South Africa. In this metropolis built on a brutal history, a new form of African modernity is developing that has little to do with what we have known before. Johannesburg draws on multiple racial legacies, a vibrant economy, a liberal democracy, and a culture of consumerism that partake directly of the currents of globalization. Through a growing ethic of tolerance, the city is likely to revive African aesthetic and cultural creativity, just as Harlem or New Orleans once did in the United States.

7

Cosmopolitan Exchanges

Scenes of Colonial and Postcolonial Reading

ELLEKE BOEHMER

This essay contends that scenes of reading staged within the postcolonial novel connect with practices of reading that colonial newspapers encouraged. These scenes and practices both call up ideas of cosmopolitan exchange, and at once appeal to and investigate transnational and cosmopolitan values. Turning to colonial India in particular, I suggest that late nineteenth-century Anglophone Indians were shaped as cosmopolitan travelers by their initial social formation in Indian cities, in particular by their colonial education and by their newspaper reading. They wrote and they read as self-conscious Westerners, in much the same way as the reading characters we find in postcolonial novels such as by Tsitsi Dangarembga (Zimbabwe) or Manju Kapur (India) read as Westerners also.

Research I have undertaken on colonial newspaper reading has shown that readers in colonial contexts, broadly conceived, for example in British India, generally saw themselves as forming part of an international reading public.[1] In other words, they were intercultural travelers even before they themselves set out traveling. They were encouraged in this approach by the forms and mode of colonial journalism, which tended to address itself to readerships at once at home and abroad, and so bolstered colonial readers' sense of their world citizenship. The same two levels of reading activity, and of self-perception, located at once at home and abroad, can be distinguished in the postcolonial novel.

Whereas colonial reading is generally seen as ideological, controlled, and regulated—we might think of Thomas Macaulay's infamous "Minute on Indian Education" (1835)—it is often assumed that postcolonial reading is subversive. My question here is to what extent this was so, and relatedly, whether colonial reading was not a great deal more uneven and layered than it is given credit for?[2] Colonial reading often produced a sense of proximity and fellow feeling, in a situation where hierarchical separation was part of everyday life, whereas scenes of reading in the postcolonial novel identify strongly across cultural and national borders, but at the same time assert a difference from local communities and contexts.

Writing in all forms, not forgetting journalism, allowed colonial Indians, especially those who were migrants, not merely to articulate their experiences of migration but also to give these journeys imaginative shape.[3] Journals and letters home, the more retrospective forms of the travelogue and the memoir, but also the colonial newspaper, provided effective forms through which colonial travelers, including from India, could reflect on the modern imperial world that they themselves were making and remaking in the process of moving through it. For instance, the linear and denotative forms of the travelogue allowed Indian migrants to plot familiar day-to-day patterns within unfamiliar spaces.[4]

The newpaper and the periodical, too, provided the colonial migrant imagination with the interpretative tools through which to make sense of the pell-mell and cosmopolitan contingencies of their experience, especially given the stark juxtapositions of geographies and social worlds their layout made possible wherever in the world they were published.[5] Therefore if, as Benedict Anderson contends, the world was conceptualized, reconceptualized, and consumed on a daily basis by way of the nineteenth-century newspaper's format and its mass production, this was something that happened not only in London or New York, but in Bombay and Calcutta too.[6]

Equipped with these powerful ways of imagining the modern world, late nineteenth-century Indian travelers, when they reached the imperial metropolis, inevitably read its public spaces through a standardized vocabulary of everyday city life acquired as part of their experience in India, which included their newspaper reading. And though London was generally seen to be far larger and more crowded than their home cities, it was still the case that the features these travelers singled out for comment, had already been formalized as codes of a global city life drawn from what they knew of urban India, or from what Partha Mitter calls their "virtual cosmopolitan" know-how.

Importantly, therefore, late nineteenth-century colonial travelers, in encountering the capital of the modern world, did not tend to see themselves as secondary or belated in relation to it. Rather they mapped and decoded the city's streets with reference to a ready-made index of pre-existing images, geographical coordinates, and spatial terms acquired as part of a colonial education and from the pages of colonial newspapers. Urban dwellers themselves, citizens of Bombay, Calcutta, Lahore, or Delhi, self-consciously modern inhabitants of a rapidly expanding imperial world, they met the world's largest metropolis on relatively equal terms, even while conceding that its bustle, traffic, and sheer scale were matched nowhere else on the planet.[7] Far from being unintelligible, London to these colonial travelers was not only cosmopolitan but comprehensible and readable in its cosmopolitanism.[8] Like Calcutta or Delhi, as Partha Mitter again writes, London was a hybrid cosmopolis that operated as a crucible for lateral modernist and global formations.[9]

The replication of an urban imaginary through print technology and through cosmopolitan reading, is persuasively illustrated in the example offered by the relatively unknown yet for all that representative provincial paper, the *Indian Mirror*, the weekly journal of the Calcutta Brahmo Samaj.[10] Like the later *Modern Review* (1907), the Calcutta monthly associated with Bengal's modernist art movement, the *Indian Mirror* was broadly liberal, nationalist, and reformist, much concerned with the measure of "Indian loyalty to the Crown." Its four-page broadsheet featured short reports on foreign news (often relating to India, such as Irish Home Rule developments) and civic notices (concerning temporary closures of the Hooghly Bridge, for example), alongside reviews of local cultural events: a performance of the Mahasheta at the Opera House, for instance, where "a well-written English synopsis of the piece" was "placed into the hands of those who could not follow it in the original." As in other metropolitan as well as regional newspapers of the day, these notices and reviews were juxtaposed with advertisements concentrated in the side columns and on the back page. Some of the ads interestingly featured businesses (publishers, opticians) with outlets in London and Bombay as well as Calcutta. So Lawrence and Mayo opticians, who advertised their "perfect pebble" spectacles in the *Indian Mirror*'s pages, boasted offices at 1A Old Bond Street in London, Rampart Row, Bombay, and 3–4 Hare Street, Calcutta.[11]

Thinking of virtual cosmopolitanism, perhaps the most interesting articles in the 1886 *Indian Mirror* were its almost daily reports on the Government of India's Colonial and Indian Exhibition in London, which highlighted both insignificant and important features and events. The detail lavished on, for example, a description of the installation of the display cases, or an address by the Prince of Wales, created a striking effect of close yet transnational focus, certainly when compared to the same paper's far briefer, broad-brush reports on Calcutta-based events. From the point of view of the *Indian Mirror* (or indeed of other Indian regional newspapers, such as the *Bombay Gazette*), it was as if the Exhibition were taking place not thousands of miles away, but in a parallel world proximate to Calcutta.

As this suggests, the imperial communications networks that sustained colonial newspapers created so dynamic a connectivity between the empire's cities that, in local readers' imaginations at least, the colonial periphery could be regarded as less distant from the metropolis than the latter's elevated status implied. Within these lively networks, Indian tourists writing on the Exhibition in London might overnight convert their travel notes into newspaper columns for Calcutta or Colombo newspapers (and subsequently into guidebooks for later travelers), and Thomas Cook and Sons set out to reinforce existing intercultural links by arranging regular tours from India to the Exhibition via the Suez Canal.

Within the "mirror" worlds of the *Indian Mirror*, therefore, the India being staged abroad could be placed cheek-by-jowl with the India being lived at home, within the time frame of a single day. The interconnected narrative world implied in the repackaged and juxtaposed reports found no gap between these different cosmopolitan Indias, just as the London-based newspapers too were conjuring into being an increasingly globalized world through intercutting stories from the colonies with reports on Britain.

The serial generation of modern meanings in the newspaper, therefore, far from moving outward from the single source of the metropolis, is more accurately described as a two-way or even multidirectional process.[12] As Indian migrants moved across the world and mingled with strangers—as did other modern travelers—their relatively stable local and regional identities and belief systems brought over from home were thrown into new, unpredictable, and quintessentially cosmopolitan mixes. In interpreting these experiences, it could not but be helpful that processes of confronting and then convening a heterogeneous world were encapsulated in the very pages of the newspapers and periodicals which they consumed, and to which some contributed.[13] Through their engagement with these pages, Indian newspaper readers became involved participants in, as well as observers of, Britain's public culture. The situation represents an interesting expansion of Benedict Anderson's largely monadic model of newspaper reading as nation making, where the primary reference is to the metropolitan reading population.

Turning now to the postcolonial novel, I would want to propose that the scene of reading often conjured within its pages (especially in the case of the Bildungsroman), retraces but also exceeds the pell-mell heterogeneous worlds called up on the pages of the colonial newspaper. The represented scene of reading in the novel could therefore be seen as world making, that is, as assuming the existence of cosmopolitan readers, or a cosmopolitan reading public, and so as forging transnational links. Drawing on the work of K. Anthony Appiah, by cosmopolitan readers and reading here I refer to the democratic consumption of texts from across cultural boundaries, and to the processes of identification that such reading encourages. Such processes are facilitated, however, by the values and also the structures that a colonial education lays down.

In Dangarembga's *Nervous Conditions*, the scene in which the character Nyasha reads D. H. Lawrence's *Lady Chatterley's Lover* and then has her book confiscated by her father, is justly celebrated in postcolonial literary studies as a resistant postcolonial act which is thwarted by conservative authority in the form of her father (75, 81, 83). By choosing to read Lawrence's once banned book, Nyasha is kicking against her own culturally mixed identity (78) and her and her parents' Anglicization (74), as symbolized also in their bedclothes and rose-patterned tea set. Yet elsewhere in the novel, and certainly when it comes to the more compliant and grateful Tambu, reading, though it involves socially subversive choices, is safely circumscribed by the Anglophone syllabus of children's and young women's reading. Taking in the colonial newspaper alongside Blyton, the Brontës, and Alcott as she does (33, 93, 117), Tambu's obedient reading backlights Nyasha's. Neither young woman in fact reads as anything other than a Westerner and a would-be or virtual cosmopolitan, identifying cross-culturally and straddling different

"English" cultural worlds, while at the same time increasingly cutting themselves off from their immediate family and local context.

As to Kapur's *Difficult Daughters*, central to this generational novel of Indian coming into being is the protracted and often painful relationship of an English teacher, called the Professor, and his student Virmati. The one reads for pleasure, and returns to India from his education in England with a trunk full of English books, "bringing as much of England as he could" (33). The other reads to improve herself, to seek a vocation rather than take her mother's route of marriage and childbirth.

In many ways, reading draws the couple together and cements their relationship. The Professor teaches Virmati about Shakespeare and English poetry; she admires his ambition and his devotion to his books, his Keats and Alfred Austin. At the same time, however, their investments in reading are quite divergent. He reads in a purposeless way, as part of his quest for "the beautiful." She reads to educate herself, so that she may be useful as a teacher outside of marriage. Both read in order to find their own ideal self-image projected back at them, an image to which they then mutually hope their lover will correspond. But though both modes of reading are profoundly egotistical and parochial, they both also involve assuming the existence of a community of like-minded Western-educated people, readers of English literature, in which the lover figure will be centrally involved.

Reading characters within these in many ways representative postcolonial Anglophone novels by Dangarembga and Kapur make an appeal to a shared cultural and literary repertoire, much as readers of colonial newspapers related to a common vocabulary of cultural and geographical reference points. The reading public to which the writers of these novels appeal, therefore, is necessarily always across the border and so in principle cosmopolitan, just as the public "called out" by the colonial newspaper was intercultural, urbane, and globally informed—or, in short, cosmopolitan. The scene of reading in both cases refers beyond national borders and as such becomes an important form of cosmopolitan self-consolidation and identity making.

NOTES

1 Elleke Boehmer, *Indian Arrivals 1870–1915: Networks of British Empire* (Oxford: Oxford University Press, 2015), especially chapters 2 and 3.

2 See, most recently, Sheldon Pollock, ed., *Literary Cultures in History: Reconstructions from South Asia* (Berkeley: University of California Press, 2003); Francesca Orsini, ed., *The History of the Book in South Asia* (New York: Routledge, 2013); Stuart Blackburn and Vasudha Dalmia, *India's Literary History: Essays on the Nineteenth Century* (Delhi: Permanent Black, 2006); Abhijit Gupta and Swapan Chakravorty, eds., *Founts of Knowledge* (Delhi: Orient Blackswan, 2015); Abhijit Gupta and Swapan Chakravorty, *Moveable Type* (Delhi: Permanent Black, 2008); Swapan Chakravorty and Abhijit Gupta, *Print Areas: Book History in India* (Delhi: Permanent Black, 2004).

3 Boehmer, *Indian Arrivals.*

4 Paul Carter, *The Road to Botany Bay* (London: Faber, 1987); Mary Louise Pratt, *Under Imperial Eyes: Travel Writing and Transculturation* (London: Routledge, 1992). See also J. M. Coetzee, *White Writing* (Boston: Harvard University Press, 1988).

5 See Paul Gilroy, *The Black Atlantic* (London: Verso, 1993), chapter 1, in particular in this context his discussion of Martin Delany's identity as formed through a "process of movement and mediation."

6 See Benedict Anderson, *Imagined Communities*, rev. ed. (London: Verso, 1991); and his *The Spectre of Comparisons* (London: Verso, 1998).

7 See Sumit Sarkar, "Rammohun Roy and the Break with the Past," in V. C. Joshi, ed., *Rammohun Roy and the Process of Modernization in India* (New Delhi: Vikas, 1975), 63.

8 Partha Mitter, *The Triumph of Modernism* (London: Reaktion, 2009), in particular 10–11, 229. Indian cities, Mitter writes, were dynamic sites where Western capital and the forces of global modernity most forcefully impacted on the subcontinent, and where, in consequence, fruitful interactions between near and far, global and local, the Western avant-garde and home-grown anticolonialists, took place. Bombay, in particular, was from its outset a cosmopolitan even more than an imperial city, its early settlement in the late 1660s having involved different diasporic communities seeking commercial opportunities, not least Gujerati Parsis, the Malabari community, and Baghdadi Jews such as the Sassoon family. Bombay's Sarasenic Gothic architecture, for example, drew influences from several different cultural sources, most prominently the Mughal Empire and the Victorian neo-Gothic. See also Preeti Chopra, *A Joint Enterprise: Indian Elites and the Making of British Bombay* (Minneapolis: University of Minnesota Press, 2011); Ramachandra Guha, *Gandhi before India* (New York: Vintage, 2015), 60–61.

9 See Felix Driver and David Gilbert, eds., *Imperial Cities: Landscape, Display and Identity* (Manchester: Manchester University Press, 1999).

10 The following commentary is based on the 1886 copies of the *Indian Mirror* held in the Asutosh Collection, National Library of India, Kolkata, read in March 2009. Brahmo Samaj-leaning, the *Indian Mirror* was at the time of the 1911 Durbar still going strong, at which point Satyendra Nath Sen, subeditor from 1886, became chief editor.

11 The May 4, 1886 issue carried an advertisement for Thacker, Spink and Co., now perhaps better known as the publishers of Charlotte Brontë's *Jane Eyre* in India. See Josephine McDonagh, "Rethinking Provincialism in Mid-Nineteenth-Century Fiction: *Our Village* to *Villette*," *Victorian Studies* 55. 3 (Spring 2013): 399–424.

12 RozinaVisram, *Asians in Britain: 400 Years of History* (London: Pluto Press, 2002) lays particular emphasis on the relative multiplicity and diversity of early Indian presences in Britain, and Antoinette Burton, *At the Heart of the Empire: Indians and the Colonial Encounter in Late-Victorian England* (Berkeley: University of California Press, 1998) on the many contingencies through which their cultural identities were shaped.

13 See Antoinette Burton and Isabel Hofmeyr, eds., *Creating an Imperial Commons: Books that Shaped the Modern British Empire* (Durham: Duke University Press, 2014).

8

The Cosmopolitan Experience and Its Uses

THOMAS BENDER

While there is not a common understanding or definition of cultural cosmopolitanism or a politics of cosmopolitanism, the phrase is understood to have a positive valence and progressive implications.[1] Certainly, in the global and multicultural 1990s many progressives turned to cosmopolitanism as a desirable cultural and political value. This association of cosmopolitanism with *ethnos* is currently understood as positive. But there is always the danger of the flip side. The word and the idea also have a darker connotation in central Europe in the late nineteenth and early twentieth centuries where it was an anti-Semitic epithet.

I want to reframe the way we think of cosmopolitanism, making it an experience and a quality. Rather than thinking of it as an idea, a political category, theory, or analytical concept, I propose that cosmopolitanism is most usefully understood as an *experience* with both cultural and political implications. I have two reasons. One is mildly theoretical, prompted by Bruno Latour's challenge to sociological concepts that have no empirical existence. For Latour the most notorious example is the sociological tradition derived from Emile Durkheim's master concept of the "social" or a "social fact."[2] The second posits that the world of difference, the foundation of cosmopolitanism, is a domain of inevitable uncertainties and recalculations about oneself and of people and places. Thus cosmopolitanism is not a thing but an active, even unsettling ongoing process. The cosmopolitan is not, as in popular usage, a person who is easy moving around the world, never uncomfortable. My notion of cosmopolitanism is at odds with the long-standing commonplace that "cosmopolitan people" are those who are "able to feel at home anywhere."[3]

Cosmopolitanism, as I understand it, is challenging, even hard work. It is best understood within the experiential and experimental framework of the pragmatism of William James and John Dewey. Both James and Dewey challenged enclosure and celebrated experience. Experience is active; it cannot be reduced to a thing. James believed that concepts and descriptions needed to be unstiffened as "experience overflows its own definition."[4] For Dewey experience is fundamental. It is used in the title of two of his most important books. Early on he trained his mind on the "processes of experiencing."[5] Dewey's article in 1894 on "The Reflex Arc in Psychology," the publication that moved James to embrace Dewey as a vital colleague, elided the mind-body problem by displacing the stimulus-response notion of mind and behavior. For Dewey, the movement from stimulus to action was not phased; it was a single event. If that argument was celebrated by James for solving the mind-body problem, it can also be understood as locating experience at the center of human knowing and action.[6]

The cosmopolitan, as I understand it, is someone for whom experience is consequential. By that I mean that new experiences are neither casually absorbed nor exoticized. New experience for the cosmopolitan is moderately unsettling. Such an unsettling stimulates inquiry into the novelty or difference. But—and this is the main point—it also prompts introspection by the cosmopolitan. The cosmopolitan is open to the unease of forming a new understanding of both one's self and of the world when invited by the confrontation of difference. Cosmopolitanism is not a seeking of universal commensurability, or what James called "monism" and Karl Mannheim characterized as the impulse of individuals and groups "to make their interpretation of the world universal."[7] The cosmopolitan, by contrast, turns inward to introspection in the face of outward difference. The issue in a world of difference is not the play between particularism and universalism, but rather that of particularism and particularism. It implies being open to a particular kind of novel experience.

Jane Addams not only embodied this sort of cosmopolitanism at Hull House in immigrant Chicago, but she explained it and its importance in *Democracy and Social Ethics* (1907). The transformative moment begins with a sense of unease, or, as she put it, "maladjustment" in the world surrounding oneself. "We are learning," she wrote, "that a standard of social ethics is not attained by travelling a sequestered byway but by mixing in the thronged and common road." Engaging and experiencing that world of difference nourishes a "democratic spirit, for it implies that diversified human experience and the resultant sympathy which are the foundation and guarantee of Democracy." For her, "social perspective and sanity come only from contact with social experience; that is the surest corrective of opinions concerning the social order." Such experience of a "wide reading of human life" enables a "new affinity for all men, which probably never existed in the world before." She places the citizen under a "moral obligation" to choose "our experiences, since the result of those experiences must ultimately determine our understanding of life."[8]

I think Addams is not too far from what Anthony Appiah calls "rooted cosmopolitanism," but she insists on more. Her understanding demands much more introspection and negotiation.[9] She expects nothing less than a serious inquiry into one's own sense of self as well as the character of the "other." My sense of what this burden implies is articulated in a passage in Clifford Geertz's *Local Knowledge*. It is a passage to which my thinking often returns:

> To see ourselves as others see us can be eye-opening. To see others as sharing a nature with us is mere decency. But it is from the far more difficult achievement of seeing ourselves amongst others, as a local example of the forms of human life locally taken, a case among cases, a world among worlds, that the largeness of mind, without which objectivity is self-congratulation and tolerance a sham, comes.[10]

Again, such cosmopolitanism is not easy. In fact, one must be aware that the cosmopolitan experience as here described is always slightly subversive of one's sense of self and one's relation to a "home" culture. A cosmopolitan must cultivate a doubleness that allows both commitment and distance, an awareness at once of the possible distance of the self and of the possibility of dialogical knowledge of the other person or group. The echo of W. E. B. Dubois is intended.[11]

As already noted, this understanding of cosmopolitanism is quite a distance from the notion of the cosmopolitan as one who is comfortable anywhere. William James warned that "whoever says that the whole world tells one story utters another of those monistic dogmas that man believes at his risk." It is easy, he added, to "see the world pluralistically, as a rope of which each fibre tells a separate tale; but to conceive each cross-section of the rope as an absolutely single fact, and to sum the whole longitudinal series into one being living an undivided life, is harder."[12]

The cosmopolitan mixes unfamiliarity and recognition. The cosmopolitan is engaged but always slightly uncomfortable, even at home. There is something of the sensibility of the migrant or exile. Tzetvan Todorov has made this point with an account of a comment *and* the pathway that brought the comment to his attention. "The man who holds his country sweet is only a raw beginner; the man for whom each country is as his own is already strong; but only the man for whom the whole world is a foreign country is perfect." The route that brought this comment to him was in a way a map of cosmopolitanism: Todorov, a Bulgarian living in Paris, took it from Edward Said, a Palestinian long resident of New York, who took it from Eric Auerbach, a refugee German Jew living in Istanbul.[13] The cosmopolitan's own world and its surround become themselves objects of inquiry and selfhood.

In recent years, a number of scholars have contrasted the nation-state and empire, with the former intolerant of difference and the latter far more tolerant.[14] This is not universally true. In fact, as Carl Nightingale has recently shown, racial residential segregation may have been invented in the cities of British India in the eighteenth century.[15] But the Ottoman Empire is the preferred example for this claim, and the imperial authorities did accommodate a large number of different cultures and polities. As long as taxes were paid to the sultan in Istanbul, different cultural and religious groups were allowed to organize their lives in ways fitting their own preferences. This is often referenced as an instance of cosmopolitanism, but I think the Ottomans supported pluralism and toleration. Tolerance is a considerable virtue, but if it is cosmopolitanism, it is cosmopolitanism lite, as it does not demand self-reflexivity.

However, the French Empire in eighteenth-century North America provided an example of what might be called a cosmopolitan world. In his celebrated book, *The Middle Ground: Indians, Empires, and Republics in the Great Lakes Region, 1650–1815*, Richard White shows how far partial intercultural understanding (or partial misunderstanding, as he describes it) created a cosmopolitan world that embraced Europeans and Native Americans. Neither the Native Americans nor the French Recollect missionaries, Jesuits, colonial officials, traders, and trappers fully understood the other, but neither did they seek to extend or impose their own worldview. In a pattern of perhaps deliberate misunderstanding that was driven by mutual need, difference and collaboration enabled each to find analogues in the other culture by looking in fresh ways at their own culture. They did not enter into the worldview of the other—though a few "went native." But they grasped enough to actually learn more about themselves and ways they could comprehend and be comprehended by the others. That, to me, is an example of cosmopolitanism. It was built on experience and it was active. It was not easy; it depended on needs (trade), and the power and resources had to be relatively equal, making for a reasonably level playing field—a "middle ground," as White characterizes it.[16]

On that ground they sought analogues, not perfect ones, but workable ones. They did not fully enter into the world of the other—or have any desire to do so. But they did enter enough to establish a working mutuality. Both practicality and discomfort prompted the self-reflection that pointed toward a Jamesian cosmopolitanism. In his discussion in *Pragmatism* of how ideas change, James made the point that rethinking or reorganizing our ideas is often the result of an "inward trouble."[17] For James this discomfort applied to the challenge of being a cosmopolitan, as he explained in a letter of 1894: "One should not be a cosmopolitan; one's soul becomes 'disintegrated.' . . . One's native land seems foreign. It is not wholly a good thing, and I suffer for it."[18]

For centuries the homes of cosmopolitanism have been cities and the sea. Melville's South Sea novels, including *Moby Dick*, reveal the cosmopolitanism of the sea.[19] Cities, like empires, but more consistently, have shown themselves more open to cosmopolitanism than nation-states, which tend to seek uniformity or sameness, whether of language, religion, skin color, or ethnicity.

If the metropolis is the natural home of cosmopolitanism, the suburb—especially the gated community version—is its opposite. The metropolis more or less enforces immediate confrontation with social difference. Of course, it is possible, even all too common, to avoid the recognition of others. But my point is that even recognition is not enough for the experience that makes a cosmopolitan. Sometimes extremely different experience produces recoil, even fear, that may be difficult to overcome. Whether intense or mild, the point is not just engagement with the other, but self-reflexivity. One has to become in some degree less at home with one's city and one's self on the way to becoming a cosmopolitan. The experience that makes a cosmopolitan is at once a partial understanding of the other and an enriching partial reunderstanding of one's self. It is not easy.

It was such an understanding that underlay the urban theories of Frederick Law Olmsted, the nineteenth-century designer of Central Park and other great urban spaces. He thought that Broadway sidewalks and those of other crowded streets produced a suspicion of others: too much rushing, too great a need for alertness, too much worry about confronting a pickpocket, too little time for reflection about those about you or yourself. "Our minds are thus brought into close dealings with other minds without any friendly flowing toward them." He added that city life produces "a tendency to regard others in a hard if not always hardening way." Most important, he felt that such "conditions" compelled urban dwellers "to look closely upon others without sympathy."[20]

Olmsted's concern about sympathy is not that of a Hallmark card. It is a potentially transforming experience. Olmsted's usage is described by Adam Smith in his *Theory of the Moral Sentiments* (1759). Smith called for an effort of imagination to understand, to feel some affinity with another person who is marked by difference.

> As we have no immediate experience of what other men feel, we can form no idea of the manner in which they are affected, but by conceiving what we ourselves should feel in the like situation. . . . By the imagination we place ourselves in his situation.[21]

Smith's example predicates a confrontation with another person in pain or distress. But his point is sympathy in the face of difference. In fact, one of Smith's examples of this act of sympathy was that of a male imagining himself in the position of a woman experiencing the pain associated with labor.

One's engagement with difference, whether marked by pain or any other condition of difference, provides an *experience* that prompts both a reaching out and a self-reflexive awareness. What Smith calls sympathy is a double action that could be characterized—as Smith does—as a moral act of recognition and engagement. That experience reorients us to the world around us, whether in a small or large way. And that is the foundation of cosmopolitanism.

Olmsted's New York was a somewhat chaotic mix of peoples and cultures, made all the more unsettling as the capitalist economy encouraged competition rather than sympathy. Alienated labor marked not only the working classes but the emerging middle classes as well. It was the city of Herman Melville's "Bartleby the Scrivener" and the urban experience that he described in the opening page of *Moby Dick* (1851):

> There now is your insular city of the Manhattoes. . . . Right and left, the streets take you waterward. . . . Look at the crowds of water-gazers there. Circumambulate the city of a dreamy Sabbath afternoon. . . . What do you see? Posted like silent sentinels all around the town, stand thousands upon thousands of mortal men fixed on ocean reveries. . . . But these are all landsmen; of week days pent up in lath and plaster—tied to counters, nailed to benches, clinched to desks. How then is this? Are the green fields gone?[22]

Olmsted had been one of those clerks, having been apprenticed to a mercantile house on the East River. After a few months of misery he escaped by sea as crew on a China clipper. But that too disappointed him. In time he made his mark as the first and foremost American urban theorist and designer.

Olmsted's vision of metropolitanism at once affirmed the possibility of a shared public culture *and* recognized the permanence of social and cultural differences based on class, ethnicity, and gender. The Central Park was to be a terrain, free of the competitiveness of the capitalist city surrounding it and open to the multicultural population of the city. The park needed to be "so attractive as to force into contact the good & bad, the gentlemanly and the rowdy."[23]

He understood that the aesthetic experience of the landscapes he designed could not erase class division, but the park offered an "opportunity for people to come together for the single purpose of enjoyment, unembarrassed by the limitations with which they are surrounded at home, or in the pursuit of their daily avocations."[24] There is in this notion an insight that points toward the experience that can open one to a cosmopolitan understanding of different ways of being in society.

Recognizing the ineradicable social, economic, and cultural structures that divided the population of the metropolis, he insisted that there was a possibility in this grand common space for moments of recognition of the "other" in a shared experience. Olmsted reported to the American Social Science Association in 1870 that at the park "you may . . . often see vast numbers of persons brought closely together poor and rich, young and old, Jew and Gentile. I have seen a hundred thousand thus congregated." And he added, there was an evident "glee in the prospect of coming together, all classes largely represented . . . each individual adding by his mere presence to the pleasures of all others."[25] Without ceasing to be who they were, the thousands he described were surely affected by not only the difference of others, but of their own difference from others—yet enjoying the whole.

In designing Central Park (and many other American parks) Olmsted sought the opposite of New York's Union Square. At the time Olmsted began work on the park, Union Square was the lively hub of the city, the meeting place of all peoples, a role it played until 1904, when Long Acre Square became Times Square and replaced Union Square. His vision for the park was a world of serenity where the diverse population of the city could experience each other in an atmosphere that encouraged openness and mutual sympathies. The resulting cosmopolitanism would, he felt, both enrich individual lives and sustain a vital public life.

Yet Olmsted was in the end too cautious. He misunderstood or failed to grasp the dynamic of the social world of Union Square. He erred in thinking that cosmopolitanism could only be enacted under the controlled conditions of the park, where rural aesthetics and heavy policing were thought to be essential reassurance for a diverse public. In fact, Union Square, which unnerved him, worked in a way that was more similar to his understanding of the park than he could imagine. The confrontation with difference was more dramatic, perhaps even harsher. Yet there was often a cosmopolitan result.

Union Square was a meeting point of many New Yorks. If immigrants flanked the Square on the southeast, to the west was exclusive Fifth Avenue. Just a block off the Northeast perimeter was the city's most gracious residential block, Gramercy Park. Nearby the Gilder-deKay "studio" was the city's most important salon, hosted by editor Richard Watson Gilder and the artist Helena deKay, where writers, theater people, and artists met every week. Next door to the Gilder home was the Century Club, where the gentry of the city gathered when they were not at the Union League Club, also on the Square.

All around the Square were restaurants, hotels, and shops of every kind. There was, of course, Delmonico's, but there was also Moretti's restaurant, where Americans were introduced to spaghetti, macaroni, and Chianti. Tiffany's, Brentano's Literary Emporium, Stewart's Department Store, and Lord and Taylor were destinations at the Square for the elite. At the counters of these department stores elite women were served by working-class women. But these women related to each other differently at the nearby Consumer's League, a cross-class organization where "shop girl" and "consumer" worked on behalf of "shop girls" and seamstresses.

If Steinway Hall and the Academy of Music anchored Fourteenth Street just east of the Square, all around there were various popular entertainments that drew the working class. Tin Pan Alley had its origin here, and the Palace Gardens provided entertainments ranging from fireworks and pagodas to mimes, magic, ventriloquism, and Indian dances. At the Hippotheatron across the street from the Academy of Music, there were acrobatics, pantomimes, and equestrian shows. A little farther east was Luchows, a German restaurant, and Hubert's Dime Museum. The Square was also the home of Tammany Hall, where elites and union leaders collaborated. Tony Pastor's Theatre (in the lower level of the Hall), was where vaudeville was invented, drawing popular audiences.

This listing—and it is partial—reveals the complexity and openness of this central space in the city. With a mix of uses and classes tugging at each other, a diverse public was formed on this terrain. It was the kind of experience that nourished cosmopolitanism. Here the particular, homogeneous cultures of the city's different populations came into contact and awareness. Out of this interaction men and women were confronted with experiences that forced both observation of the "other" and self-reflection. Each contributed to the whole of a distinctive "public," and each brought back to the *gemeinschaftlich* world of their local community something new and different to think about—providing the foundation for a more cosmopolitan sensibility.

Such experiences as I have pulled out of history are harder to find today. If cosmopolitanism is defined as a lived relation to difference that both reaches out to others and into one's own self, an era of making urban cosmopolitans may be coming to an end. Both the definition and the making of the cosmopolitanism I have emphasized here has been dependent upon spaces and interactions that characterized metropolitan cities between roughly 1850 and 1950. Since then urbanism has vastly changed, as massive migrations of peoples on every continent have moved into sprawling and divided megalopolises, where the conjunctures that were once at Union Square are unlikely. The spatial reorganization of our lives and the vast expansion of digital relations together radically limit social experience. The dissolution of that experience will either weaken, even dissolve, the ideal and experience of cosmopolitanism or invite us to create and locate new experiences that will nourish a new cosmopolitanism and the cosmopolitan experience.

NOTES

1 For a recent analysis of the complexity of the language of cosmopolitanism, see Giles Gunn, *Ideas to Die For: The Cosmopolitan Challenge* (New York: Routledge, 2013).

2 Bruno Latour, "Gabriel Tarde and the End of the Social," in Patrick Joyce, ed., *The Social in Question: New Bearings on the History of the Social Sciences* (London: Routledge, 2002), 117–32.

3 Harriet Prescott Spofford, *Art Decoration Applied to Furniture* (New York: Harper & Brothers, 1877), 162, referring to the incorporation of "Oriental" materials and themes in domestic settings.

4 Quoted in Ross Posnock, *The Trial of Curiosity: Henry James, William James, and the Challenge of Modernity* (New York: Oxford University Press, 1991), 10.

5 John Dewey, *Experience and Nature* (LaSalle, Ill.: Open Court, 1925), 10. He also used experience in the title of *Art as Experience* (New York: Minton, Balch & Company, 1934).

6 John Dewey, "The Reflex Arc Concept in Psychology," *Psychological Review*, 3 (1896), 357–70.

7 Karl Mannheim, "Competition as a Cultural Phenomenon," in his *Essays on the Sociology of Culture* (London: Routledge & Kegan Paul, 1956), 196–98.

8 Jane Addams, *Democracy and Social Ethics* [1907], ed. Anne Firor Scott (Cambridge: Harvard University Press, 1964), 7, 9–10.

9 K. Anthony Appiah, *Cosmopolitanism: Ethics in a World of Strangers* (New York: W. W. Norton, 2006). Addams and Appiah are closer if she is compared with his earlier book, *In My Father's House: Africa in the Philosophy of Culture* (New York: Oxford University Press, 1992).

10 Clifford Geertz, *Local Knowledge: Further Essays in Interpretive Anthropology* (New York: Basic Books, 1983), 16.

11 See his *Souls of Black Folk: Essays and Sketches* (Greenwich, Conn.: Fawcett, 1961), chap. 1.

12 William James, *The Writings of William James*, ed. John J. McDermott (Chicago: University of Chicago Press, 1977), 411.

13 Tzetvan Todorov, *The Conquest of America: The Question of the Other*, trans. Richard Howard (New York: Harper & Row, 1984).

14 See especially the impressive book by Jane Burbank and Fred Cooper, *Empires in World History* (Princeton: Princeton University Press, 2010) for an argument for empire in respect to the matter of the politics of difference in empires.

15 Carl Nightingale, *Segregation: A Global History of Divided Cities* (Chicago: University of Chicago Press, 2012).

16 Richard White, *The Middle Ground: Indians, Empires, and Republics in the Great Lakes Region, 1650–1815* (New York: Cambridge University Press, 1991).

17 William James, *Pragmatism and Other Writings*, ed. Giles Gunn (New York: Penguin, 2000), 31.

18 Letter to Carl Stumpf, "Familiar Letters of William James—II," *Atlantic Monthly* (online), August 1920.

19 See also Marcus Rediker and Peter Linebaugh, *The Many-Headed Hydra: Sailors, Slaves, Commoners, and the Hidden History of the Revolutionary Atlantic* (Boston: Beacon, 2000); Greg Dening, *Beach Crossings: Voyaging across Time, Culture, and Self* (Philadelphia: University of Pennsylvania Press, 2004); Mauricio Tenorio-Trillo, *I Speak of the City: Mexico City at the Turn of the Twentieth Century* (Chicago: University of Chicago Press, 2012).

20 Frederick Law Olmsted, "Public Parks and the Enlargement of Towns," *Journal of Social Science* 3 (1871), 11, 22.

21 Adam Smith, *The Theory of Moral Sentiments* (Oxford: Oxford University Press, 1976), 9.

22 Herman Melville, *Moby Dick, or the Whale* (Boston: Houghton Mifflin, 1956), 1.

23 *The Papers of Frederick Law Olmsted*, eds. Charles Beveridge and Charles Capen McLaughlin (Baltimore: Johns Hopkins University Press, 1981), vol. 2, 236.

24 Albert Fein, ed., *Landscape into Cityscape: Frederick Law Olmsted's Plans for a Greater New York City* (Ithaca: Cornell University Press, 1967), 101.

25 Olmsted, "Public Parks and the Enlargement of Towns," 18–19.

9

Cosmopolitanism and the Claims of Religious Identity

JEAN BETHKE ELSHTAIN

In many discussions of the topic, the word "cosmopolitan" carries an undertone of moral superiority, especially in relation to claims of faith. It does not advance the discussion, however, to locate religious faith and commitment *prima facie* on the parochial and particularistic side of the ledger, and enlightenment, universal consciousness, and other high-sounding things on the other. Rather, one should acknowledge this attitude of moral superiority and move past it. In an attempt to do so, I will approach the topic of the cosmopolitan idea and religion from an angle informed by political history and thought.

Among the eighteenth-century intelligentsia in Europe, the notion of the cosmopolite was often that of the *Luftamach*, the person who was at home anywhere, which is to say nowhere in particular. The cosmopolite could drop into cultures, be there for a period of time, and then move on. He or she traveled very lightly. This notion of the cosmopolite brings to mind Milan Kundera's great novel *The Unbearable Lightness of Being*. Some of those interested in cosmopolitanism surely know the novel. One of the female protagonists, Sabina, is very light indeed. She is born in Prague but finds a home in Switzerland. She sheds part of her identity as she goes, just as she sheds relationships. Her heavy identity is associated with her tragic homeland, Czechoslovakia, and she rids herself of much of that, winding up on the northeastern shores of the United States. The other female protagonist, Tereza, is very heavy. When Russian troops march into her homeland during the Prague Spring in 1968, she has to be there. It is her home and her native soil clings to her. She cannot be at home—truly at home—anywhere else. Thus the novel presents a contrast between two ways of inhabiting identities.

In terms of this contrast, one could ask, as an aspect of identity is religion light or heavy? To answer, certain religious identities are inhabited lightly, while others are heavy. American Protestantism is a very light religion that can be quite comfortable with a kind of thin universalism, indeed, that historically has been one of the bearers of that kind of universalism. But heavier religious identities represent a more difficult proposition. Evangelical Christianity, Catholicism, Islam, and several forms of Judaism are all strong faiths, with strong claims of adherence. Most often we think of the claims of religion in relation to the claims of nationality. How do faith and citizenship comport? How is religion enacted in the public sphere? For the devout Christian, Muslim, or Jew, circumscribing the practice of their religion to the private sphere runs directly counter to requirements of faith that involve forms of public expression.

My experience as part of an ongoing dialogue with Arab Muslim scholars called the "Malta Forum" for half a decade is instructive in this respect. During our second meeting, we made something of a breakthrough. In our previous discussions we scholars from the United States heard that a thoroughly secularist society was unacceptable from a Muslim perspective. Our response was that there is secularism—and then there is secularism. Not all forms of the secular are the same.

We insisted that the American mode of dealing with the issues of faith and civic life is significantly different from the French tradition of *laicité*, for example. French *laicité* involves a hard separation not only between church and state, but between politics and religion on the level of civil society and civic expression. These principles of the secular, interestingly enough, are not in the name of *no* religion, but in that of a religion of the state. The notion of *laicité* anticipated that there should be a kind of civic religion. Certainly that was the project of the makers of the French Revolution and the ardent defenders of the *laicité* tradition in its aftermath. Atatürk's revolution in Turkey also reflected these principles of *laicité*. But in America, the development of secularism was a different story. There was a juridical separation of church and state. There was no religion of the state, no establishment faith, but plenty of intermingling of religion and politics on the level of civil society, part of the freedoms protected by the First Amendment. This demonstrated, we insisted, that there can exist a secular state and at the same time a society that was not totally secularized. That is to say, there can exist a civil society in which concepts and ethics, concerns and enthusiasms inspired by faith might find a home, and indeed historically did so. At this point we would usually cite part of the enormous list of great civic movements inspired by faith in American history, including of course Martin Luther King and the Southern Christian Leadership Conference.

Where does cosmopolitanism enter into any of this? Perhaps we can work by analogy from *laïcité* and the contrasting American experience. Certainly there is one version of cosmopolitanism that is openly hostile to any and all particular claims, whether they are the claims of a particular national, ethnic, religious, or other identity. According to this version of cosmopolitanism, we will meander in the darkness until we shed particularisms in favor of global consciousness, universal citizenship, or some such idea that is often presented in quite vague terms. But this is not the only option, surely. There is also a form of universal identity and consciousness, whether cosmopolitanism is the best name for it or not, that cherishes particular commitments and in fact views them as steps toward more inclusive identities that are infused with instances of universality—"universal moments"—and mutual interdependency.

Human beings certainly do not start out in a universal "someplace." Rather, everyone starts out as a helpless infant in a very particular place, usually called home. As one grows older, one's horizons expand, one's vision extends, and one comes to see others in a variety of new contexts. The most robust universalism, however, never loses touch with the particular; there is a back and forth between it and strong particular commitments. In an essay from some years ago, the political theorist Michael Walzer wrote of thick and thin identities. On the one hand, if identity is too thick one can become mired in a kind of dogged nationalism or ethnocentrism, or a very defensive and bristling understanding of faith. That is, one may become not only an adherent of one's own faith but also hostile toward the claims of the faiths of others. But on the other hand, if identity is too thin then one has no real commitments at all. The great political philosopher Hannah Arendt once insisted that one cannot be a citizen of the world, as one is a citizen of a particular polity. She was referring to concrete forms of responsibility and accountability. To say that one is a citizen of the world has a nice ring to it, but what does it mean in terms of concrete requirements or responsibilities? It might mean, for example, that if one thinks of citizenship in a more universalist way one wants to extend certain rights under the rubric of hospitality, or through some other understanding, to those who are not citizens of one's own polity. But that very extension turns on a strong notion of civic standing. Thus one sees the back-and-forth relationship between the universal and the particular. One can also think of attempts to create a universality without reference to a particular, on the level of language with the project of Esperanto, for instance. The project of a universal language failed, and failed miserably, because it was entirely invented. It was not thick with life like our mother tongues. They are called mother tongues for a reason: they nurture us, they help us to grow up, and they help to orient us within a particular place.

In my own work in the past, I have suggested that cosmopolitanism is a way to try to connect moral intuitions and concrete recognitions to certain claims that are broader than those of the self. I have suggested that one of the reasons we can respond, for example, to the cries of the homeless, is that we know what a home means, and therefore have some idea of what it means to be homeless. We can respond to the orphan because we know what a family means. We can respond to the dilemma of being stripped of citizenship because we know what citizenship means. Everything we know about moral development demonstrates that we have to begin with strong, particular, concrete recognitions. We do not begin our moral development at the heights of abstraction with some Kantian categorical imperative.

Interestingly enough, this has implications for what we usually call ecumenism as well. For some, ecumenism means that one has to dilute every religious commitment until it becomes something that everyone can agree upon, but then one is left with only very weak commitments. Far more interesting is the version of ecumenism that challenges those who adhere to strong religious commitments to engage with one another, to share a world with one another, and to learn from one another without requiring one another to relinquish some vital belief. For example, if one were to ask a Christian to give up the belief in Jesus as the son of God in the name of ecumenism, the serious Christian could only shake her head in disbelief. Just as the belief in Christ as the son of God is central to Christianity, there are beliefs that are essential to Islam, Judaism, and all other religions that cannot be compromised without compromising the religion itself. If cosmopolitanism requires discarding strong, particular commitments and beliefs, then it is not compatible with serious faith. But if one imagines a more capacious and complex cosmopolitanism, then one can imagine a dynamic understanding that can accommodate both thick and thin religious identities. We can find ways to accommodate these identities and ways in which to enrich one another so that certain universal ideas and claims penetrate our understanding of the particular and conversely, our understanding of the universal is penetrated by concrete, particular recognitions that have some thickness.

PART III

Power

10

The Cosmopolitan Idea and National Sovereignty

ROBERT J. C. YOUNG

What is the relation of the cosmopolitan idea to national sovereignty? The connection between them goes back at least two centuries, but it has been changing as the links between them have mutated under the pressure of the politics of different times. Historically, the cosmopolitan idea was originally an idea directed *against* the idea of the nation and its claims for sovereignty. The first formulations in this arena were largely German, made in a dramatic counterspirit against French nationalism before the nation-state of Germany was created. Goethe, Kant, Heine, Schiller—all affirmed their loyalty to the cosmopolitan idea of a universal humanity rather than a national identity. In an ironic twist, a unified Germany then subsequently developed instead the most extreme form of nationalism, in the course of which the term "cosmopolitan" was downgraded from its original meaning of belonging to the society of humanity to being widely used to designate the undesirable enemies of the state, rootless aliens, particularly communists and Jews. The cosmopolitan was transformed into the inmate of the camp.

The decline of the prestige of European political concepts in the aftermath of fascism provided the context for Hannah Arendt's comment on what she characterized as "the bankruptcy of the nation state and its concept of sovereignty."[1] Sovereignty, which Arendt associated with "the claim to unchecked and unlimited power in foreign affairs," legitimates a state violence, uncontrolled and uncontained by law, that eventually turns inward.[2] In this situation, the concept of cosmopolitanism has been reversed back into a positive term, offering a new international perspective and order that could establish legal and ethical standards for a world in which the sovereign state, the guarantor of the rights of the citizen, is seen to have failed. Cosmopolitanism offers a new form of internationalism: in the nineteenth century, nationalism had been opposed by the internationalism of Marx and socialism, which had spoken for, without being able to ensure, the rights and welfare of the international working class, who were frequently more subjects than citizens, with few guarantees of rights of any kind. The new cosmopolitanism anticipated by Arendt no longer operates in a binary opposition with nationalism, nor with the complementary emotion of patriotism.

The shift has taken place not merely because the system of nation-states is by definition already international—you cannot have a nation without other nations—but also because, as Seyla Benhabib has argued, the UN Universal Declaration of Human Rights in 1946 signaled a profound transformation of the concept of the international itself. The rights and sovereignty of nations, established through international treaties and so on, were shifted to the rights and claims of individuals: "This is the uniqueness of the many human rights agreements signed since World War II. They signal an eventual transition from a model of international law based on treaties among states to cosmopolitan law understood as international public law that binds and bends the will of sovereign nations."[3]

This profound transformation facilitated the development of a new cosmopolitanism. Cosmopolitanism—with its claims for universal human rights, including the rights of those who legally have no state to guarantee such rights, such as stateless refugees, migrants, child soldiers, or women and children ensnared in human trafficking—does not so much operate in opposition to ideas of national sovereignty but has transformed the status of sovereignty itself, so that the sovereign state (and any of its officers), instead of being the guarantor of rights, becomes answerable morally and in international law to the universal rights of humans. Cosmopolitanism, we might say, names a new form and practice of mediation, between the sovereignty of the state and the claims of the universal, between nation and individual, between the sovereign state and the ethics of human hospitality.

Is it possible to formulate a "transnational" or, in Homi Bhabha's terms, "vernacular" cosmopolitanism that can reconcile the competing and often conflictual claims that cosmopolitanism attempts to mediate today? In this context, cosmopolitanism has become less a contemporary idea that needs to be defined than an idea that encapsulates a series of questions that may or may not have an answer. Here, in no particular order, are just five of them:

1. How can the relation of the universal claims of cosmopolitanism to human values be mediated with the internal workings of the state, particularly in democracies? How can the universal claims of cosmopolitanism be mediated with the still autonomous rights of local democracy and with the disjunctive experiences of marginalized or minority communities—differences that may require us to rethink the form of the universal itself? One thinks in this respect of Anthony Appiah's argument that for the most part, the problem is not that one part of the world is claiming as universal something that another part of the world sees as alien, because in fact most ethical concepts claimed as universal such as "justice" or "hospitality," would be acknowledged by all.[4] In that sense, relativists fail to recognize that universals do exist. The problem is less their existence as universals than the fact that their interpretation, and hence their implementation, differs, as in the idea of justice, or, we might add, even democracy and freedom. Everyone more or less agrees on the idea of justice and a just world, but the problem, as Amartya Sen has pointed out, is that different people or societies inevitably have different ideas of justice.[5] How can we reconcile them, or establish a conversation that may begin to mediate if not resolve their differences?

2. Whereas the coalescence of nation and state meant the consolidation of citizenship with forms of ethnic or cultural belonging, the identification for individuals and groups of the one with the other, cosmopolitanism raises the question of how new forms of belonging in a world marked by migration, diaspora, and transnational labor might be understood in relation to those older forms of singular cultural identification. Nationalism's now largely abandoned utopia (or perhaps rather dystopia) of a homogeneous nation has allowed the articulation of different forms of identification that more resemble a Venn diagram with overlapping constituencies, some of which may fall inside the state, some outside, others in its hitherto unacknowledged peripheries. This situation is particularly true for minorities who are the product of relatively recent immi-

gration; their identifications are not a matter of choosing between identifications but of having multiple, simultaneous identifications.

In times past, such overlapping loyalties were considered a threat to the state: for example, loyalty to Rome among Catholics in early nineteenth-century Britain was regarded as a menacing disavowal of loyalty to the nation. In the modality of nationalism, you either identified with your nation or you did not, as in the British politician Lord Tebbit's famous test for national belonging formulated more recently in the Thatcher era: which cricket team do you support—England, India, or Pakistan? But the modality of minoritarian status in today's nation is that you do not have to choose between your nation and your cricket team—you can identify with both, a new kind of relation that we live every day and that governs our diasporic identities. Can the cosmopolitan idea enable a new theorization of the relation of the sovereign state to forms of transnational identification, a move that will involve breaking down the inside-outside dichotomy on which the nation-state is predicated and on which many of its policies are formulated? Can the sovereign state find modes of inclusivity for those legal or illegal aliens within its borders, whose lives are lived within its polity and on whose labor the polity often depends?

3. German sociologist Ulrich Beck has argued that the difference between Kant's cosmopolitan idea of 1784 and that of today is that the cosmopolitan is no longer an idea; indeed, Beck would deny the validity of the title of this essay.[6] He argues that both at the level of human rights treaties and the international institutions that attempt to enforce them, and at other levels of what he calls banal cosmopolitanism, the cosmopolitanism in which we live every day as a result of the international forces of globalization, cosmopolitanism has today become materialized and institutionalized. It is no longer merely an idea. For instance we could think of NYU Abu Dhabi in this sense as a typical phenomenon of our cosmopolitan era. As both an independent university in the Middle East and at the same time an integral part of New York University, its structure also characterizes what Beck, heavily influenced by the writings of Homi K. Bhabha, calls the "both/and" structure of cosmopolitanism, which replaces the "either/or" structure of nationalism.[7]

Cosmopolitanism has become materially realized at the level of what in postcolonial theory we call the subaltern, the often invisible people at the bottom of society. In this context, we should acknowledge the other cosmopolitanism of Abu Dhabi: the vast pool of migrant workers and laborers from the Middle East and South Asia who are actually building NYU Abu Dhabi and who embody a very different version of the cosmopolitan experience. What is the relation of such cosmopolitans to the sovereign state in which they work, without the rights of citizenship? How can our academic disciplines, many of which are predicated on the form and boundaries of the nation-state, reconceptualize their objects of knowledge so as to take account of the changing human and material formations of the world that no longer correspond to national borders?

4. The reach of cosmopolitanism forces us to ask how we should formulate the relation of the sovereign state to the ethos of humanitarian intervention, where issues of human rights, or of genocide, legitimate intervention from outside. Will it be taken, as now seems to be the practice, as a case-by-case issue, according to the political pressures of the day? Somalia, yes, Rwanda, no. Is it possible to formulate more cogent and ethical rules for such situations?

Without such a framework in place, the danger has been that humanitarian cosmopolitanism has become a means of political and military intervention against a sovereign state when it suits the powers that have the power to intervene, whether in the name of destroying claimed weapons of mass destruction, or allegedly saving Muslim women from the burqa—but then, as a result, subjecting them, their children, and their families to the destructions of ongoing war. What, we might ask simply, are the politics of humanitarian cosmopolitanism in relation to national sovereignty? What do we make of the masculinist discourse that often seems to be at play in such discourses of cosmopolitanism that speak in the name of humanity?

5. How far has the cosmopolitan idea also reached out to include the new global social movements that have enabled the rise of new forms of politics, such as the global ecology movements, trans-

national women's movements, religious movements, or those of indigenous peoples who have utilized the possibility of transnational organizations and technology to articulate their claims with other comparable groups against their own individual sovereign states? To the extent that such activism could be seen to embody the continuing legacy of the anticolonial struggles of the twentieth century, what is the relation of the cosmopolitan idea to an older Left internationalism?

The questions that the relation of the cosmopolitan idea to sovereignty pose require us to broach many of the most fundamental political issues of our time. One further insistent question remains: how can we translate the cosmopolitan idea into a transformative reality?

NOTES

1 Hannah Arendt, *On Violence* (Orlando: Harcourt, 1970), 6.
2 Ibid., 5.
3 Seyla Benhabib, *Another Cosmopolitanism* (New York: Oxford University Press, 2006), 16.
4 Kwame Anthony Appiah, *Cosmopolitanism: Ethics in a World of Strangers* (New York: W. W. Norton, 2007).
5 Amartya Sen, *The Idea of Justice* (Cambridge, Mass.: Harvard University Press, 2009).
6 Ulrich Beck, *Cosmopolitan Vision* (Cambridge, Mass.: Polity Press, 2006).
7 Ibid., 57.

11

Spectral Sovereignty, Vernacular Cosmopolitans, and Cosmopolitan Memories

HOMI K. BHABHA

In keeping with the representational style and practice of taking the genre of the photograph, the snapshot as a kind of cosmopolitan exercise, I will present a text which consists of three snapshots: the first section of my essay is called "spectral sovereignty," the second "vernacular cosmopolitans," and the third "cosmopolitan memories." I do this in the spirit of one of the earliest cosmopolitical projects, the photographic archives of the Musée Albert-Kahn in Paris, that great "Archive of the Planet" for which Kahn sent photographers all across the world to take photographs (in Autochrome color) and to film. It's a remarkable archive of the way the world looked between 1909 and 1931, and it demonstrates the cosmopolitan interconnections at that time.

Before I start, I'd like to echo a point touched on by Robert Young in "The Cosmopolitan Idea and National Sovereignty." I have tried to answer some of Robert's questions, not in the order he's posed them, but as part of a narrative. It is of course true that certain cosmopolitan acts in the world can actually intensify national and ethnic relations, almost make them artificially intimate. In Dubai that is one of the issues for South Asian migrant workers. They literally live closer together than they would ever live otherwise. If you go a little bit outside cosmopolitan Dubai, you see a very different Dubai. This is something we should not forget: cosmopolitanism of various kinds produces its own artifices of ethnic identification, its own politics of identity, which of course you have to go and look for. But when you look for it, you find it. And what you find is one of the problems with the way in which a certain kind of market cosmopolitanism works transnationally.

Let me start with a few words from an article by Avishai Margalit which I'm very fond of, called "The Lesser Evil." It's a rather cryptic paragraph, an enigmatic set of rather deep ideas. I've tried in different ways to work with them, today and in other places. Margalit writes: "It is injustice, not justice, which brings us into normative politics; despotism, not freedom. Moral political theory should start with negative politics: the politics that informs us how to tackle evil before it tells us how to pursue the good."[1]

Spectral Sovereignty

Robert Young's finely crafted questions follow the dark trajectory of Margalit's thought. How often in the past century, and in this present one, have we not found ourselves stranded on the Via Dolorosa in any number of towns, countries, and villages, saying "Never Again"; and how often has human history responded with a sly, startling echo: "Again and Again and Again". Young invites us into the normative realm of cosmopolitanism by recalling Hannah Arendt's passionate condemnation of "the bankruptcy of the nation state and its concept of sovereignty" after Auschwitz.[2] And yet, almost half a century later, the Arendtian echo lives on in Agamben's statement, "The refugee should be considered for what he is, that is, nothing less than a border concept that radically calls into question the principles of the nation-state and, at the same time, helps clear the field for a no-longer-delayable renewal of categories."[3] What is the nature of the crisis of the nation-state today? Or to put it another way, in what sense does cosmopolitanism clear the way for a renewal of our human rights; the representation of global justice; and the construction of a polity of "equality-in-difference" that protects and propagates the interests of minorities, individuals, collectives, and groups—what Etienne Balibar has called "equaliberty"?[4]

To start with the negative politics of the nation-state—to move from injustice to an idea of justice, from tyranny to tolerance and beyond—should not turn us into gleeful undertakers busily burying the remains of the nation's tattered sovereignty. The sovereignty of the nation-state may have lost its ethical authority after Jim Crow or after Auschwitz or, more recently, after Rwanda, or after Gujarat. Its political sovereignty may have been compromised and displaced by some of the financial structures of neoliberal global markets, just as its territorial sovereignty has become permeable to nongovernmental organizations and, I must say, the generally weak enforcement of international legal regimes. These losses of sovereignty have also manifested themselves in new compromise-formations—the avatars of spectral sovereignty—that exercise a furious affective and imaginative sense of "national" belonging, often theological and political at the same time, among transnational and diasporic populations. There are those who believe that the sway of Hindutva stretches from India to New Jersey; others who see the *umma* as a global phenomenon capable of generating "an ethical life" commensurate with the cohesive intimacy of an Islamic national community wherever and whenever they may be living. For the Kashmiris, the Palestinians, and some First Nations peoples, the nation form is at once and ever a proleptic promise—the fulfillment of a future that knows no end in the sacrifice of lives and the loss of goods in the cause of a passionate patriotism.

Such spectral sovereignty must certainly not be understood as the national mimesis of minorities or the disposed alone. Powerful Western nations use the empowered prerogatives of "security"—Preemption, Redemption—to claim for themselves corners of a foreign field that are forever England, or France, or the United States. The ghosts of sovereignty are capable of reappearing in many garbs and speak in strange tongues. Gunboat democracy in Iraq was repeatedly justified as a cosmopolitical act that sought to go beyond "national consciousness" (which was abundant in Iraq), toward creating a model "civil society" that, as they put it, would stabilize the entire Middle East region and unify it so that the Euphrates would flow gently and docilely into the Thames, the Seine, and the Mississippi. What I am calling spectral sovereignty is not a leftover remnant of the Westphalian system that has somehow been resistant to the transformative forces of globalization or cosmopolitanism. It is a hybrid constellation of affect and political effect; a semblance of the past as it passes into the history of the present. Spectral sovereignty is produced in the asymmetrical and interstitial conditions of global disjunction and it is absolutely contemporary with attempts of globality to create market-based consumer cosmopolitanism.

Cultural theorists like ourselves—hypocrites lecteurs, mes semblables, mes frères—have rightly taken "sovereignty" to task, without sufficiently acknowledging the iterative and affective part of spectral sovereignty, whose global-cosmopolitical ambitions, adhesions, and affiliations are magnified and accelerated multiple times through new, digital technologies. It is as if an aching phantom limb (the notion of sovereignty) even though it has been severed, had found its perfectly fitting "virtual" prosthesis. When cultural theorists argue that "postmodernism" is the logic of global capital, or that "the world market establishes a real politics of difference,"[5] they equate the conceptual language of cultural studies with select aspects of the global political economy—commodification, financial flows, capital transfers, outsourcing, flexible accumulation. These economic and financial processes that seem to resonate with aspects of a kind of Deleuzian deterritorialization are then mobilized for a wider political and ethical argument.

The aim of empire-assisted cosmopolitan citizenship lies, Michael Hardt and Antonio Negri argue, in "the struggle against the slavery of belonging to a nation, an identity and a people, and thus the desertion from sovereignty and the limits it places on subjectivity—is entirely positive. Nomadism and miscegenation appear here as figures of virtue, the first ethical practices on the terrain of empire."[6] Such an emancipatory ideal—so affixed on, so fetishizing of, the flowing, borderless, global world—neglects to confront the fact that the migrants, refugees, or nomads do not merely circulate just because the signifier suggests that they should. They need to settle, claim asylum or nationality, demand housing and education, assert their economic and cultural rights, and seek the status of some form of citizenship. It is salutary, then, to turn to less "circulatory" forms of the economy, like trades and tariffs, or taxes and monetary policy—much less open to metaphoric appropriation or deconstruction—to see how they impact on the global imaginary of diasporic cultural studies. At a rough estimate, almost 90 percent of all worldwide trade policies of tariffs are still controlled by nation-states rather that interregional bodies. There are some exceptions like the EU and Mercosur, even though the figures are not spectacularly different. Positive global relations depend on the protection and enhancement of these national "territorial" resources, which should then become part of the "global" cosmopolitical economy of resource redistribution and participate in a transnational moral economy of redistributive justice. It should be seen in that way. These are complex relationships, and I think it does no good at all to follow certain notions of borderlessness for their own sake: it is very important to be able to see the tensions between what remains, because what remains fixed is not always what was fixed. There are new fixities, new borders. Just as with globalization, there are new pockets of polity. The fact that, for example, in India literacy levels have not changed dramatically cannot simply be read as part of an on-going history. These have to recalculated, reconjugated, if I may use the verbal term, in current conditions.

Vernacular Cosmopolitanism

Pursuing the theme of "negative politics" in a more positive direction leads us into a shadowy realm just prior to the cosmopolitan claims of normative political community. This is a moment in the making of Ethical Life that Hegel describes as an unresolved contradiction, or as Jean Hyppolite puts it, a "tormented opposition between sensuousness and duty. . . . We must therefore postulate an indefinite life in order for the subject continually to make moral progress."[7] It is the torment of this indefinite life—which introduces indeterminacy, anxiety, and contingency into the practices of ethical life and into the idea of prog-ress itself—that enables us to take our first steps toward an everyday vernacular cosmopolitanism. When I talk about negative politics, I'm focusing on that moment before the normative comes to be constituted, the disturbed moment before, the moment that in his work on ethical life Hegel sees as the indefinite moment of a kind of subsumption. I'm suggesting that if you bracket out that subsumption and spend a little more time with this moment of the indefinite, then you reach something that allows you to think about the cosmopolitical in a useful way.

Our nation-centered view of sovereign citizenship can only compre-hend the predicament of minoritarian "belonging" as a problem of a political ontology—a question of belonging to a race, a gender, a class, a generation that becomes a kind of "second nature," a primordial iden-tification, and an inheritance authenticated by tradition, a naturalism and a naturalization of the problem of citizenship. The vernacular cos-mopolitan view takes the position of a negative political ontology and suggests that the commitment to a "right to difference in equality" as a process of constituting emergent groups and affiliations has less to do with the affirmation or authentication of origins or "identities," and more to do with political practices and ethical choices. Minoritarian affiliations or solidarities arise in response to the failures and limits of democratic representation, creating new modes of agency, new strategies of recognition, new forms of political and symbolic, as well as affective, representation—NGOs, antiglobalization groups, Truth and Reconciliation commissions, international courts, local agencies of transnational justice (such as the gacaca courts in rural Rwanda). Vernacular cosmopolitanism represents a political process that works toward the shared goals of a democratic rule, works toward them again from that negative moment of process, rather than simply acknowledging already constituted "marginal" political identities or entities.

The torment of the indefinite, as I am calling it, in the creation of vernacular cosmopolitanism often presents itself as an existential and ethical anxiety that is at the heart of any cosmopolitical relationality. If, as Seyla Benhabib argues—and Young agrees—the Universal Declaration of Human Rights in 1946 "signaled a profound transformation of the international itself whereby the rights and sovereignty of nations established through international treaties was shifted to the rights and claims of individuals," then even this world-changing document is not free from the marks of what I have called "the indefinite," precisely at the point at which it makes claims to be universal. The unsettled universality of the Declaration is not primarily a matter of its inability to deal with cultural pluralism, otherness, or relativism, as problems that face it from the outside, or indeed of its inability to respond to whatever "Asian values" are. There is a more fundamental structural issue—differentiation as an internal problem—that is visible even in as seemingly singular and universal a phrase as "a member of society" in Article 22: "Every person as a member of society is entitled to the realization of the economic, social, and cultural rights enumerated below."

The "subject" of rights in the Universal Declaration is an ongoing articulation of representations and repressions—a Gordian knot of ideologies and beliefs, or a web of beliefs about culture, identity, and agency that are absorbed into the draft, into the rhetoric itself, or erased from it. This great cosmopolitical instrument must be read, as I've suggested, with the nation, as much for its substance as for its spectral authority. The rhetoric of the Declaration is an iterative practice of drafting and erasure, and must be grasped as a process of instantiation and incompletion (the torment of the indefinite) that is part of any serial archive. For instance, the travaux préparatoires, that give you the discursive and archival history of Article 22, attest that the innocuous, abstract-sounding phrase "as a member of society,"—who could disagree with it?—is the denomination of a "subject" of second-generation rights that is a strange composite of divergent historical strategies of that time of "subjectivity" that cast their shadows on the very drafting of the phrase. There are all sorts of controversies there, which allowed them to come to this distillation which has this universal, resounding sound but is in fact a battleground itself, a profound indeterminate place. The liberal individual subject versus the Marxist subject of collective rights; the citizen-subject articulated with the subject of international law; the (failed) attempt by Western governments to damage the cause of social rights by designating Article 22 as an "umbrella" article—these are some of the contradictory forces that created the mise-en-scène for second-generation social rights. Ideologies at odds with each other; concepts of agency conceived in the overlap, the Venn diagram, between the national and the international; the ontology of rights balanced precariously between transcendence and effective territoriality.

To reveal the indefinite structure of the modern cosmopolitical subject is to understand the uses of negative politics as the tentative, yet tenacious, stage or phase before—or indeed in anticipation of—the normative status and politics of the Declaration. And this attention to that which is not as yet concretized or instrumentalized makes possible another important move in constructing a cosmopolitical ethics. Julia Kristeva eloquently makes the case in elaborating her concept of cosmopolitan societies as paradoxical, side-by-side communities consisting of subjects who are simultaneously the same and the other:

> Such an ethics should reveal, discuss, and spread a concept of human dignity, wrested from the euphoria of classic humanists and laden with alienations, dramas, and dead-ends of our condition as speaking beings. [...] That being the case, as social as that strangeness might be, it can be modulated—with the policy of achieving a polytopic and supple society, neither locked into the nation and its religion nor anarchically exposed to all of its explosions.[8]

To propose an ethics of cosmopolitanism not based primarily on our dignity as human beings—the assumption of the Universal Declaration—but on our psychic and social alienations, moral ambivalences, and personal agonisms as speaking-subjects raises questions that go far beyond Kristeva's own semiotic and psychoanalytic ends. What does it mean to locate the authority of recognition, or the endowment of dignity, in the very act of annunciation? In the scene-shifting, self-positioning regimes of discursive address? Does the immanent, time-worn value of universality have to be renounced in order to accommodate the alternative perspective of what Seyla Benhabib calls our necessary "democratic iterations": "The deconstruction of the sovereign nation that confronts its authority with a process of fluid, open, and contentious public debate, the lines then separating we and you, us and them, more often than not rest on unexamined prejudices, ancient battles, historical injustices, and sheer administrative fiat."[9] The act of enunciation, which represents the ongoing processes and performances of the speaking subject—very different from the speaking subject as Kristeva announced it—is the imminent domain of discourse. Enunciation is the ongoing articulation of language that always tries to capture the present as it is passing into the future; and as such, I believe, it is intimately related to the assertorial and aspirational basis of rights, the ethics of rights which are often prior to their institutionalization and their legislative power. This a very important area, that part of negative polity before the right becomes a right, all that happens before—the solidarity, the construction of a party or a group. The symbolic and ethical power of rights, Amartya Sen argues in *The Idea of Justice*, lies in their rhetoricity, not their propositionality—in their acts of enunciation. It is their rhetorical and conceptual structure as ethical assertions—"not propositions about what is already guaranteed"—Sen argues, that ensures that "the public articulation of human rights (and recognition) are invitations to initiate some fresh legislations . . . and not just one more human interpretation of existing legal protections."[10] The "enunciative" ethics of cosmopolitanism are phrased in what I would call "quasi" or "proto" universals, not because they are abstractly true for all time, nor, like dignity, are they ends in themselves. Ethical enunciations in relation to rights and rhetorical assertions make a claim to a peculiar universal-cum-alterity, only because we repeatedly return to them, translate them ceaselessly, and extend them proleptically.

This is a different way of thinking about universalism, not by saying it is a plural universalism, which actually doesn't do the work at all because what's the point of having that, but by saying that there is an iterative logic to universality, particularly in this area, that repetition and translation continually open universality to the problematics of alterity and difference. Universals are instrumentally efficacious not because they are incontrovertible "truths for all time"—as we know from their success or otherwise in legal challenge—but because their constant iteration and repetition is part of the revisionary temper of "negative politics" as it aspires to the truth of normative politics. Universals are not "ends." They continually, however, send us back to the beginning to relocate, re-pose our starting questions, and to retool our originating assumptions.

Cosmopolitan Memories

It was an unsettled wet morning in late May. The rain skidded across the windscreen, blinding us for a moment and then suddenly clearing, giving us no kind of hint of what kind of day we were to expect. My host, a German professor from Munich, suddenly suggested that we make a stop in Nuremberg. "You must see Nuremburg, I must take you there."

"Where?" I stuttered, really meaning "Why?' and then, of course, I quickly recovered: "Yes certainly, what an excellent idea." I vaguely remembered a film about the Nuremberg trials with Spencer Tracy and Marlene Dietrich, *Judgment at Nuremberg*, seen as a child in Bombay, much before I knew anything about Albert Speer or the millions of Nazis who frequently gathered in what Hitler called "The City of the Rallies." Just these distant recollections, the heinous echolalia of Hitler's high-pitched ravings, and a tired, overused phrase from Hannah Arendt—"the banality of evil"—trailed along in my mind as we drove off the Autobahn, and after some innocuous suburban maneuvering, arrived at the Zeppelinfeld, Hitler's massive parade ground.

The vast stadium of soaring stone and empty, crumbling terraces was soundless. Where hundreds of thousands once stood to rapturous, roaring attention, today, in the rain, there were only a few of us—a man scraping the rust off his car, children baiting a dog—a few of us, tourists and visitors, at a loss for words, and what was far worse, without any sense of how to behave, or what really to look at, or what truism of history to utter. This sight was neither background nor foreground. It was strangely there, etched strongly in history and memory, and somehow nowhere.

How do you "dis-possess" a cultural space, a heritage site that has developed a global resonance, a cosmopolitan reference? How do you "dis-possess" a sight or subject of the past that is at once tangible and intangible—and yet preserve and protect something of the traumatic, barbaric heritage of its memory, something of that anxiety which has to be preserved, without which history is silenced and memory is made mute. Guilt, Reparation, Apology, Truth and Reconciliation—these are important moral dispositions and political strategies that strive to surmount the internecine violence of nations and states "in transition" by practicing the virtue of public confession and the balm of collective introspection. But there is nothing in the ethic of ameliorative witnessing, however sincere in its pursuit of human "fairness" and historic justice, that prepares you for the "vacuum" that such dis-possessed cultural monuments create—"the half-life of heritage," on the other side of which lies the death of culture and the destruction of humanity. As I stood in this place of barbaric cultural transmission I was startled to hear a loud triumphant roar, a raucous chorus of celebration that rose from behind a bank of trees. I froze. Was I hallucinating? Alexander Kluge's remarkable film *Brutality in Stone*, that explores the architectural tomb of the half-dead Zeppelintribune, flashed before my eyes. It brought back those voices—Hitler, Himmler, anonymous camp commandants—that Alexander Kluge had dug up from the Nazi archive to accompany his silent visuals. These "dis-possessed" moments and monuments, merely mortar and marble, are not free of the morality of human choice.

In the lengthening shadows of the Zeppelintribune I felt a gathering sense of being in the midst of many unresolved experiences and narratives. At first I shrank away from this dispossessed site of shame—Noli me tangere, What did all this have to do with me? And then I realized that there was no way out of it. The half-life of heritage was also mine to embrace. Only by identifying with this conflictual ambivalence between cultural appropriation and cultural alienation—between enunciation and erasure—could I make a moral alignment between what we know now and what we should have done then, between the cosmopolitical here and the global then and there. But who is the cosmopolitan "we"?

Why me? I, who was not even there, born in another country, years after the event?

To enter the realm of cosmopolitan memory is to place oneself—and others—within the orbit of a question posed by Margalit in a discussion of *The Ethics of Memory*: "Is the moral witness a forward-looking creature even when his [or her] testimony is about the past?"[11] The moral witness is caught in a double time frame of cosmopolitical memory, surviving the testimony of the past while striving to possess the freedoms of the future. This complex temporal layering of memory consists, one might say, of a past that refuses to die, confronted by a future that will not wait to be born. You are faced with an open, onrushing future that demands a kind of ethical confidence that only comes from looking back from the future, as if one had the advantage of retrospection and afterthought.

What makes the moral witness a "forward looking creature"—what allows her to exclaim, Never Again—is the anticipatory, proleptic nature of moral consciousness itself. In *Thinking and Moral Considerations*, her beautifully wrought meditation on "the banality of evil," Hannah Arendt argues: "conscience appears as an afterthought. . . . What makes a man fear [it] is the anticipation of the presence of a witness who awaits him only if and when he goes home."[12] The future-looking nature of global memory—which is neither redemptive nor tragic—is both an "afterthought" (the projection of a traumatized past) and an "anticipation" (a proleptic future). Memory's cosmopolitan reach is not merely a spatial extension of ethical attention that crosses cultures, moves beyond borders, and converges upon new maps of the global world-picture: new internationalisms, new financial sectors, new technologies. Such vanities are short-lived and shortsighted. The ethical project of cosmopolitan memory is a negative politics: the perception of public virtue and progress seen through the dark, sometimes distant glass of human survival.

NOTES

1 Avishai Margalit, "The Lesser Evil," *Royal Institute of Philosophy*, vol. 54, March 2004, 187.

2 Hannah Arendt, "On Violence," in *Crises of the Republic* (San Diego: Harcourt Brace & Co., 1972), 108.

3 Giorgio Agamben, "We Refugees," trans. Michael Rocke, *Symposium* 49:2 (1995), 117.

4 Etienne Balibar, *Equaliberty: Political Essays* (Durham, N.C.: Duke University Press, 2014).

5 Michael Hardt and Antonio Negri, *Empire* (Cambridge, Mass.: Harvard University Press, 2001), 151.

6 Ibid., 362.

7 Jean Hyppolite, *Genesis and Structure of Hegel's "Phenomenology of Spirit"* (Evanston, Ill.: Northwest University Press, 1979), 478.

8 Julia Kristeva, *Strangers to Ourselves* (New York: Columbia University Press, 1991), 154.

9 Seyla Benhabib, *The Claims of Culture: Equality and Diversity in the Global Era* (Princeton: Princeton University Press, 2002), 177.

10 Amartya Sen, *The Idea of Justice* (Cambridge: Harvard University Press, 2009), 359.

11 Margalit, op. cit., 152–53.

12 Hannah Arendt, "Thinking and Moral Considerations: A Lecture," *Social Research* 38:3 (1971), 444.

12

Cosmopolitan Prejudice

PAULO LEMOS HORTA

The contradictions of cosmopolitanism came into focus in the summer of 2016 as commentators struggled to explain both the triumph of Brexit and the populist appeal of Donald Trump's presidential campaign. In this shifting political landscape, the conservative columnist Ross Douthat sought to disabuse readers of the *New York Times* of the notion that the cosmopolitanism of the economic and cultural elites in New York and London amounted to a genuine openness to difference. Taking issue with a media narrative that opposed tribalism and cosmopolitanism, Douthat suggested that this new species of "global citizens" behave much like a tribe. Sharing the same set of values and defining themselves against the same out-groups, these cosmopolitans take advantage of the new technologies of globalization to circulate within a zone of "comfort and familiarity."

One might readily agree that "[g]enuine cosmopolitanism is a rare thing" and that the "global-citizen bubble" distinctly limits encounters with real cultural difference. Cosmopolitanism in its most vigorous form should entail a willingness to be transformed by an experience of the foreign rather than just the comfort of belonging to a global elite. When Douthat searches for historical examples of a more meaningful engagement with cultural difference, however, his choices represent a new set of contradictions. "There is," he claims, "more genuine cosmopolitanism in Rudyard Kipling and T. E. Lawrence and Richard Francis Burton than in a hundred Davos sessions." This abrupt turn to the age of empire for examples of a more authentic cosmopolitanism suggests an odd nostalgia for a time when the world seemed to offer examples of impenetrable strangeness to be mastered by daring feats of exploration and cultural immersion. This era may provide an antidote to the increased homogeneity of our contemporary world, but the mixture of tolerance and prejudice in this model of imperial cosmopolitanism does not provide a solution for the challenges of our contemporary political culture. Douthat's suggestion that empire "made cosmopolitans as well as chauvinists—sometimes out of the same people" is certainly applicable to figures like Richard Burton,[1] but what does this mean for our understanding of the limits of cosmopolitan tolerance?

A more nuanced understanding of Burton's status as a cosmopolitan is offered by the liberal philosopher Kwame Antony Appiah, who uses the famous explorer and translator as a point of departure to consider questions of ethics and belonging in his seminal study of cosmopolitanism. Appiah marvels at Burton's ability to "go native" again and again during his travels in South Asia, Africa, Arabia, and the Americas, but is also attentive to the distinct limits of Burton's empathy—most evident in his acceptance of the institution of slavery. Thus Burton takes on two roles in Appiah's work: both the cosmopolitan who seeks out the experience of difference and the counter-cosmopolitan who cannot quite escape the residual prejudices of his early upbringing.[2] A closer look at the remarkable feats of immersion and impersonation that characterized Burton's time abroad, however, suggests that the acquisition of bias was a critical part of Burton's cosmopolitan self-fashioning. If Burton provides a remarkable example of the empathetic adoption of foreign cultural values, he also provides an example of the way in which tolerance and prejudice are intertwined within cosmopolitan experience.

Burton's reputation as a poster boy for cosmopolitanism rests upon the extraordinary feats of travel, language acquisition, and cultural immersion that characterized his career as a colonial officer, explorer, and diplomat. From his first postings in colonial India, Burton deliberately sought to fashion himself in the image of the foreigner to pursue his goal of undermining the complacent sense of superiority of "John Bull" abroad. The key to this exercise in self-fashioning was Burton's remarkable acquisition of foreign languages—in his estimate, more than thirty. Passing six language exams in seven years, Burton attempted to rival the achievements of those Anglo-Indian officers and diplomats who sought to rule Britain's Indian empire through their expertise in "Oriental" languages, but he also self-consciously set himself apart from this class of administrators. Claiming that those "who prided themselves most on their conversancy with native dialects and native character, are precisely those persons who have been the most egregiously, the most fatally, outwitted and deceived by the natives,"[3] he deliberately cultivated the perspective of the cosmopolite who could move effortlessly between multiple vernacular languages and imperial cultures to achieve a more accurate understanding of this protean environment.

The most impressive of Burton's deeds was arguably his plan to complete the pilgrimage to Mecca and Medina in 1853 in the guise of Mirza Abdullah, an Arab-Persian from the north shore of the Persian Gulf. This was the persona that Burton established during his service with the East India Company and which he resurrected as he set off on his most challenging experiment in foreign cultural immersion, hoping to surpass the achievements of earlier European "pilgrims" like Jean Louis Burckhardt. In 1853, Burton disembarked in the port city of Alexandria en route to Mecca in his "old character of a Persian wanderer," boasting in his travelogue that local servants would mistake him for an *Ajami*, a Persian Muslim. Yet the stranger had miscalculated. Mirza Abdullah found himself unwelcome in Cairo due to the prejudice against Persians, who were thought to be "clever and debauched." To salvage his trip, Burton decided to dispense with one identity and reemerge as a Pathan, an Afghan born and raised in India. Mirza Abdullah thus became Sheikh Abdullah. In the *Personal Narrative of a Pilgrimage to El-Medinah and Meccah*, Burton elaborated upon the fine adjustments necessary to inhabit this new identity. Even the simple act of drinking water as a Muslim raised not in Persia but in India required "no fewer than five novelties." This tour de force—taking on not one but two distinct Muslim personae in quick succession—would make Burton famous.[4]

Against the benefits of cultural immersion in any one culture, Burton consistently asserted the importance of the cognitive expansion that extensive travel provided. He conceived of his practice of disguise as enabling a cosmopolitan experience that would disrupt familiar patterns of thought. To travel was to be stripped of one's illusions about home and educated in un-belonging. Viewed from the perspective of Scinde, Burton contended, the English attachment to romantic conceptions of English identity rooted in rural belonging appeared ridiculous. "I regret to say," Burton wrote, "that the Scindians . . . having no word to explain your 'home,' attach none of those pretty ideas to the place in question."[5]

Burton would promote the translation of foreign works into English as an essential means of introducing the same cognitive dissonance into the national culture, allowing readers "the enormous advantage of being capable of comparing native with foreign ideas and views of the world."[6] In his own translations, he sought to deprovincialize English concepts about what constituted literature, good taste, and good style. Determined to "foreignize" the English language, Burton displayed an uncompromising commitment to neologisms, foreignisms, and the preservation of the sound effects of the original text in his translations.[7] He sought to mirror the impact of foreign travel by unsettling expectations with unknown vistas, like undiscovered countries.

Appiah admits to a lifelong fascination with the figure of Burton, generated after encountering his translation of *The Thousand and One Nights* as a child. At fourteen, he read a biography of Burton and was struck by his apparent ability to be "a Mohammedan among Mohammedans, a Mormon among Mormons, a Sufi among the Shazlis, and a Catholic among Catholics." In Appiah's *Cosmopolitanism*, Burton is presented as being "something of a freak of nature in his ability to penetrate different cultures—to 'go native,' as we say, and do so time and time again." In this capacity, Appiah deploys Burton as exemplary of the kind of openness to other cultures that he sees as essential to the cosmopolitan. He thus emphasizes the "voracious assimilation of religions, literatures, and customs from around the world" that mark Burton "as someone who is fascinated by the range of human invention, the variety of our ways of life and thought," to the point that "he could see the world from perspectives remote from the outlook in which he had been brought up."[8] Burton thus embodies the second defining feature of Appiah's model of cosmopolitanism: the ability to recognize "that human beings are different and that we can learn from each other's differences." While few are capable of Burton's freakish gift for cultural immersion, Appiah contends that "most of us have the ability to some lesser degree: we can often experience the appeal of values that aren't, exactly, our own."[9]

If Burton's talent for cultural immersion serves the purposes of Appiah's argument in some respects, other examples of the Victorian traveler's perspective are more difficult to reconcile with the concentric circles of belonging that characterize cosmopolitanism in the philosopher's work. While Appiah's model of cosmopolitanism serves to affirm his own affiliation with multiple overlapping communities defined by relationships of kinship and love (as an Asante, a Ghanaian, an American, and as the bearer of his mother's British heritage), the cognitive dissonance that characterizes Burton's experience seems to lead instead to a sense of loss and un-belonging. This aspect of Burton's cosmopolitanism appears as an important undercurrent in the insightful psychological reading by biographer Fawn Brodie, who suggests Burton felt a "restlessness" and a "fluidity of his identity" that meant that he "felt at home no place." Jean-François Gournay likewise interprets the "frenzy of Burton's activity as translator" as the continuation of a series of disguises that speak to an elusive quest for identity.[10] In a reversal of the familiar sense of the cosmopolitan at home everywhere, Burton seems to have been at home nowhere.

Like Douthat, Brodie links Burton with T. E. Lawrence, another cosmopolitan known for his ability to sympathetically engage with Arab culture. Lawrence's autobiography indicates that he mirrored Burton in recognizing the cognitive gains of immersion in a foreign culture: "The effort for these years to live in the dress of Arabs and to imitate their mental foundation, quitted me of my English self, and let me look at the West and its conventions with new eyes; they destroyed it all for me." However, what was lost was not easily replaced: "Easily was a man made an infidel, but hardly might he be converted to another faith. I had dropped one form and not taken on the other. . . . Sometimes these selves would converse in the void; and then madness was very near, as I believe it would be near the man who could see things through the veils at once of two customs, two educations, two environments."[11] For Burton too, the adoption of a new cultural persona provided him with a lens to see through the conventions of his late Victorian era. It was this unraveling of familiar English assumptions about culture, and in particular sexuality, that constituted the cosmopolitan education he sought to provide readers of his travelogues and translations. In his commentary on *The Thousand and One Nights*, he declared his intention to shock contemporary Englishmen out of what he termed their nineteenth-century prejudices—cultural, religious, and sexual.

The worlds through which Burton moved were not as easily reconciled as the concentric circles of belonging described by Appiah. More illuminating of Burton's cosmopolitan practice, and his self-fashioning as Mirza Abdullah, is the notion of cosmopolitanism offered by American historian Thomas Bender. Drawing upon the pragmatism of John Dewey and William James, Bender reverses the usual experiential meanings associated with cosmopolitanism. While some might argue that the cosmopolitan is comfortable in all settings and in all cultures, Bender suggests that cosmopolitan experience should entail some degree of discomfort. The cosmopolitan is someone prepared to be unsettled by an encounter with difference, which should prompt not only an inquiry into this novel experience but also a reevaluation of one's own identity. This is the cosmopolitanism that we seem to encounter in Burton's writings—a cosmopolitanism with the potential to transform.[12]

The progressive potential within foreign immersion is most evident in Burton's critical comments on the practices of British imperialism. In his travelogues of Scinde, for instance, Burton launched a scathing attack of British policies designed to stamp out indigenous practices and to force local subjects to assimilate to English manners, laws, beliefs, and dress.[13] Burton objected to any quest to rid the territory of traditional practices such as *sati*, and he argued that Britain, as the greatest Muslim empire of its age, should govern its territories with a more sympathetic understanding of Muslim mores. Burton's mockery of British imperial policy as a crude form of plunder uninformed by the needs of local populations has led scholars to dub him a critic of empire. Yet Fawn Brodie, who remains the most incisive of his many biographers, was closer to the mark in observing that he was "not so much against Empire and imperialism [as] frustrated with a second-rate, amateurish, bumbling, arrogant, mismanaged Empire." Even as he railed against English imperialism, he praised French, Dutch, and Portuguese examples of colonial rule. What Burton wanted to see was a form of imperialism that was more knowledgeable of and sympathetic to local mores and more successful in raising local standards of living through modes of industrialization that might alleviate "chronic poverty."[14] He sought a more cosmopolitan imperialism that was both more attentive to local values and bolder in its use of this knowledge to pursue the objectives of colonial rule. Burton thus suggested that the British administrator in India keep his Muslim subjects in line by threatening them with cremation, an unthinkable punishment that would have precluded an afterlife according to Muslim belief.

Again and again Burton asserts the value of immersing oneself in alternative cultural practices, but in ways that lead to problems in applying contemporary definitions of cosmopolitanism. While Appiah holds on to some notion of a universal, Burton's repeated reinvention of his own value system in different cultural contexts seems to lead into a relativism that excuses too much. This position is perhaps most provocatively stated in Burton's travelogue of the Congo: "Conscience is a purely geographical and chronological accident. . . . And what easier way to prove that there is no sin however infamous, no crime however abominable, which at some time or in some part of the world has been or is still held in highest esteem?"[15] Burton's descriptions of black Africans as "hideous" and "bestial" encapsulate the racism that underpins his acceptance of the institution of slavery in Central Africa, and in this respect he fails what Appiah deems the other essential imperative for the cosmopolitan—to recognize "our responsibility for every human being." In Central Africa, Burton seemed to reach the limits of a cosmopolitanism based on sympathetic identification. As Dane Kennedy argues in his recent biography, Burton tended to react with hostility when he encountered a context in which he could not pass as an insider.[16] Racial difference proved to be an impenetrable barrier to achieving a sense of solidarity during his travels in Central Africa.

For Appiah, Burton's example serves to illustrate the sobering recognition that prejudice is not derived solely from ignorance, and that intimacy need not lead to "amity."[17] In the end, however, he attributes Burton's failings to a counter-cosmopolitanism rooted in the biases left over from his early education in Englishness. I would argue in contrast that one should not so quickly abandon the idea that these prejudices were a product of Burton's successive cultural immersions—that they were part of a cosmopolitanism produced in intimate contact with the foreign rather than being a residue of resistance to the cognitive impact of cultural difference. The adoption of local biases was essential to Burton's attempt to fashion new identities that would allow him to insinuate himself in a new ethnic, national, or religious community.

This interplay between going native and internalizing native prejudices is an overlooked constant in Burton's attempts to articulate a distinctive cosmopolitan perspective. In his earliest South Asian travelogues, Burton expressed a firm rejection of what he perceived to be the prevalent biases among British Orientalists and colonial administrators against Muslims and in favor of Hindus. Reversing this valuation, he developed a strong preference for the Persian "race" as he developed a deep friendship with his Persian language teacher, Mirza Mohammad, and began to cultivate his own identity as a Persian Muslim in a series of local expeditions. "The gifted Iranian race," Burton claimed, was "physically the noblest and the most beautiful of all known to me." The Sindhis, in contrast, were described as a "semi-barbarous race"—a "half-breed between the Hindoo, one of the most imperfect, and the Persian, probably the most perfect specimen of the Caucasian type." As Fawn Brodie observes of these South Asian travelogues, "Burton is always involved; he admires, he disapproves, he hates, he loves; he judges; he scoffs; he scorns."[18] If, as the biographer notes, he always "feels, passionately and intensely," I would add he does so *with* particular communities, and against other communities defined in terms that replicate local categories.

Burton's desire to contest conventional judgments of religious communities outside the Anglo-American mainstream is on display once again in the travelogue that chronicles his nine-month trek across America in 1859–60. Highlighting a three-week stay among the Mormons of Salt Lake City, *The City of the Saints* displays the intertwining of tolerance and prejudice characteristic of much of his travel writing. Rejecting contemporary portraits of Mormonism as "venomous," Burton seeks to normalize the position of the "Mormon Mecca" among the many holy cities that he has visited over his lifetime of travel, placing it alongside the Muslim sites of pilgrimage as well as Memphis, Benares, Jerusalem, and Rome.[19] The description of Burton's arrival in Salt Lake City—his first sight of the valley after emerging from the Wasatch Mountain canyon—is one of his most lyrical pieces of writing and may be placed alongside his record of his first sighting of Medina in the *Personal Narrative*, where he seems to share the pious enthusiasm of the pilgrims. The "lovely panorama of green and azure and gold" seemed to him "fresh as it were from the hands of God," and the view of the lake, "bounding the far horizon, like a band of burnished silver," made him understand why believers felt the "Spirit of God pervades the very atmosphere."[20]

Appiah's liberal theory of cosmopolitanism may be seen as a rejection of the claims of such religious communities given the opposition it sets up between the liberal values of tolerance, epistemic modesty, and open-mindedness and what he terms the "toxic" cosmopolitanism of evangelical Christianity, the colonialist's civilizing mission, and the "apocalyptic nihilism" of the terrorist.[21] In Burton's writing, global religions and their capitals are not presented as the antithesis of cosmopolitanism, but rather as representative of an alternative set of values too readily dismissed in mainstream England. Burton marshals statistics to demonstrate Salt Lake City to be a site of immigration for many thousands of Europeans, rather than an isolated refuge for castoffs and renegades. While he emphasizes the sizable British presence in the city, he would concur with a French traveler's depiction of Salt Lake City as a place where "English, Scotch, Canadians, Americans, Danes, Swedes, Norwegians, Germans, Swiss, Poles, Russians, Italians, French, Negroes, Hindoos, and Australians" converge "to live more than brothers in perfect harmony."[22]

There is evidence that Burton sought to immerse himself in the distinctive perspective of the Mormons and hence to write about their community from an insider's perspective. He spent at least three days in September 1860 taking copious notes in the Historian's Office of the Church of Jesus Christ of Latter-Day Saints. Brigham Young himself granted Burton more than the customary attention due to a famous foreign visitor and personally showed him the city. Burton's travelogue presents the Mormon leader as singularly capable and without pretense or vanity, and offers a defense of the practice most condemned in contemporary portraits of Mormonism—polygamy. Drawing from a comparative perspective nurtured by his many journeys, Burton presented polygamy among the Mormons as natural and moral. While the "Mormon household has been described by its enemies as a hell of envy, hatred, and malice, a den of murder and suicide," Burton argues that the "same has been said of the Moslem harem." He asserts that both these assessments reflect "the assertions of prejudice or ignorance," and provocatively ventures that "in point of mere morality the Mormon community is perhaps purer than any other of equal numbers."[23] Burton mocks the absurdities reported in other travelogues of Utah, such as the report of outdoor stables where Mormon wives would have been stored like animals. Contemporary reviews of *The City of the Saints* in London would interpret Burton's sympathy for the Mormons as credulity.[24]

While distinctive in his sympathy for the Mormons and impassioned in his defense of polygamy, Burton also used his travelogue of America to articulate sharp opinions of a series of other groups: Western Americans, "mountain men," French Canadians, and Native Americans of thirty different named tribes. Burton claimed to be eager to meet the native peoples in peace and in battle and boasted of having acquired knowledge of the practices of scalping and totem carving, but in reality, as biographers have observed, he had minimal if any contact with native peoples. His references to natives as deceitful, lying, and thieving are largely derived from his fellow travelers. Biographer Edward Rice concludes that in this case Burton's opinions were "formed, sadly, not by experience but by the prejudices of his companions."[25] Historian David Wrobel contends that Burton generally avoided contemporary stereotypes of the noble savage and the uncivilized barbarian, but he seems to have drawn on the conventional wisdom of other travelers to write with assurance of the various merits of different native tribes. If his interest in the spiritual beliefs of Native Americans signals that Burton possessed some degree of sympathy, he was not above volunteering military advice on how to best subjugate rebellious tribes.[26]

When Burton sought to inhabit a foreign identity—whether that of the Arab or the Mormon—he tended to internalize the quarrels, sympathies, and antipathies of that group—in sum, its biases. This proved to be a difficult match with his role as a British diplomat, which began in 1861 with a minor posting in Fernando Po, an island off the west coast of Africa, but eventually took him to Brazil, Damascus, and Trieste. Burton's writings from his diplomatic postings in Brazil once again reflect the intermingling of openness and bias that characterized his efforts to navigate foreign ground. In South Asia he had already developed a fascination with the Portuguese as representative of an alternative mode of cosmopolitan empire—embodied for Burton in the poetry of Camões.[27] In Brazil this identification became even more intense as he sought to reverse what he saw as an English bias in favor of the Spanish and against the Portuguese with characteristic vehemence. He took great umbrage at the description of Brazil as "[b]irds without song, flowers without perfume, men without honour, and women without honesty." Such a sentiment could only be spoken by "a stranger, after a few months' residence, who can hardly speak a connected sentence of Portuguese."²⁸ Finding in print the observation, "Strip a Spaniard of all his good qualities and you have a Portuguese," Burton caustically rejoined, "Strip a Portuguese of his thrift and industry, supply him well with bigotry and a pride which has nothing to be proud of, and you have a Spaniard."²⁹ Burton not only championed the Empire of Brazil, but he mocked the legacy of the Spanish conquistadores, extending sympathy to the "wondruous physical civilization[s]" of the Aztecs and Incas vanquished by "a band of . . . Barbarians."³⁰

Not surprisingly, Burton's championing of the Empire of Brazil was manifest politically in his support for its continued practice of slavery. Burton's thoughts on its survival in Brazil after its abolition elsewhere represent the corollary to his support for a cosmopolitan ideal of empire adapted to local norms. Burton was not making a universal and universalizing argument for the continuance of slavery in the world, but rather a particular apology for the Brazilian imperial government's rationale for the continuation of slavery. It is a defense of cultural exceptionalism of a piece with his case for polygamy among the Mormons in America or for the Hindu rites of *sati* that British colonial administrators abhorred. In Brazil, Burton sided with majority local opinion against the fashion of Europe and the instructions he received from the British Foreign Office. In cultivating a special kinship with the local inhabitants rather than the British government and the citizens he was supposed to be representing, Burton publicly jettisoned those elements of British public opinion and foreign policy that might have made him less welcome among the local elite.

In Brazil, Burton parlayed a relatively modest posting as consul at Santos into sojourns at the imperial court in Petropolis, where he befriended the Brazilian emperor, Dom Pedro II. Long after Burton was posted elsewhere, the two men remained friends, and in the last year of his life, the former emperor, living in exile in Paris, would even attempt a translation of the *Thousand and One Nights* into Portuguese. Would this degree of favor and intimacy have been possible had Burton fulfilled his obligation as a diplomat to articulate British policy on the contentious issue of slavery? Can one infiltrate cultures, be accepted as a foreigner, without embracing local prejudices? Is not the sharing of prejudices, the recognition that a bias is reasonably held, one of the first thresholds to be passed for any degree of cultural immersion and social acceptance? Appiah observes that anthropologists tend to accept and explain practices that metropolitan readerships find shocking—from genital mutilation to cannibalism—but what of embracing a tribe's hatred for a neighboring tribe, or endorsing its enslavement of it?

The controversial issue of Burton's anti-Semitism may be the most important test of how the experience of cultural immersion might impact the balance of tolerance and prejudice in the cosmopolitan traveler. Burton's early letters demonstrated his sympathy and even his repeated identification with the predicament of Jews in Europe. As late as his Brazilian sojourn in the 1860s Burton would observe, in a confession that reflects the odd contradictions of his cosmopolitanism, "Had I choice of race, there is none to which I would belong more willingly than the Jewish—of course the white family."[31] Accusations of anti-Semitism crystallized around Burton's time as British consul in Damascus, where his identification with the local Muslim population was accompanied by a critical attitude toward Jewish merchants and Christian missionaries.

Burton arrived in Damascus with a well-established affinity for Arab culture and Islam and an ability to pass as an Arab sheikh that he continued to put to use on the streets of the city. Whether or not he was simply adopting the perspectives of his Muslim subjects, Burton's inclination was to question the policies of previous British consuls who had offered support to the local Jewish and Christian population. Predictably, the "first unpleasantness" that Burton protested to the Foreign Office was the distribution of "Christian tracts" among the Muslims of Damascus by the superintendent of the British Syrian school at Beirut.[32] In addition to alienating Christian missionaries, Burton angered the Jewish community by refusing to aid Jewish creditors under British protection because he deemed that they had acted as usurers "in ruining villages and imprisoning destitute debtors upon trumped charges."[33] This was despite his earlier assessment of the majority of the Jewish population as "hard-working, inoffensive, and of commercial integrity, with a fair sprinkling of the pious, charitable, and innocent people." The letter of protest prepared by London's Chief Rabbi Sir Francis Goldsmid suggests that the perceived anti-Semitism of Burton's actions was seen as a newly acquired prejudice and speculates that perhaps it was the influence of his new Roman Catholic wife, Isabel.[34] Suspicions would turn into virulent accusations of hatred as Burton was accused of torturing Jewish boys suspected of marking crosses next to mosques to incite anti-Christian sentiment. The result was a parliamentary inquiry that led to Burton's recall from Damascus. In this context, Burton's mode of cosmopolitan identification was of little help in managing the tensions between religious communities.

Anthony Appiah faults Burton for the perceived insufficiency of his cosmopolitanism. In this view, Burton is cosmopolitan in some respects, counter-cosmopolitan in others. This insufficiency might be more accurately termed an asymmetry: Burton is remarkably receptive and open in his attitude to some foreign cultures, but not to others. Appiah's assessment dovetails with the observations of Edward Said and Dane Kennedy, who conclude that however much time Burton might have spent abroad, he ultimately inhabited bubbles of Englishness and inherited English prejudice. However cosmopolitan Burton's views might have been in relation to Islam, in other respects the Englishman and the Victorian showed through, along with attendant prejudice about black Africans or Jews. Applying Said's framework, it might be argued that Burton inherited assumptions from the texts produced by earlier generations of Orientalists. Even those who did travel were beholden to assumptions inherited from previous scholars and travelers and broader English attitudes toward foreign cultures and faiths.

But what if the remarkable malleability and openness to foreign cultures and practices that led Burton to be more tolerant than his London-bound contemporaries in some respects also contributed to his being more prejudiced in others? Why assume that the cosmopolitan ethic that calls for openness and receptivity to foreign mores and the possibility of being transformed by cross-cultural encounter will lead to tolerance rather than bias? Why not regressive prejudice as well as avant-garde tolerance? Appiah himself notes that coexistence leads to enmity as well as amity. I would contend that Burton's ability to "go native" in many different contexts entailed a certain talent for absorbing and articulating foreign beliefs and prejudices. Burton's identification with the host cultures he privileged as civilized reflected a lack of concern with other local constituencies that had been victimized or oppressed. Part and parcel of Burton's cosmopolitanism was the impulse not to criticize slavery, or sati, or polygamy. In his strong identification with particular foreign cultures, Burton also took pride in reproducing and rationalizing their low opinion of perceived rival and enemy cultures. Burton took sides with the Persians against the Turks, with the Portuguese against the Spanish, and in general with Muslims against proponents of other faiths (inclusive of Christianity). Most controversially, he sought in his posting in Damascus to justify local prejudice not only against missionaries but also against Jewish creditors under British protection. Burton—"the collector of worlds"—seems to have picked up prejudices as quickly and as vociferously as he collected languages.[35]

Rather than rejecting Burton's biases as counter-cosmopolitan, they should be understood as integral to his self-fashioning as a cosmopolitan. Why assume that prejudice is inherited from one's home culture and tolerance learned from travel and experience of the world abroad? Why interpret Burton's biases as representative of the Victorian Englishman, and his tolerance as a result of his experience of other cultures? What Anthony Appiah identifies as Burton's extraordinary malleability in foreign cultural environments does indeed make him an important test case for cosmopolitan ethics, but any attempt to excise the acquisition of prejudice abroad from our study of cosmopolitan experience impoverishes our analytical vocabulary. A consideration of prejudice showcases the limitations of holding out Kipling, Lawrence, and Burton as foils to metropolitan elites in an era that assumes an opposition between nativists and cosmopolitans. Another project, as Thomas Bender suggests, is to seek out historical and contemporary examples of cosmopolitan practices more open to introspection and the reevaluation of core allegiances and assumptions. Given the concerns expressed from a variety of political vantage points in recent commentary on Brexit and Trump, we must be attentive to the risks of complacency and self-mythologizing in our assumptions of cosmopolitanism and seek other models in the practices of a broader range of social groups not only in New York and London but in Accra and Rio de Janeiro.

NOTES

1 Ross Douthat, "The Myth of Cosmopolitanism," *New York Times*, July 3, 2016, SR9. The column elicited a series of influential responses, among them Daniel Drezner, "The Truth of Cosmopolitanism," *Washington Post*, July 5, 2016.

2   K. Anthony Appiah, *Cosmopolitanism in a World of Strangers* (New York: W.W. Norton, 2006), 1–8.

3   Richard Francis Burton, *Scinde: or, the Unhappy Valley*, 2nd ed. (London: Richard Bentley, 1851), I: 3.

4   Richard Francis Burton, *Personal Narrative of a Pilgrimage to El-Medinah and Meccah* (London: Longman, Brown, Green, and Longmans, 1856), I: 10–18.

5   Burton, *Scinde*, I: 182.

6   Richard F. Burton, "Translators," *Athenaeum*, February 24, 1872, #2313, 241–43. He felt Oriental literatures were well taken care of due to the demand determined by British imperial and foreign office priorities. In his argument for translation Burton stressed the need to fund translations from "smaller" languages, ranging from Flemish to Brazilian Portuguese.

7   On Burton's philosophy of translation, see Paulo Lemos Horta, *Marvellous Thieves: Secret Authors of the Arabian Nights* (Cambridge: Harvard University Press, 2017), 245–247.

8   W. H. Wilkins, *The Romance of Isabel Lady Burton* (New York: Dodd Mead, 1897), 712, quoted in Appiah, *Cosmopolitanism in a World of Strangers*, 6. Appiah's lifelong interest in Burton shared in conversation at the old Downtown Campus, New York University, Abu Dhabi, March 1, 2013.

9   Appiah, *Cosmopolitanism in a World of Strangers*, 4–11.

10 Fawn Brodie, "Notes on Burton," Huntington Library; Jean-François Gournay, *L'appel du proche-orient: Richard Francis Burton et son temps, 1821–1890* (Paris: Didier-Erudition, 1983), 124.

11 Quoted in Fawn Brodie, *The Devil Drives: A Life of Sir Richard Burton* (New York: W. W. Norton, 1984), 104.

12 Thomas Bender, "The Cosmopolitan Experience and Its Uses," in this volume.

13 Respectively Burton, *Scinde*, I: 182 and II: 278.

14 Brodie, "Notes on Burton," Huntington Library. On imperial policy, see Burton's review of D. Mackenzie Wallace, "Egypt and the Egyptian Question," *Academy*, January 19, 1884, no. 611, 46. He expressed a similar enthusiasm for industrialization in his commentary to *The Lusiads*.

15 Richard F. Burton, *Two Trips to Gorilla-Land and the Cataracts of the Congo* (London: Sampson Low, Marston, Low & Searle), I: 185–186.

16 Dane Kennedy, *The Highly Civilized Man: Richard Burton and the Victorian World* (Cambridge: Harvard University Press, 2007), 89.

17 Appiah, *Cosmopolitanism*, 4–11.

18 Burton, *Scinde*, I: 283, 284; Fawn Brodie, "Notes on *Scinde: or The Unhappy Valley* [London: 1851]," Huntington Library.

19 David M. Wrobel, *Global West, American Frontier: Travel, Empire, and Exceptionalism from Manifest Destiny to the Great Depression* (Albuquerque: University of New Mexico Press, 2013), 57.

20 Richard F. Burton, *The City of the Saints and Across the Rocky Mountains to California* (New York: Harper & Brothers, 1862), 240–241.

21 K. Anthony Appiah, *The Ethics of Identity* (Princeton: Princeton University Press, 2005), 220.

22 Quoted in Wrobel, *Global West, American Frontier*, 59.

23 Quoted in Brodie, *The Devil Drives*, 186.

24 As the *Athenaeum* complained, in its review of *The City and the Saints* of November 30, 1861, quoted in Brodie, *The Devil Drives*, 187–188.

25 Edward Rice, *Captain Richard Francis Burton: A Biography* (Boston: Da Capo Press, 2001), 431, 436.

26 Wrobel, *Global West, American Frontier*, 55.

27 Paulo Lemos Horta, " 'Mixing the East with the West': Cosmopolitan Philology in Richard Burton's Translations from Camões," in *A Sea of Languages: Rethinking the Arabic Role in Medieval Literary History*, ed. S. Akbari and K. Mallette (Toronto: University of Toronto, 2013), 82–99.

28 Richard F. Burton, *Explorations of the Highlands of the Brazil*, 2 vols. (London: 1869), 1: 409.

29 Richard F. Burton, "Review of A. B. Ellis West African Islands," *Academy*, March 7, 1885, no. 670, 163.

30 Richard F. Burton, *The Lands of the Cazembe. Lacerda's Journey to Cazembe in 1798*, translated by Captain R. F. Burton (London: Royal Geographical Society, 1978), 38 n.

31 Burton, *Exploration of the Highlands of the Brazil*, I: 402–3 n.

32 "Damascus, the Case of Captain Burton, late H. B. M.'s Consul at Damascus." London, March 1972. Foreign Office Blue Book on Burton, 3.

33 Quoted in Brodie, *The Devil Drives*, 256. The Huntington Library preserves a copy of Burton's eight-page letter on the subject of his recall from Damascus to Her Majesty's Secretary of State for Foreign Affairs, dated 14 Montagu Place, Montagu Square W. October 16, 1871. B. J. Kirkpatrick, ed., *A Catalogue of the Library of Sir Richard Burton, K. C. M. G. Held by the Royal Anthropological Institute* (London: Royal Anthropological Institute, 1978), 34.

34 Brodie, *The Devil Drives*, 256.

35 The quoted phrase is Iliya Troyanov's from his fictionalized biography of Burton, *The Collector of Worlds* (London: Faber & Faber, 2006).

PART IV

Critique

13

A Stoic Critique of Cosmopolitanism

PHILLIP MITSIS

In the sum of the parts, there are only the parts.
—Wallace Stevens, "On the Road Home"

The Stoics lately have become poster boys for various kinds of benign
cosmopolitan theorizing. They also, however, have become philosophical heroes for Wall Street and for the American military.[1] Although it is
no doubt true that philosophers often become more important for what
they are thought to have said rather than for what they thought they
were saying, the incongruity of these two receptions of Stoic thought is
particularly ironic—and not only from the vantage point of the ancient
Stoics themselves, who could be so tiresomely ostentatious about their
not wanting to be all things to all people. Although a few moments'
reflection on the central tenets of Stoicism should make it pretty clear
why neither of these particular receptions carries much historical plau-
sibility, the notion of liberals on safari, apostles of universal brotherly
concern, CEOs, and generals all waking up and discovering themselves
to be philosophical bedmates certainly seems ripe for a certain kind of
wry ideological exploration. We will leave these ironies, however, for
others to explore and here focus instead on a few more limited questions
about why cosmopolitanism and ancient Stoicism make for such strange
bedfellows. In so doing, I hope to make this not just an entirely pedantic and depressing exercise of exposing instances of willful misreading,
sloppy history, clubby scholarly conformity, and so on—although there is
certainly plenty of blame to go around. Rather, this exploration will turn
some common arguments about Stoics as cosmopolitans on their head
and suggest why the ancient Stoics actually provide an important point
of departure for criticizing many of the going forms of contemporary

cosmopolitanism, indeed, often the very forms that most insistently claim them as intellectual forbears.

First, though, to get our bearings, it might be useful to take a tour of the remaining ancient evidence, which by any measure is exceedingly meager. Our single most reliable and detailed piece of evidence, by far, is provided by Diogenes Laertius (fl. c. 3rd century C.E.), who is writing more than half a millennium distant from the founders of Stoicism:

> [S]ome people, including the circle of Cassius the Sceptic, criticize Zeno [the founder of Stoicism] extensively: first, for declaring at the beginning of his *Republic* that the education curriculum is useless; and secondly, for his statement that all who are not virtuous are foes, enemies, slaves, and estranged from one another, including parents and children, brothers and brothers, relations and relations. They criticize him again for presenting only virtuous people in the *Republic* as citizens, friends, relations, and free, so that for the Stoics, parents and children are enemies, since they are not wise.[2]

We have good independent reasons for thinking that Zeno strictly limited citizenship in his *Republic* to the wise, but whatever precise form of a non-cosmopolitan political view one decides this particular passage evinces, it really is striking how little airplay it gets from those scholars—many of whom should know better—who claim the ancient Stoics as forerunners of cosmopolitanism. The Stoics, moreover, held that the appearance of a wise man is exceedingly rare—as rare as the Ethiopian Phoenix; hence, this vision of the great mass of humanity being endlessly condemned to relations of enmity at every stratum of personal and public life suggests a more dismal view of human political possibilities than that of even, say, the anti-cosmopolitan Carl Schmitt, who mainly restricts himself to *political* enmity and creates, rather optimistically from the perspective of this passage, an important space in political life for relations of friendship. Thus, given this darkly cacotopic fantasy about human relations rising up out of our best evidence about ancient Stoic politics, one might reasonably wonder whence cometh all the recent fuss about Stoic cosmopolitanism.

Before turning to this question, however, it might be helpful to continue Diogenes's report, since it rounds out the correlative vision of Zeno's best society:

> and [they criticize him again] for his doctrine, set out there concerning community of wives, and his prohibition at line 200 against the building of temples, law courts and gymnasia in cities. They also take exception to his statement on currency: "The provision of currency should not be thought necessary either for exchange or travel," and for his instruction that men and women should wear the same clothes and keep no part of the body completely covered."[3]

These further features of life in Zeno's *Republic* serve as essentially a kind of antinomian laundry list aimed at eradicating from the Stoic city of the wise the most important traditional features of life in a Greek *polis*. Of course, a Stoic sage, unlike the philosopher king in Plato's *Republic*, is able to live in any kind of city and still be perfectly happy, since he can be blissfully happy even on the rack. But, if a group of wise Stoics did live together—and again, in contrast to Plato's account, it is not exactly clear why they would either need or want to—their dwelling place, according to Zeno, would have no temples or statues of gods, no law courts, no gymnasia for training young men for the military, no weapons, no money, and presumably no private property. This is because the wise have no need of such external things in order to be morally virtuous. General education too would be abolished and with it, the need to memorize Homer and, more important, the possibility of imbibing the traditional Homeric worldview, with all its supporting institutions. For the Stoic, such institutions are based on irrational religious fears, on unnecessary worries about material goods and status, and on mistaken anxieties about defending one's life or goods from the incursions of others. As such, they should be eliminated.

It has sometimes been suggested that by eliminating specifically *Greek* political and religious institutions, the Stoics are envisioning a more cosmopolitan conception of political arrangements that goes beyond the narrow confines of the Greek city-state. Such a claim strikes me as dubious, since what Zeno conceives of instead is insufficiently inclusive to support any tenable conception of cosmopolitanism. He offers sole membership in his *polis* to a perhaps nonexistent group of the wise, and their invulnerable virtue is sufficient in itself to vitiate the need for common institutions, even of a very tepid sort that can help coordinate common efforts, much less those that on a grander scale attempt to protect differences and ameliorate potential conflict.

By the same token, Chrysippus (an early successor of Zeno who is presumably following him doctrinally) advocates in his *Republic* total sexual polymorphism. Sex, for the Stoic, is a matter of moral indifference and involves nothing more than bits of flesh rubbing against one another. Such rubbing might involve the flesh of one's mother, daughter, sister, or anyone else male or female. From the perspective of the Stoic wise man, Oedipus and Jocasta should just kick back and dote on the fine children they produced,[4] though given that neither is wise, they still are likely to become embroiled with their children in familial hatreds unconnected to their particular history of rubbing. In Plato's *Republic*, sexual communism is carefully controlled as a means of breeding the best citizens and there are built-in riders aimed at avoiding incest. The Stoics disagree. For them sex is an indifferent external consideration of the flesh that in no way touches inner moral autonomy or has any relevant political consequences.

Not surprisingly, their unconventional views on this score attracted much attention in antiquity and often proved an embarrassment to later Romans who, in trying Stoicism on for size, were attracted, like Stockdale, to the more muscular side of Stoic virtue. I mention these rather sensationalist features of their doctrines, however, not in the spirit of the tabloids, but because it can be useful to keep such Stoic attitudes in mind when reading recent claims about their careful attention to practices rooted in local familial and gender justice.[5]

This studied indifference to the body as a site of cultural construction or signification led the Stoics to further claim that institutions surrounding the burial of the dead are also to be eliminated. Giving members of the community a proper burial was taken throughout the Greek tradition to be one of the most crucial sociopolitical functions of the city-state.[6] Thus, Herodotus, for instance, argues that what marks Greek culture off from Indian culture is that the Greeks burn their dead while the Indians have the custom of eating them.[7] The Stoics argue, on the other hand, that the treatment of the dead is a matter of utter indifference. The dead are just so much flesh and, if one does not want to waste the meat, it is perfectly in keeping with nature to eat them. Notice in this context, however, that although at first glance the Stoics might seem to be endorsing the indigenous religious practices of Herodotus's reputed Indians against those of their own culture, in fact they are keen to reject a Herodotean conclusion about the importance and divergence of rooted local customs. They are not, that is, recommending eating the dead out of any regard for the religious beliefs of others. For Herodotus, custom (*nomos*) is king and with that recognition comes toleration for the ways of others and a lack of chauvinism about one's own. For the Stoics, conversely, reason is king, and the variability of custom is merely a matter of indifference. Indeed, they linguistically override such particularist claims by arguing that *nomos* is to be identified only with God's rational moral law, which is the same everywhere. We will need to take up their conception of the moral law more fully, but for now some of these further details of the Stoic position can serve to provide an initial glimpse of what I would characterize as a uniform Stoic hostility to arguments based on local or "rooted" customs, attitudes, and institutions.

Readers not conversant with the details of ancient Stoicism should now be in a better position to approach the two main ancient texts that are most frequently trotted out as evidence for their cosmopolitanism, typically in isolation from this more reliable evidence. Both come from authors already deeply embedded in a Roman imperial context and while I do not necessarily agree with Anthony Pagden's claim that so-called cosmopolitan thinking in this period is strictly in the ideological service of Roman imperial goals,[8] it is doubtlessly misleading to read these passages entirely independent of their Roman intellectual and political context.

We can turn to the first of these passages insofar as it has become the main prop for attributing a kind of "rooted" cosmopolitanism to the ancient Stoics. Martha Nussbaum, for example, has leaned on it heavily in lauding the Stoics' attempt to combine what she describes as a rich recognition of individuals' local affiliations with their universal respect for each individual *qua* human being. For the moment, I will bypass the question of whether this kind of picture of cosmopolitanism with a communitarian face is even coherent, but Nussbaum anchors her argument in a passage from Hierocles, a later Neo-Stoic (1st–2nd cent. C.E.), who describes each of us as being surrounded by an extending series of concentric circles beginning with our innermost self, family, relatives, neighbors, and so on, and ending with a final circle embracing humanity as a whole. On the basis of her interpretation of this particular image, she argues that the Stoics insist that we do not "need to give up our specific affections and identifications, whether ethnic or gender-based or religious. We need not think of them as superficial, and we may think of our identity as being partly constituted by them."[9]

To begin with, as far as I can tell, the passage says absolutely nothing about religion or gender per se, but let me first set out the relevant excerpt. The text, it is worth noting, is from a treatise entitled *How Should One Behave toward One's Relatives?*

> For each of us, most generally, is circumscribed by many circles, some smaller, some larger, some surrounding others, some surrounded, according to their different and unequal relations to one another. The first and closest circle is that which each person draws around his own mind, as the center: in this circle is enclosed the body and whatever is employed for the sake of the body. For this circle is the shortest and all but touches its own center. The second after this one, standing further away from the center and enclosing the first, is that within which our parents, siblings, wife, and children are ranged. Third, after these, is that in which there are uncles and aunts, grandfathers and grandmothers, the children of one's siblings, and also cousins. After this comes the one that embraces all other relatives. Next upon this is the circle of the members of one's deme, then that of the members of one's tribe, next that of one's fellow citizens, and so, finally that of those who border one's city and that of people of a like ethnicity. The furthest out and largest one, which surrounds all the circles, is that of the entire race of human beings. Once these have been thought through, accordingly, it is possible, starting with the most stretched-out one, to draw the circles—concerning the behavior that is due to each group—together in a way, as though towards the center, and with an effort to keep transferring items out of the containing circles into the contained. For example, in respect to love of one's family it is possible to love parents and siblings and therefore, in the same proportion, among one's relatives, to treat the more elderly men and women as grandparents

or uncles and aunts, those of the same age as cousins, and the younger ones as children of one's cousins. Thus, a clear recommendation has been set forth, in concise terms, for how one should treat relatives, since we have already taught how people should behave towards themselves, and how parents and siblings, and further toward wife and children: the charge is that one must honor, in a way similar to these last, those from the third circle, and must in turn honor relatives in a way similar to these latter. Indeed, a greater distance in respect to blood will subtract something of good will, but nevertheless we must make an effort about assimilating them. For it would arrive at fairness if, through our own initiative, we cut down the distance in our relationship toward each person.[10]

Hierocles has sometimes been taken to be offering an example of the Stoics' theory of social *oikeiosis*—though the word does not occur in the passage—and as such the account has gathered both praise and blame. This claim is dubious, but for the sake of argument, let's suppose this passage reflects a Stoic belief that we begin with a feeling of kinship, recognition, and the like to ourselves (*oikeiosis*) and then in the course of our psychological development begin to extend it to others. We have touched on Nussbaum's praise,[11] but it is easy to see how less communitarian minded critics would find much to criticize in a view that appears to base moral regard on relations of distance from one's own personal desires and interests. As a social mechanism, such a tactic seems problematic if it merely involves projecting one's self-regard onto others or of identifying with others only to the extent that they mirror one's inner needs and self-concern. The worry, of course, is that such an account fails to give proper recognition to other individuals as being worthy of respect in their own right.[12] Moreover, it is hard to see how this tactic of viewing others from the perspective of one's own self-regard is supposed to underpin the psychological development of one's sense of rational impartiality and the recognition of the equal dignity of every human being.[13]

Complaints against such a view of social *oikeiosis* are arguably justified, but they are aimed in this instance, I would argue, at a phantom, since only a reading driven by very particular theoretical goals could lead one to conclude that Hierocles is claiming that every group in an outer circle should eventually be brought into the innermost circle of one's own identity and that this can be a method for achieving an all-encompassing rational impartiality. Hierocles merely says that one should always try to treat those from an enclosing circle as we do those from the circle it encloses and his primary focus seems to be on relations among relatives, which after all, is the topic of his treatise. What Hierocles envisions in each case, is trying to reduce distance, not to eliminate it entirely. He concedes, moreover, that even in relations among close relatives, goodwill is related to distance in blood, thus apparently recognizing grounds for obligation that are independent of any commonly shared rationality or humanity. Indeed, it is precisely for this seeming innovation that many scholars have thought that Hierocles has moved well beyond Stoic doctrine, perhaps under the influence of the Peripatetics in giving relations based on purely contingent relations and affection any moral grounding. But bracketing such scholarly niceties, this passage seems much more plausibly read as just a bit of homespun ethical advice of the sort we might expect to find in such a nontechnical, rhetorical work that has all the hallmarks of a popular self-help manual. Rather than propounding any deep claims about the nature of our cosmopolitan social identity, Hierocles's image of the circles seems to be merely a vivid way of illustrating a commonplace bit of general, if not particularly taxing, practical advice about how to go about treating one's family relations somewhat better. Accordingly, however much we think that such claims about the importance of family cohesion are driven by a larger Roman imperial agenda, it at least should be evident how far Hierocles has moved from Zeno's and Chrysippus's original Stoic conception of wise men having wives in common, indiscriminately rubbing their flesh against all and sundry, and of virtuously enduring the ineliminable enmity of their family relations, all of whom are mere fools. It is perhaps an interesting scholarly question for specialists how strains in Neo-Stoicism developed that wished to transform *No Exit* into *The Brady Bunch*; but the actual relevance of any of this to larger questions of cosmopolitanism is rather tenuous to say the least, and certainly does not portend a conception of "rooted" cosmopolitanism.

Our second passage is even more notorious and controversial, at least among classical scholars, but for all that it is fairly easy to defuse its relevance to discussions of cosmopolitanism. Again, we can begin with a view of the passage that Martha Nussbaum has thrown her support behind. In the course of arguing against Richard Rorty's call for Americans to give up the politics of indifference and to embrace both patriotism and a common feeling of national identity, Nussbaum argues that we would do much better to adopt "the very old idea of the cosmopolitan, the person whose allegiance is to the worldwide community of human beings."[14] Appealing to a two-sentence summary of the main point of Zeno's *Republic* by Plutarch (46–120 C.E.) for the Stoic notion of a world citizen, she claims that it is "the source and ancestor of Kant's idea of the 'kingdom of ends', and has a similar function in inspiring and regulating moral and political conduct. One should always behave so as to treat with equal respect the dignity of reason and moral choice in every human being."[15] Such a notion, she insists, can be appealed to in order to help ward off the many potential harms fostered by nationalism and partisan loyalties.

Here is the passage:

And, indeed, provoking much amazement, the *[R]epublic* (*politeia*) of Zeno, who founded the Stoic school of thought, strives to make this one main point, that (a) we should not dwell in cities and *demes* each (of us) isolated by distinct legal ordinances (*dikaiois*), but (b) that we should hold all men to be demesmen and citizens, and that there should be one form of life and organization (*kosmos*), just like a herd grazing together and brought up in a common pasture (or in a common custom or law).[16] Zeno, for his part, wrote this down, having imagined it to be unreal or as a mere image of the lawful orderliness (*eunomias*) of the philosopher and of the *politeia*, whereas Alexander provisioned talk with deeds.[17]

First, consider a few brief features of its respective context. Our opening passage from Diogenes, like a work of modern scholarship, cites line numbers from Zeno's text to support its argument, quotes parts of it apparently verbatim, and it occurs as part of a larger philosophical doxography whose intent is to describe and criticize ancient philosophical works. This passage from Plutarch, on the other hand, is from an essay on Alexander the Great's accomplishments in which one of Plutarch's passing leitmotifs is to contrast the actual deeds of a great man with the mere words of ineffectual philosophers (whose positions he regularly misdescribes). Plutarch, moreover, is also a vehement and often unreliable critic of Stoicism elsewhere in his more straightforwardly philosophical essays and there is no evidence that he ever had a text of Zeno's *Republic* at hand. Given these differences in context and argumentative goals, it is easy to see why there are grounds for suspicion about the trustworthiness of Plutarch's comments when they conflict with those of Diogenes.

It might be helpful to begin with one contrast between the two passages that is central for questions of cosmopolitanism. The passage from Diogenes claims that Zeno does away with law courts; wise men do not need them since they do not commit injustice, nor can anyone do anything to a wise man in ways that would need to be redressed in a court. In Plutarch's telling, on the other hand, all men, rather than being subject to distinct legal ordinances, are to be subject to a common law. What seems abundantly clear, at least, is that the particular details of Plutarch's comments are being driven by the comparison to Alexander, since unifying the world under one law is exactly what Plutarch claims Alexander actually managed to do. In making this claim, he is doubtlessly being anachronistic and reading back Roman imperial ideology onto Alexander's conquests, since it seems fairly clear that Alexander was not hoping to realize some unified political ideal through his program of conquest. But for our purposes, it is sufficient to note that he discusses both Alexander and Zeno in the light of Alexander's role as a conqueror and what resulted from it. It is therefore not especially surprising that his deeply Platonic and deeply unstoic simile of sheep grazing together seems to cry out for a shepherd—in this case, Alexander. It is almost impossible for us to imagine Zeno portraying his hyperrational sages who care only for their moral autonomy grazing together like a herd of sheep in their *polis*.

There is, moreover, a larger problem of interpreting the point of Plutarch's contrast between Alexander and Zeno. The initial problem we face is that this text, when taken out of its context, might misleadingly seem rather exciting, as in Nussbaum's cosmopolitan reading. When one reads it in the context of its comparison to Alexander, however, we must content ourselves with a much more deflationary reading. This is because in accordance with Plutarch's overall conclusion, what Alexander accomplished historically was to break down distinct legal ordinances and to make everyone members of his empire. That Alexander was instrumental in joining communities together exactly in this way is one of Plutarch's most common refrains in the work. Elsewhere he claims that whereas only a few have read Plato's *Laws*, the myriads who previously were either living brutishly without laws or living under their own laws came to make common use of Alexander's laws.[18] Plutarch's primary concern is to illustrate these characteristic results of Alexander's actions. He makes a reference to an ineffectual philosopher like Zeno either on the basis of some rather tenuous and mostly irretrievable similarities, or in the same arbitrary way, for instance, that he does in the above reference to Plato's *Laws*.

For those defending the kind of cosmopolitan reading Nussbaum offers, there are a host of formidable obstacles. When taken out of its larger context, it is easy to see how (b), for instance, might conjure up moral and political attitudes such as a cosmopolitan respect for universal justice, equality, and the intrinsic mutual respect of all individuals by reason of their common humanity—especially when one is looking back through the lens of the later history of political theory. This is indeed heady stuff, of course, but I doubt that a careful reading of the passage as a whole can support any of these claims. First, Plutarch hardly can be seriously concluding that what Alexander accomplished historically through his conquests is such an earthly realization of the kingdom of ends. Moreover, it would severely undercut his own argument to show that Alexander only accomplished something that is a pale reflection of what Zeno was imagining. In fact, it is Zeno, he claims, who is capable of imagining only an image of what Alexander has achieved. The direction of explanation, then, goes from Alexander to Zeno, and those who support a high cosmopolitan reading leave Plutarch with the odd result of making Alexander's achievements rather second-rate compared with Zeno's moral vision, which can hardly be Plutarch's point.

By the same token, we have to be careful about how we read the moral claims in "we should not dwell in communities isolated by legal ordinances" and "we should consider all humans as fellow citizens." Proponents of cosmopolitanism typically interpret this as distinguishing two communities, "the local community of our birth, and the community of human agreement and aspiration . . . that is fundamentally the source of our moral obligations."[19] They then assume that Plutarch must be referring to the latter. But here Plutarch is surely making a different point that is in line with his central goal of favorably contrasting Alexander with philosophers. Philosophers say that people should live in a particular manner, but Alexander through his actions makes it the case that people actually live in that manner. Plutarch is not signaling a distinction between a natural and conventional community. Rather, he is claiming (no doubt tendentiously) that Zeno could at best urge people in words to live in a way that Alexander made possible in deeds.

Similarly, Nussbaum interprets (a) as a deep moral command enjoining that we should consider all human beings our fellow citizens with respect to such basic moral values as justice. What Plutarch actually says, however, is far less morally dramatic and again, something readily achievable through territorial conquest rather than any deepened sense of moral recognition, that is, that people dwell together under a common law.

Of course, it might be objected that there must be some basis of comparison with Zeno's views for Plutarch to be referring to him in this context. This is not necessarily the case, since Plutarch's comparisons are often merely arbitrary. But one possible candidate in this passage is the Stoic notion of the *koinos nomos*, or common natural law pervading all things. Plutarch shows an awareness of this central Stoic doctrine elsewhere and may be alluding to it here.[20] In Diogenes Laertius, we find a typical instance of this Stoic claim, for which there is much evidence:

> living in agreement with nature comes to be the end, which is in accordance with the nature of oneself and that of the whole, engaging in no activity forbidden by universal law (*ho nomos ho koinos*), which is right reason pervading everything and identical to Zeus, who is the director of the administration of existing things. And the virtue of the happy man and his good flow of life are just this: always doing everything on the basis of concordance of each man's guardian spirit with the will of the administrator of the whole.[21]

The Stoics think that the universe is governed by a divine providential law and that one will be both virtuous and happy only if one follows it. But even if we grant that (c) makes an allusion to the Stoics' claim that we should live by the divine commands of natural law, we still need to be careful about how we approach the claims in (a) and (b), and also about the political conclusions we draw from the passage. First, it is clear that for Zeno only the wise and the gods can live in accordance with the *koinos nomos*. Everyone else, of course, is still subject to the *koinos nomos* and thus *should not* dwell in isolated judicial districts (a) and *should* regard all humans as members of the same community and as fellow citizens (b). However, it is not at all clear that living according to divine law requires from the Stoic the kinds of generalized moral attitudes to others that characterize Kant's kingdom of ends, since although everyone may have the potential to take part in this moral community, precious few actually do—only the wise and gods. The rest remain in a condition of mutual enmity and irrational foolishness. Nor, as a consequence, does obedience to the *koinos nomos* necessarily require the kinds of political commitments Nussbaum links to a more generalized cosmopolitanism.

Moreover, it should be remembered that Plutarch's main emphasis is on the difference between what Zeno could only imagine in words and what Alexander actually achieved through his conquests—bringing people to live together in common like a grazing herd. The Platonic image of grazing sheep, however, is consonant with Plutarch's emphasis on how Alexander's conquests helped to bring peace and order to a chaotic world. In other contexts, moreover, such an image typically suggests a Platonic notion that sheep graze most harmoniously and safely under the eye of a benign and watchful shepherd/ruler. So we should be wary about the political message we can draw from this image and from the passage in general. The fact that someone is a fellow member of my community or a fellow citizen does not by itself guarantee that I view him as my equal, if my community is arranged in various social and political hierarchies. While it is true that, for the Stoics, we are all rational sparks of god and equal in that basic sense, this does not lead them to make any straightforward inferences to universal *political* equality. Indeed, just the opposite seems to be the case. The surviving Stoic texts we have using the terminology of *isotes* or *aequalitas* all aim at capturing a notion of the impartial administration of law among individuals who are clearly assumed to belong to different levels of political and social hierarchies. Modern attempts to enlist Stoics in the ranks of cosmopolitan thinkers often merely assume that their cosmopolitanism entails a range of other political attitudes and ideals as well. The Stoics, however, typically argue that we may be given different social and political roles to play by fate, but it is a matter of moral indifference whether we play the role of, say, an Agamemnon or a Thersites.[22] No matter the role we play, king or slave, we can still perfect our inner moral autonomy.

It is probably time to ask, however, what the upshot of this kind of philological detective work contributes to our understanding of cosmopolitanism. At the risk of trying the patience of those not familiar with the field, this examination has tried to offer a glimpse of the nature of the evidence that remains and the sorts of assumptions and arguments that surround it. I have argued that it is not very likely that this passage from Plutarch can carry the burden of even bland forms of political cosmopolitanism. But even if we granted a stronger cosmopolitan reading of the passage, we would still be left at best with a certain kind of thin, selective moral regard for others that may be ethically commendable, but that leaves questions of political engagement and state institutional power untouched. Nothing in this passage, therefore, is incompatible with a traditional view derived from Hegel that in the Hellenistic period philosophers turned inward, giving up their interest in questions of political participation, political goals, and non-individualistic forms of social relations.

This is, no doubt, a deflationary view of the Stoics' political thought and perhaps much less interesting than what is on offer from several modern reconstructions. But since the ancient Stoics have been injected into contemporary debates about cosmopolitanism, I would like to raise in conclusion what I see as a strong objection on their part to an influential recent defense of cosmopolitanism by Anthony Appiah. For Appiah, friendship offers an important test case for thinking about cosmopolitan relations and the possibility of successfully negotiating between ethical obligations that "invoke community founded in a shared past or collective memory" and so-called thin moral obligations that "are stipulatively entailed by a shared humanity."[23] The Stoics too think that friendship is important for their city of the wise, but the difference in their respective conceptions offers an important window into a problem lurking for Appiah's project. For Appiah, friendship is a particularist good. "*My friend Mary* is not simply an instantiation of the general good represented by *friendship*; she's not like one first-class stamp on a roll of first-class stamps."[24] To think of friendship in this postage stamp way, Appiah asserts, is to confuse social goals based on impartiality with personal ties based on shared history and community. Invoking Debbie Boone ("It can't be wrong/ When it feels so right") to illustrate how we reject moral theories that don't track actual existing empirical norms, Appiah attempts to carve out a space for friendships that elicits strong sets of obligations not reducible to those demanded by moral impartiality.

We can consider in passing the Stoics' strong reservations about Debbie Boone's feelings of rightness. As is well known, they reject decisions grounded in ordinary emotions because they think that most emotions, apart from a few special Stoic emotions, arise from mistaken views of one's own good. It may feel right, but if those feelings are based on Johnnie's dimple, his shiny Corvette, and the way he wears those Levis, Debbie may be letting herself in for some trouble down the line. The Stoics think that what is right must be grounded in attitudes that are neither contingent in this way nor based on false views of virtue and the good. To take another example from Appiah, we all, he suggests, can recognize the bonds of friendship among thieves. True, the Stoics reply, but we also recognize how we think someone is better off leaving a gang and graduating to pursuits that are better both for themselves and for society. Why is that? Like most theorists of friendship in antiquity, the Stoics believe that friendship worthy of a name requires a mutual commitment to virtue. Indeed, taking Aristotle's conception to its logical conclusion, they argue that your best friend might be someone you have not yet met, since only virtue matters. Of course, we might find such a view that jettisons all claims of a mutually shared history deeply counterintuitive, but the Stoic view responds directly to a seemingly intractable dilemma facing any account of friendship. Derrida, reviving an ancient philosophical quandary from the Greeks, poses the following basic question. Why is it that we value friends? For themselves or for their qualities? If we value friends for their qualities, that is, for their abstract properties—Appiah's postage stamp worry—it seems that we do not value our friends *qua* themselves as individuals. This is because if we value friends only for their abstract properties we might find ready substitutes. Sure, Sally has a good sense of humor, but Dolly has a better one, so why not trade up, if what I really value in my friends is a sense of humor? One might object that we value friends not just for one property, but for their uniquely individual set of properties. But it doesn't take much imagination to see

that once we concede that what we value in friends are abstract properties and not individuals *per se*, we still have reasons to trade up from
one particular grab bag of properties to another, if in it we find more
instantiations of those properties that we like. Appiah clearly would not
be happy with such a view of friendships, but he fails to offer any explicit
justification of friendships based on shared experience and community.

One possibility that might arise from a Debbie Boone justification is
that "I love Johnny just because he is Johnny"—that unique individual
who is Johnny. But in making this claim, one runs into the other horn
of Derrida's dilemma. How is it possible to love something without any
properties? Or at the metaphysical level, how do we conceive of a bare
particular with no properties? To love people for themselves alone also
raises a further ethical and moral worry. Let's call it the battered wife
worry. "I love Johnny for himself alone. Of course, he beats me, is an
alcoholic, and runs around, but aren't I, as a good wife, supposed to love
him for who he is?" If we are inclined to say no, we have to appeal to
abstract properties, good and bad, over and above Johnny *qua* Johnny.

Appiah, of course, wants to maintain a delicate balance between particularist values and those of moral impartiality, but the Stoics would
claim that the so-called particularist value of friendship he relies on
quickly falls apart into its Derridean disjuncts of abstraction and bare
particularism upon further analysis. Ironically, moreover, the particularism of the kind of friendship that Appiah defends turns out to be
the particularism of the bare individual, and the values of community
and history that he defends are therefore only defensible when they are
grounded—or rooted, if you will—in those very abstract, postage stamp
values that he rejects as explaining the value of friendship. This is the
reason, in fact, that the Stoics maintain that the only friendships that are
justifiable are those between virtuous friends who actually know how
to benefit one another in light of the good. You may not have met that
virtuous person yet, but if there is such a good person in the world, he
is benefiting you more, as the Stoics say, by moving his finger, than all
the Johnnies you may have grown up with and hung around with for
reasons having nothing to do with the good.

The Stoics thus offer an austere and pessimistic reminder that many of
the values that contemporary theorists build on, especially in attempting
to separate an ethical sphere of personal obligation in contradistinction

to a thin moral sphere of universal obligation, rest on fragile foundations that are often merely assumed from empirical intuitions, common
sense, and the like—the Debbie Boone syndrome. When we scratch the
surface, they insist, we are likely to end up falling onto the other horn of
Derrida's dilemma, that of having to ultimately justify so-called personal
"ethical" relations by appeal to thin moral abstractions.

Moreover, to the extent that the Debbie Boone syndrome spills over
into political theorizing, of which one worrying instance are the many
hybrid forms of contemporary cosmopolitanism that rest on it "just feeling right," we are likely to face the impossible task of what the Stoics saw
as founding a city made up of enemies and fools. In their view, even the
thinnest forms of cosmopolitanism can only include a few virtuous wise
friends, and the chances of that are, unfortunately, as rare as the Ethiopian phoenix.

NOTES

1 See the vivid book of Vice-Admiral James Bond Stockdale, *Courage under Fire:
   Testing Epictetus's Doctrines in a Laboratory of Human Behavior* (Stanford: Hoover
   Institute, 1993). The laboratory referred to here is the infamous Hoa Loa prisoner
   of war camp ("Hanoi Hilton"). Stockdale's account of his lived Stoicism often
   captures far more of the spirit of the ancient doctrines than that typically found in
   what he no doubt would describe as the tepid world of scholarly "yackety-yack."
   However, while ancient Stoics are very adept at exerting their moral will in the
   face of adversity and at withstanding torture, they are also committed peaceniks
   and deny the need for weapons, military training, or organized combat even to
   save one's own life or goods, much less to halt the spread of communism or to
   secure oil.
2 Diogenes Laertius 7.32 ff=LS 67B.
3 Diogenes Laertius 7.32 ff=LS 67B, continued.
4 Sext. Emp. 3.246; 1.491.
5 E.g., Martha C. Nussbaum, *For Love of Country? A New Democracy Forum on the
   Limits of Patriotism* (Boston: Beacon Press, 1996).
6 Cf. Antigone, Pericles's funeral oration at Thucydides, 2.35 ff, etc.
7 3.228.
8 Anthony Pagden, "Stoicism, Cosmopolitanism, and the Legacy of European
   Imperialism," *Constellations* 7 (2000): 3–22. Pagden argues that the conception
   of cosmopolitanism that arose in this period is inextricably tied to the Roman
   imperial goal of imposing one political order on the world. Although such a view
   provides an important counterweight to those who extract cosmopolitanism
   from its historical context, it lacks nuance. Cf. Melanie Subacus, who shows how
   political cosmopolitanism arises in Rome from, among other things, particular

worries about the nature of kinship ties and the extension of citizenship within the empire. Melanie Subacus, "*Duae Patriae*: Cicero and Political Cosmopolitanism in Rome," Ph.D. dissertation, New York University, 2014.

9 M. C. Nussbaum, "Patriotism and Cosmopolitanism," *Boston Review* 19.5 (1994), 9.
10 Stobaeus, *Anthology*, 4.84.23, trans. Konstan.
11 Cf. Kristeva, *Strangers to Ourselves* (New York: Columbia University Press, 1991), 56 ff.
12 M. M. McCabe, "Extend or Identify: Two Stoic Accounts of Altruism," in R. Salles (ed.), *Metaphysics, Soul, and Ethics in Ancient Thought* (New York: Oxford University Press, 2005): 413-443.
13 Nussbaum, *For Love of Country?* 9.
14 Nussbaum, *For Love of Country?* 9.
15 See Nussbaum, "Patriotism and Cosmopolitanism," 8.
16 There is a pun here on nó-mos (law) and no-mós (pasture).
17 Plutarch, *De Alexandri magni fortuna aut virtute*, i 329a8-b7, trans. my own.
18 328e5-8.
19 Nussbaum, *For Love of Country?* 9.
20 See Vander Waerdt 1994: 272 ff.
21 Diogenes Laertius.7.88, trans. Long and Sedley, 63C.
22 Diogenes Laertius.7.160.
23 Kwame Anthony Appiah, *The Ethics of Identity* (Princeton: Princeton University Press, 2005), 229–230.
24 Appiah (2005), 230 ff. On Stoic friendship, see Glenn Lesses, "Austere Friends: The Stoics and Friendship," *Apeiron* 26.1 (1993), 57–75.

14

A Cosmopolitanism of Connections

CRAIG CALHOUN

Cosmopolitanism is an ancient idea, typically traced back to Diogenes of Sinope, who aspired to be a citizen of the world partly to avoid the laws and social norms of any particular place. Instead, he affirmed, one should simply live in accordance with nature. He dressed badly, slept in a tub, and advocated public sex and unrestrained belching. The citizens of Athens thought the self-declared citizen of the world was simply uncivilized.

Fortunately, one does not have to be uncivilized to be a cosmopolitan. Diogenes gave us a term that we translate as "citizenship of the world," but we use it less to describe a political status, like citizenship in a nation-state, than a sense of appreciation and responsibility for the whole world. Some people follow Diogenes in imagining that advancing cosmopolitanism is a matter of shedding local cultures because they are all restrictive. Others, however, more usefully imagine cosmopolitanism as something we achieve in and through culture, on the basis of resources provided to us about the history of civilizations, the teachings of religions, and the intellectual contributions of scholars. This is the perspective I advance here. We do not have to think of cosmopolitanism in terms of the lowest common denominators of human nature. We can think of it in terms of the highest aspirations of human culture. This is what makes it appropriate as a theme for this occasion, which celebrates communication and collaboration between countries embodied precisely in an institution of learning.

Here is the moral of my story, stated up front: learning to be an effective and responsible citizen of the world—a cosmopolitan—is not simply a matter of absorbing universal truth. It is a matter of learning to navigate cultural difference and differences of basic values and orientations—and doing so with respect for people who navigate those differences less.

The idea of being a citizen of the world has gone through many per-
mutations since Diogenes. It was important to the Stoic philosophers of
Rome and has surfaced, not always under precisely the same name, in
a range of empires and world religions. It flourished among Arab philosophers in Al-Andalus and other Europeans in both the age of Shakespeare and that of the more rationalist Enlightenment.

More recently, the term *cosmopolitan* has come into fashion since the
late 1990s. It is the topic of best-selling books and numerous academic
anthologies. This reflects three different stimuli.

First, there was the fall of Soviet communism. This encouraged high
hopes for the possibility of achieving a new global order. Cosmopolitanism became an important name for this agenda, encompassing human
rights, the proliferation of nongovernmental organizations, hopes for
the spread of democracy, and attempts to strengthen the United Nations
and other global institutions. There was more unalloyed optimism for
this agenda in the 1990s. Terrorism, wars, financial collapse, and the
evident weakness of our global tools for dealing with these events have
made the 2010s a more sobering time. We worry not just whether the
global order will be just, but whether it will in fact win out over chaos.
But hope remains widespread that it will be possible to realize higher
standards of international, cosmopolitan justice.

Second, there has been growing recognition that people around the
world are joined in a common community of fate. Should massive climate change occur, it will affect the whole world. Even without climate
change, there are serious ecological dangers that create transnational
and even global risks, and infectious diseases that do not respect
national or cultural boundaries. Or consider the implication of nuclear
weapons (or other weapons of mass destruction). They make warfare
something the whole world has to worry about, not just a problem for
combatant countries. Cosmopolitanism here names the need for transnational collaboration to confront these challenges—and the expectation that it will emerge because people of many countries share in the
sense of need.

Third, globalization calls forth cosmopolitanism. Economic integration, migration, the spread of world religions, the capacity of electronic
media to transcend distance—all spread awareness that no nation stands
alone. Contact among cultures enriches knowledge and encourages

appreciation of different kinds of artistic beauty and expression. Globalization, however, is not simply a single phenomenon spreading everywhere. It is a host of different patterns of interconnection. No market is simply the universal market. Great religions seek the universal in different ways. Globalization is not an entirely new phenomenon but is shaped by histories of empire and war, trade relations that long predate modern capitalism, and efforts to build better relations among countries. Discussions of cosmopolitanism or world citizenship need to take this into account. The learning offered in a great university needs to provide students with resources for understanding these different situations and perspectives.

An orientation to other cultures and to all the world's people is ethically and intellectually important. In cosmopolitanism we can see an embrace of human diversity that enriches life by incorporating knowledge and creativity from other cultures. Equally we can see the sense of an underlying commonality because all are human, and as the Roman playwright Terence put it, "nothing human is alien to me." This can extend into an idea of responsibility that each of us should care about others distant from us. How we approach this makes a great deal of difference.

It is easy to be too casual about cosmopolitanism because the word is used to mean too many different things. I suggest three ways that cosmopolitanism can be discussed. The first, I suggest, reduces cosmopolitanism to style—a style associated especially with global elites. Possibly attractive, and in many ways empowering for those who learn it, this is mainly a distraction from more basic ethical, social, and political concerns. The second approaches cosmopolitanism as a universalistic ethics based on ideas like human rights that stress the equivalence of every human being. Valuable to theories of justice, this is nonetheless a limited perspective because it abstracts persons too much from social and cultural contexts and often blinds us to the implications of material inequality. The third approach sees cosmopolitanism not only in equivalence but in connections. It emphasizes that although we are growing more connected, the patterns of our connections are varied and incomplete, not universal. It reminds us that we engage the larger world through our specific localities, nations, religions, and cultures, not by escaping them.

Cosmopolitanism as Style

"Cosmopolitan" is a compliment for the suave and debonair. It is praise for those who know how to pick out an Italian suit, who read the *Economist* and *Financial Times*, who can discuss the merits of Nobel Prize–winning novelists from Egypt, Portugal, or Nigeria. It is a term of self-congratulation for those who can eat Asian food with chopsticks, Ethiopian or Indian food with fingers, and pick the right fork for each course at an elegant European banquet. In both popular culture and political science, cosmopolitanism often figures as an attitude, a style, a personal commitment; this is not necessarily political or even ethical. Contrast the significance of the phrases "citizen of the world" and "man of the world." The former may hint at humanitarian commitments or leadership in global business or diplomacy. The latter is as likely to be about expanded tolerance for ethical lapses—or simply about more fashionable clothes.

For many people, cosmopolitanism denotes a world that is simply an object of consumption, there for individuals' pleasure. "The goal of cosmopolitanism is self-expression and self-realization," writes feminist lawyer Kimberly Yuracko. "Cosmopolitanism presents individuals with a wide range of options; they choose the one that will bring them the most pleasure and gratification."[1] This consumerist perspective on cosmopolitanism is widespread.

In the world's global cities, and even in many of its small towns, certain forms of cosmopolitan diversity appear ubiquitous. Certainly Chinese food is now a global cuisine—both in a generic form that exists especially as a global cuisine and in more "authentic" regional versions prepared for cultivated global palates. And one can buy Kentucky Fried Chicken in Beijing. Local taste cultures that were once more closed and insular have opened up. Samosas are now English food, just as pizza is American and Indonesian curry is Dutch. Even where the hint of the exotic (and the uniformity of the local) is stronger, one can eat internationally—Mexican food in Norway, Ethiopian cuisine in Italy. Consumerist cosmopolitanism can even extend to marriage choices. "Cosmopolitan" is the first category in the advertisements posted by would-be husbands seeking brides (and vice versa) in the *Sunday Times of India*.[2]

As many people use the word, *cosmopolitanism* suggests a personal attitude or virtue that can be assumed without change in basic political or economic structures—which are external to the individual. Much of its appeal comes from the notion that cosmopolitanism (a version of ethical goodness) can be achieved without such deeper structural change. But cosmopolitanism is not simply a free-floating cultural taste, equally accessible to everyone; it is not just a personal attitude or a political choice, although it can inform these. Cosmopolitanism is also a matter of material conditions that are very unequally distributed. What seems like free individual choice is often made possible by capital—social and cultural as well as economic. Take the slogan in Sony's recent computer advertisements: "C is for Choice, Color, and Cosmopolitanism." Surely C is also for Capital.[3]

Take Singapore's president, who spoke of the island's "cosmopolitans" and "heartlanders." After his speech, a local blogger responded sarcastically: "Many Heartlanders think that to become a Cosmo, you need a lot of money. Nothing could be further from the truth. Being a Cosmo is essentially a state of mind, and has nothing to do with that overdraft that keeps you awake at night."[4] He continued with mock advice on wines and watches, cars and condos. But as blogger Mahesh Krishnaswamy said, "Travel is the true measure of a Cosmo. 'Been there, done that' is their motto." Sadly, he fears his readers are "those of us who haven't been, primarily because we haven't a bean."

In short, cosmopolitanism is not equally available to everyone. Some have more money and get more choices. This is a limit to the consumerist path to global harmony. Beyond this, the dominance of the English language in global discourse privileges native speakers. The influence of Western culture and institutions opens access to some more easily than to others. A disproportionate number of the world's meeting places are in Europe and America—the United Nations in New York, Paris, Rome, and Geneva; the Bretton Woods institutions in Washington, D.C.; and the academic centers that are not only strongest but also most richly international.

Ethical Universalism and Cosmopolitanism

The cosmopolitan attitude need not be understood primarily through consumer choices. It is represented also by concern for universal human rights, action in response to humanitarian emergencies in distant countries, and efforts to promote a more just global economy.

Kant is pivotal to the tradition of understanding cosmopolitanism as universalism, relying on a logic of categorical equivalence. For Kant, cosmopolitanism would start with recognizing the rights of all human beings and on this basis set limits on the ambitions of all states. It would extend to a notion of "universal cosmopolitan existence" as "a perfect civil union of mankind."[5] In the seventeenth and especially the eighteenth centuries, such cosmopolitanism reflected the rise of a new faith in reason and hopes that this would provide a way to overcome conflicts based on more directly religious faiths. Kant's cosmopolitanism was shaped centrally by concern for peace and justice; engagement or appreciation across lines of cultural difference was not a prominent focus for him. This theme was central to the Enlightenment and has been basic to discussions of cosmopolitanism in political philosophy ever since.[6]

Thus, cosmopolitanism is commonly associated with abstract equivalence, the equal value of human beings considered as individual tokens of a global type: humanity.[7] In religious terms, each human has a soul; in a more secular vocabulary, each has rights. This understanding underwrites most philosophical accounts of ethical universalism. But categorical equivalence among all human beings describes only an abstract whole, not the more complicated and heterogeneous world in which human beings differ for cultural and other reasons, claim identities and forge solidarities and enmities. It underwrites minimal ethical obligations but cannot grasp fully the importance of human embeddedness in culture or social relationships.

Indeed, much recent liberal cosmopolitan thought proceeds as though belonging is a matter of social constraints from which individuals ideally ought to escape or temptations to favoritism they ought to resist. Claims of special loyalty or responsibility to nations, communities, or ethnic groups are subordinated or fall under suspicion of illegitimacy. To claim that one's self-definition, even one's specific version of loyalty to humanity, comes through membership in a more particular solidarity is, in Martha Nussbaum's words, a "morally questionable move of self-definition by a morally irrelevant characteristic."[8] Nussbaum holds that the highest and strongest obligation of each person is owed to humanity as a whole.[9] Her cosmopolitanism is thus about the equivalent value of individuals and the aggregate good of all persons.

For universalists, cosmopolitanism is centrally about how well or poorly we relate to strangers—those we do not know and those outside our political and communal solidarities. A cosmopolitan cares about people to whom he or she does not have a strong personal connection and about the world as a whole. Ethicists like Nussbaum and Anthony Appiah put the stress on orientations to individual action and considerations of justice and equity. From the perspective of justice, there are certainly strong reasons to think that all human beings should be considered equal. Why should an accident of birth—being born in one country any more than being born light-skinned or male—confer any special privilege? Should not those of us who benefit from global trade have obligations to consider whether the products we buy are produced by coerced or child labor? One can approach these ethical issues in narrowly individual ways—for example, by taking care not to buy certain products. Seeking to have a bigger impact requires considering political or at least institutional remedies and changes.

For many who use the term, cosmopolitanism signals a direct connection between the individual and the world as a whole.[10] This may be taken as the basis for an ethics that says each is obligated to all. The implication is that local cultures, nations, and perhaps even religions stand in the way of recognizing the essential equivalence of all human beings. In cosmopolitan discourse, it is thus common to assume that an open, enlarged view of the world must be a matter of transcending strong ties to other people in favor of commitment to humanity as a whole.

Starting from the perspective of abstract equivalence, seeing essential similarities as the main ground for cosmopolitanism tends to make differences appear as potential problems. They may be occasions for tolerance—as members of one religion tolerate adherents to others—but this is hardly a source of cosmopolitan unity. Likewise, nations are often understood by universalistic cosmopolitans as only self-interested sectional loyalties—preferences for one's own group. Strong cultural loyalties appear as prejudices.[11] But this leaves out at least half the story. For thick or strong cultural loyalties not only join people to each other and enable both individual and collective life but also, along with creativity, offer variety to the world. The development of nations—and the social institutions that organize national societies, including but not limited to government—is also a cosmopolitan achievement. Nations knit together smaller regions and provinces, however imperfectly; some provided structures of assimilation and citizenship for large numbers of immigrants. Likewise, although religions divide human beings, they also offer some of the largest scale and most influential forms of transnational, cosmopolitan solidarity.

A Cosmopolitanism of Connections

Instead of grounding cosmopolitanism in the categorical equivalence of human beings, we might ground it in our relationships to each other. An element of this may be incorporated into the notion of a common relationship to God, the creator of all. A similar notion can also be extended to all living things, whose lives would all be extinguished by a cataclysmic environmental tragedy, for example. The unity then lies in the potential of disaster so great it would end all, the mirror image of creation radical enough to create all. Being part of a "community of fate," with its orientation to a future to be achieved or averted, may be an important bond among diverse people.

Fully grasping the lateral connections humans create with each other requires situating them in history. That is, we might say that connections among people and places (and animals and plants and flowing waters or indeed buildings and machines) are forged not only by external causes like divine creation or fate but also by human action in history. Nations are *not* always the enemies of cosmopolitanism; they are often agencies of integration among different regions, classes, religions, and ethnicities. In this view, humans are joined not just by abstract equivalence but also by the interpersonal relationships and the social institutions—from language to states to religions—that we have created. The capacity for such creation is basic to humanity.[12] Everyone is connected to others and through them to all. But the connections are partial and incomplete, however dense and important they may be. History has connected us in some ways, more to some others than to all. We have the possibility to create a new future but, as Marx put it, not under conditions of our own choosing. What we can create is always shaped by our situation in history. This seems a more robust way to ground cosmopolitan thinking than the universalism of abstract categorical equivalence.

Think of Christianity and Islam—universal religions but also threads of connection across nations and regions, along migration routes, and through common projects of learning. Sometimes cohesion is stressed—we speak of Christendom or the *umma* of Islam. But the great world religions do not resolve differences into simple unity; rather, they provide common languages, sets of aspirations, and occasions for connecting. So too, think of cities, especially the great international cities that bring together travelers on different missions of business or cultural exploration, immigrants, citizens of different backgrounds. These cities connect to each other, not just to their hinterlands; they connect different parts of the world. How many languages are spoken on a daily basis on Manhattan? How many are spoken in Abu Dhabi?

Consider different ways of speaking about the environment. We might stress the equality of all humans and use a notion of equal entitlement to judge the unequal distribution of natural resources. We might stress not that we are the same but that we are in the same boat, and focus on the risks we all share from degradation or catastrophic destruction of that environment. But we might also locate ourselves in relationships forged with or through the environment. A single river flowing hundreds of miles may feed fishing villages and challenge sport fishermen, irrigate farmland, water grassy lawns, provide drinking water to a city, and drive a turbine. It may entertain kayakers and raise the value of property with scenic views. Both transportation and pollution may connect people at different points. Both equality and community of fate are real issues. But deeper understanding and practical solutions alike depend on grasping the ways in which people are related to each other through their dependencies on the river. Moreover, each of those ways of depending on the river has a history, is shaped by culture and habit, and is informed by a specific location. Again, think of bodies of water— the Indian Ocean, the Red Sea, the Mediterranean. The world's regions are not just landmasses or places of common culture. They are also the different lands touched by common bodies of water that provide connections and mutual influence.

We are connected, but incompletely. We have responsibilities because of our connections, because we are affected by and affect others, not just because of abstract similarities. At the level of both individuals and culture more broadly, we are transformed by the historical processes of social action and interaction; these give us capacities for mutual understanding. These capacities are always in some degree specific to the cultural and historical circumstances in which they are forged; they are not simply universal. We should not confuse the experience of roaming the world and appreciating its constitutive differences with grasping it as a whole.

The dominant strands of cosmopolitan theorizing draw heavily on the experience of frequent travelers, roaming freely across borders and sometimes creating expatriate communities where businesspeople, academics, and aid workers of several nationalities mix in formerly imperial cities. The theories sometimes also make reference to less privileged border crossers. Bolivian musicians play on street corners around Europe. Filipina housekeepers serve locals and expatriates alike in Southeast Asia. Pakistanis build skyscrapers in the Persian Gulf. Sikhs drive taxis in Toronto and New York. Mexicans migrate to Spain and the United States. Migrants are agents of interconnection in a global world and sources of multicultural diversity in societies that cannot readily understand themselves as homogeneous even if some of their members—or their governments—want to. They are often cosmopolitan in the sense of having loyalties and connections that cross national borders, but for them globalization is not the abstract universalism of cosmopolitan theory. It is not that globalization is only for the rich, or powerful, or privileged; rather, it is experienced very differently with different resources. Of course globalization also affects those who do not travel, or travel far, and we need to ask what responsibilities educated cosmopolitans have toward them.

Cosmopolitanism needs to be explored in terms of webs of specific connections that position us in the world—from friendship and kinship through national states or religions to markets and global institutions. These are not just nested at different scales; they cross-cut each other, and it is good that they do so, for differences on one dimension are met by connections on another. A central part of what a university experience does is open up new connections. It does this literally by introducing people to each other—students and professors alike. It does this also by introducing students to great products of different cultural traditions. This is a basis for analyzing both what they have in common and how they differ. It also does this by providing students with intellectual and cultural resources for confronting future challenges. These are skills, habits, perspectives—an attitude of openness and a confidence in building new relationships—as well as the accumulated knowledge of science and scholarship. Learning entails a capacity to translate and a willingness to be transformed. This is a matter not so much of shedding culture as of finding new resources in culture.

NOTES

1 Kimberly Yuracko, *Perfectionism and Contemporary Feminist Values* (Bloomington: Indiana University Press, 2003), 91; also see Jon Binnie and Beverley Skeggs, "Cosmopolitan Knowledge and the Production and Consumption of Sexualised Space: Manchester's Gay Village," 220–45, in *Cosmopolitan Urbanism*, ed. Jon Binnie, Julian Holloway, Steve Millington, and Craig Young (London: Routledge, 2006), 223.

2 Although "cosmopolitan" is the first category listed, the ads go on for many pages organized also (for the less explicitly cosmopolitan) by caste, community, language, religion, profession, and previous marital status. International educational credentials are noted throughout, but only in the "cosmopolitan" section are alliances invited specifically in terms like "cultured, cosmopolitan, Westernized" or "smart, Westernized, cosmopolitan working for MNC [Multinational Corporation]." http://timesofindia.indiatimes.com.

3 "C is for Choice, Colour & Cosmopolitan: Introducing the Sony VAIO C-Series," *Business Wire*. www.allbusiness.com.

4 Mahesh Krishnaswamy, "How to Be Cosmopolitan," blog post available at http://mahesh.sulekha.com.

5 Immanuel Kant, "Idea for Universal History with Cosmopolitan Intent," in *Perpetual Peace, and Other Essays*, trans. Ted Humphrey (Indianapolis: Hackett, 1983). It is worth noting that Kant spoke of states as well as individuals being citizens of a universal state of humankind.

6 It is worth noting, though, that political philosophy has not always discussed cosmopolitanism very much. Its core concerns have usually been the internal organization and sometimes the external relations of states and in the modern era, especially national states. Cosmopolitanism has lately come back on the agenda because of renewed attention to globalization.

7 For important and forceful recent statements of cosmopolitanism as universalism, see Seyla Benhabib, *Another Cosmopolitanism* (Oxford: Oxford University Press, 2006) and Martha Nussbaum, *Frontiers of Justice: Disability, Nationality, Species Membership* (Cambridge, Mass.: Harvard University Press, 2006).

8 Martha Nussbaum, *For Love of Country?* (Boston: Beacon Press, 1996), 5.

9 Nussbaum, *For Love of Country?*; Martha Nussbaum, *Cultivating Humanity: A Classical Defense of Reform in Liberal Education* (Cambridge, Mass.: Harvard University Press, 1997).

10 In this as in other ways, it echoes rather than transcends nationalism; see Craig Calhoun, *Nationalism* (Minneapolis: University of Minnesota Press, 1998), on this presumption of directness rather than mediation. Of course there are exceptions to this general tendency in cosmopolitan thought, efforts to understand cosmopolitanism from various scales of relationships across lines of difference rather than categorical similarity on a global scale. For a noteworthy example, see Sheldon I. Pollock, "Cosmopolitan and Vernacular in History," *Public Culture* 12, no. 3 (2000): 591–625. Much more abstractly, David Held has seen recognition of diversity as a hallmark of what he calls "cosmopolitan democracy." But he has also seen the issue more as finding appropriate representative mechanisms on a variety of scales than of shifting the idea of cosmopolitanism away from global categorical similarity to the multifarious and heterogeneous making of connections, which is necessarily at least partly local. See especially David Held, *Democracy and the Global Order: From the Modern State to Cosmopolitan Governance* (Stanford: Stanford University Press, 1995).

11 See Samuel Schleffer's critical discussion in *Boundaries and Allegiances: Problems of Justice and Responsibility in Liberal Thought* (Oxford: Oxford University Press, 2001).

12 See Hannah Arendt, *The Human Condition* (Chicago: University of Chicago Press, 1958). Arendt's account of the creative capacity at the heart of being human is inspired largely by ancient Greek thought. Christians and Jews may also draw similar ideas from the biblical book of Genesis, where creative potential is part of what humans derive from being created in the image of God.

15

The Pitfalls and Promises of Afropolitanism

EMMA DABIRI

It was with something of a sense of trepidation that I delivered a version of what would become "Why I'm Not an Afropolitan."[1] during the 2013 Africa Writes Festival. I never anticipated the response that my intervention would receive, nor did I foresee the ripple effects that would be generated in the then as yet burgeoning Afropolitan discourse.

My sense of trepidation stemmed from the fact that I had encountered next to nothing voicing concern about the particular direction in which Afropolitanism seemed to be developing. At that time there was little written about it beyond the celebratory. Notable exceptions were the art historian Okwunodu Ogbechi's (2008) "Afropolitanism—Africa without Africans"[2] and Bosch Santana's (2013) "Exorcizing Afropolitanism,"[3] an account of Binyavanga Wainaina's (tragically) unrecorded 2012 keynote speech delivered to the African Studies Association U.K. conference in Leeds, U.K. While both these reassured me that there existed at least some small minority who, like myself, remained unseduced by the veneer of sophistication, but also by the promise of African "progress," which the Afropolitan peddled, it is worth noting that they were written five years apart. There was as yet nothing that could be conceived of as a sustained critique of Afropolitanism. However, the ideas circulating in 2013 appeared to signal something of a watershed. My trepidation apparently had been unwarranted. Post Africa Writes I was overwhelmed by responses both from the audience and the online discussions that followed. It was immensely encouraging to see how many people shared my reservations about the term, but had felt silenced by the hype, by the expectation that we were all grateful for this seemingly celebratory way of approaching African identities. By late 2013 the voices of dissent had swelled in volume and frequency: from the insightful "Is Afropolitanism Africa's New Single Story?"[4] in which Brian Bwesigye reads Helon

Habila's review of No Violet Bulawayo's *We Need New Names* through the truncated version of Afropolitanism that he argues Habila represents, to Marta Tveit's "The Afropolitan Must Go,"[5] in which Tviet focuses on critiquing the term and its relationship to identity politics, while sidelining the issue of commodification that I develop as one of the central challenges to Afropolitanism. In January 2014, Africa is a Country republished the piece that had appeared on my blog the previous summer. Carli Coetzee discusses the genesis of the term during this period:

> While it is not a definitive source, it is instructive to see that Google trend cites 0 references of the term Afropolitanism in print and online in February 2012; by April 2012 there is a definite spike with 72 references logged. By mid-2014, the graph shows that uses of the word Afropolitanism reached an all-time peak.[6]

The critiques that emerged invited varied responses. In regards to my own a small number of commentators seemed to have misinterpreted my argument as some kind of attack on Selasi's attempt at forging an identity within the complexities of Diaspora, or as an outright refutation of the potentiality of Afropolitanism altogether. I would urge such commentators to a more considered reading of the essay. "Why I Am Not an Afropolitan" does indeed subject Afropolitanism to analysis within the framework of a Fanonian ethics, and is undoubtedly a critique on what I believe to be a particularly unhealthy streak of neoliberal ideology running throughout much of that which is billed Afropolitan. However, I remain bone-achingly intimate with the "stranded place"[7] (2015) from which Selasi explains she wrote "Bye-Bye Babar."[8] The pursuit of "belonging" and "home" have been central themes throughout my life. Which is why, as I explain, the concept of "Afropolitan" first excited me. I am always looking for spaces that can accommodate my position as an Irish/Nigerian woman who remains deeply connected to her Nigerianness, but who was raised first in the United States and then Ireland, and has spent her entire adult life as an immigrant. I would rather refrain from describing myself as *half* anything, and I detest the word "mixed-race." I thought perhaps "Afropolitan" presented an alternative to this terminology and, interestingly, positioned me with others through a shared cultural and aesthetic leaning rather than a perceived racial classification. Moreover, the term suggested that one could be black or African without having to subscribe to the depressingly limited identities widely perceived as being authentic.

In addressing claims that I am simply dismissing Afropolitanism, I would highlight the considerable attention I pay to Achille Mbembe's articulation of Afropolitanism. The enduring insights of Afropolitanism as interpreted by Mbembe should be its promise of vacating the seduction of pernicious racialized thinking, its recognition of African identities as fluid, and the notion that the African past is characterized by "mixing, blending, and superimposing." In opposition to custom, Mbembe insists that the idea of "tradition" never really existed and reminds us that there is a "pre-colonial African modernity that has not been taken into account in contemporary creativity."[9] Minna "Ms Afropolitan" Salami and founder of the eponymous MsAfropolitan blog writes that Africans should be as free as anybody else to have multiple subcultures.[10] This goes without saying. For me the problem with Afropolitanism isn't some aversion to subculture, but rather that the insights on race, modernity, and identity appeared to be increasingly ignored in favor of the consumerism Mbembe also identifies as part of the Afropolitan assemblage. The dominance of fashion, luxury, and lifestyle in Afropolitanism—at the expense of some of its other components—is noteworthy due to the relationship between these industries, consumption, and consumerism.

The rapacious consumerism of the African elites who claimed to make up the ranks of the Afropolitans is well documented. Frantz Fanon's prophetic words once again resonate. In the foreword to the 2004 edition of *Wretched of the Earth*, Homi Bhabha asks: "[W]hat might be saved from Fanon's ethics and politics of decolonization to help us reflect on contemporary manifestations of globalization?"[11] He reminds us that the economic landscape engineered by the IMF and the World Bank continues to support the compartmentalized societies identified by Fanon. No matter how much wealth exists in pockets, "a dual economy is not a developed economy," writes Fanon. The pockets of the mobile Afropolitan class hold much of the wealth.

I want to ask: in what way does Afropolitanism go about challenging the enduring problematics of duality and compartmentalized society identified by Fanon as one of the major stumbling blocks to African postcolonial independence? To be honest, when I look at the launch of OK Magazine Nigeria (although I don't know whether Afropolitans would claim OK magazine—I'm not sure it's chic enough), or hear about palm wine mojitos and fashion shows at the Afropolitan V&A event, it leaves me feeling somewhat depressed. Our value is not determined by our ability to produce African-flavored versions of Western convention and form. Such an approach will surely only leave us forever playing catch-up in a game the rules of which we did not write. The whole life-style of *Sex and the City* feminism, cocktails, designer clothes, handbags, and shoes is not particularly liberating in an Anglo-American context, so I see no reason why we should transfer such models to Africa and declare it progress. I'm not saying there is no place for such activities in the African context, but that it represents less of a departure from the behavior of postcolonial elites than a repetition of the same behavior.

In an era such as ours, characterized by the chilling commodification of all walks of life—including the commodification of dissent—we should be especially vigilant about any movement that embraces commodification to the extent that Afropolitanism does. In her eloquent piece "Exorcizing Afropolitanism," Bosch Santana outlines Binyavanga Wainaina's "attempt to rid African literary and cultural studies of the ghost of Afropolitanism." Bosch Santana explores the way in which Afropolitanism has become "a phenomenon increasingly product driven, design focused, and potentially funded by the West." She recognizes that "style, in and of itself, is not really the issue," but fears rather that it is "the attempt to begin with style, and then infuse it with substantive political consciousness that is problematic." In an online response to "Exorcizing Afropolitanism," Salami argued that Bosch Santana was taking umbrage at African agency. Salami framed the debate as a choice between African victimization and Afropolitanism, asking ironically, "[H]ow dare Africans not simply be victims, but also shapers of globalisation and all its inherent contestations? How dare we market our cultures as well as our political transformations?"[12]

This was the context in which I stepped into the debate, accompanied by my sense of aforementioned trepidation. I argued that our options are not reduced to one or the other (nor does Bosch Santana suggest they are). In countering Salami's interpretation of the debate, I challenged the position that defining ourselves as Afropolitan was the only alternative to the Afro-pessimism narrative. Furthermore, then as now, I continue to harbor serious reservations that the duality identified by Fanon is challenged by a small group of Africans who are in a position to be able to "market their cultures." Salami herself admits that Afropolitanism possibly goes "overboard in commodifying African culture." This statement is not one from which we can glibly turn. Rather it remains a continuing cause of concern. In 2013 I wrote that the centrality of capitalism and the importance of commodification are confirmed when one searches for "Afropolitan" on Google. Back then it was all online shops and aspirational luxury lifestyle magazines. In addition to these, the Internet is now littered with any number of "think pieces." Unfortunately a number of these seem to frame the debate according to the very binaries my vision of Afropolitanism, drawing on Mbembe, would seek to subvert. You are either *for* or *against*. Such reductive analysis fails to engage with the spaces in between, the fact that you can be critical of the direction a movement is taking while also acknowledging that it is possible to imagine alternative possibilities for it.

Providing the backdrop for these online discussions, the links to "African" art, jewelry, and ankara toys still remain. These items too are recognizable from Fanon, who writes: "The bourgeoisie's idea of a national economy is one based on what we can call local products. Grandiloquent speeches are made about local crafts." With the exception of a few well-positioned individuals of African origin, who now have a larger market to which they can "sell" this image of Africa, who are the real beneficiaries of this commodification?

Paul Gilroy has argued that commodity culture has resulted in the loss—to the advantage of corporate interests—of much of what was wonderful about black culture.[13] Afropolitanism can be seen as the latest manifestation of planetary commerce in blackness, or can be read as a type of "sanctioned blackness" (Dabiri and Gabay, forthcoming).[14] It seems as though after the consumption of so much black American culture, there is now a consumer demand for more authentic, virgin black culture. That demand turns to the continent as a fresh source ripe for the picking. Then as now, I still need to position myself with a more radical countercultural movement. For me Afropolitanism is too polite, corporate, glossy—it reeks of sponsorship and big business, with all the attendant limitations of such a culture. Should we be taking comfort in the fact that the world's eyes are again on Africa? Headlines declare, "Africa is the world's fastest growing continent" and the "hottest frontier" for investments. *Time Magazine*'s cover of "Africa Rising" announces, "[I]t is the world's next economic powerhouse," while the *Wall Street Journal* dubs it "a new gold rush." Here's a headline of my own: "The Scramble for Africa."

It's no surprise that Western media are supportive of Afropolitanism. As Fanon reminds us, "In its decadent aspect the national bourgeoisie gets considerable help from the Western bourgeoisie who happen to be tourists enamoured with exoticism." [15] Afropolitanism is the hand-maiden of the "Africa Rising" narrative and I suspect its championing by Western media runs the risk of leading us ever further astray from the "disreputable, angry places" noted by Gilroy, "where the political interests of racialized minorities might be identified and worked upon without being encumbered by an affected liberal innocence." [16] "Africa Rising" and its cohorts should not be allowed to obscure the fact that Africa has lost $1.2 to 1.4 trillion in illicit financial outflows—more than three times the total amount of foreign aid received. Africa gives more to the rest of the world than it receives and is in fact a net creditor through illicit means.

The term Afropolitan continues to be used in the art world. Okwun-odu Ogbechi was one of the first to flag the problematics of Afropolitan art. In a 2008 blog post he questioned the art world's championing of Afropolitanism, arguing that it supported a bias that only views African artists working in the west as relevant, while the artists living and working on the continent are largely ignored. He reminded us that despite the international lifestyle enjoyed by the Afropolitan, most Africans have almost absolute immobility in a contemporary global world that works very hard to keep Africans in their place on the African continent. He points out there is no immigration policy anywhere in the Western world that welcomes Africans and a major bias against African global mobility abounds in international media. Most African-based artists would find it difficult if not impossible to get a visa to visit Western museums or to show their works abroad! [17] As Europe experiences what is being referred to as the "worst refugee crises since World War II," stories of African migration could hardly be timelier. Those attempting to access Fortress Europe share chilling parallels with the Afropolitan:

like the Afropolitan these Africans too cross continents, but in contrast to the Afropolitan narrative centered on an Africa *rising*, these Africans are all too often drowning. Meanwhile, the Afropolitan comes and goes, continent hopping at leisure. Yet this disparity is not reflected in the Afropolitan narrative, characterized as it is by an international lifestyle of access and privilege.

Our provocations have, I think, forestalled the danger of an uncontested version of Afropolitanism becoming the single story of Africa. But we must remain alert to the dangers such a development would pose. The limits of the Afropolitan voice might be compared with those of second-wave feminism, where white middle-class women failed to identify their privilege while claiming to speak for all women. While we may all be Africans, there is a huge gap between my African experience and that of my father's houseboys. It is great that there are a minority of Africans whose family backgrounds and connections insure that they can traverse the world with ease (and again this is not a new development) but it is crucial that this not disguise the fact that there is a global system very much committed to keeping the vast majority of Africans *in their place.* We are now well versed in the danger of the single story. While Afropolitanism may appear to offer an alternative to the single story, we must remain vigilant against this becoming the dominant narrative for African success. The traditional Afro-pessimistic narratives, while obsessed with poverty, denied the poor any voice. While Afropolitanism may go some way toward redressing the balance concerning Africans speaking for themselves, the problem lies in the fact that we still don't hear the narratives of Africans who are not privileged. The problem is not that Afropolitans are privileged per se—rather it is that at a time when poverty remains endemic for millions, the narratives of a privileged few telling us how great everything is, how much opportunity and potential is available, may drown out the voices of a majority who continue to be denied basic life chances. While Afropolitans talk and talk about what it means to be young, cool, and African, how many of them are concerned with addressing the world beyond their own social realities, the issues that concern other Africans?

Perhaps we need to have more consensus on what constitutes Afropolitanism. Salami says in the comments section of her response to "Exorcizing Afropolitanism" that Afropolitanism means "being African without detouring through whiteness," which seems somewhat at odds with Mbembe's vision. For him Afropolitanism is a way of being African that is "open to difference" and transcending race. In a 2013 *Guardian* interview, Taiye Selasi, who popularized the term "Afropolitan" in her 2005 essay "Bye-Bye Babar or What Is an Afropolitan?" presented an image of an Instagram-friendly Africa. Her interpretation of Afropolitanism seemingly went beyond being "open to difference" to something resembling African versions of American or European cities. Afropolitanism, it appears, is grounded in the ability to engage in the same pastimes one could expect to enjoy in a Western capital. In Burkina Faso she danced until 5:00 a.m. in a Western-themed club and watched movies at a feminist film festival. Adama, her charming host, was an "Afropolitan of the highest order" by virtue of his Viennese wife and the fact that he was studying German at the Goethe Institute. To her Togo was a seaside treat which she likens to Malibu with *motorini*. Later she gushes about hanging out on the beach with hundreds of supercool Togolese hipsters.[18] Such an itinerary would be acceptable to any self-respecting inhabitant of hipster capitals like Hackney or Williamsburg and it's wonderful that one can now have the Hipster Africa Experience, but I fail to see how this represents anything particularly progressive. It seems that again African progress is being measured by the extent to which it can reproduce a Western lifestyle, now without having to physically be in the West. This doesn't appear to signal any particular departure from the elites' enduring love affair with achieving the lifestyles of their former masters. As a result, in my first version of Why I'm not an Afropolitan I mused that many of those who defined themselves as Afropolitan had evacuated much of the rich potential the term may once have suggested.

Whether devotee, detractor, critic, or convert, the furore generated around Afropolitanism demonstrates how emotive and necessary discourse around black identities continues to be. The reality is that many of Africa's children—dispersed throughout the world by the twin agents of history and economics—continue to grapple with the negotiation of our identities and the search for home.

Regularly included in academic conferences, with a growing number of books and journal editions dedicated to it, as well as becoming an emergent literary troupe, Afropolitanism seems set to establish its place within the canon of black social movements and the seemingly perennial search for a black aesthetic, spanning negritude, Pan-Africanism ,and Afrocentricity. The heated debate evoked by Afropolitanism demonstrates that for many of us, the concept of home remains complex. Afropolitanism reflects the conditions of our times. In this moment it proves tricky for a social movement—although this can be applied to almost anything—to establish itself before it is seized upon by forces committed to selling something to someone. If Afropolitanism can develop in a space beyond marketing, aspirational living, and consumerism what might be achieved? Perhaps instead of online shops, glossy magazines, and consumable products, revisiting ideas about African tradition might represent a renewed Afropolitanism. Let us really consider the precolonial modernity Mbembe names. Uncover it, allow its spirit to guide our work. When contemporary African innovation is credited to the old adage "necessity is the mother of invention," or the idea, common in many circles, that African creativity is some sort of by-product of poverty born out of desperation to survive, let it be known that Africans were creative long before they were (made) poor. So-called "illiterate" cultures that disavowed the written word, did so not out of some sort of cultural deficiency but because of the existence of alternative epistemologies that allowed them to conceive of reality in ways unimaginable to us, and which, by organizing the very concept of time, past, present and future, so differently from us, expanded the scope of human imagination in ways inconceivable within the limits of our "positivist," "empirical," and "historical" fantasies. Let us consider the human condition beyond and before binaries, acknowledging the fact that:

> In pre-colonial Africa far from the existence of single "tribal" identities, most Africans moved in and out of multiple identities, defining themselves at one moment as the subject of a particular chief or initiate of a religious society while at yet another moment as a member of a certain professional guild.[19]

Moreover:

> The ethnic paradigm thus reconfigured becomes less a matter of restrictive labelling and more of choosing between various semantic classifications dependent on the particular contexts and identities involved.[20]

In addition to broadening our understanding of how identity operated before European meddling, this is an Afropolitanism that can be more inclusive of life *on the continent*—engaging with cosmopolitan processes often neglected in the public imagination—those that occurred in African countries themselves rather than those that are the result of migration *outside* the continent. This in turn addresses concerns that Afropolitanism is a resource mainly for those of African descent in the Diaspora.

If we can salvage some of these *other* constituent elements from the Afropolitan assemblage, there remains much that could prove of value to our twenty-first century understandings of Africa and what it once meant, means, and might yet mean, to be black, to be African, in all its glorious, messy complexity. Moreover, let us think about what it might look like to organize society beyond the rigid binaries bequeathed us as our Enlightenment legacy. These metaphysical African resources might prove of far greater value to civilization than those other—far more fabled African resources—so violently fought over by the forces of global capital.

NOTES

1 E. Dabiri (2015), "Afro-Rebel (or Why I Am Not an Afropolitan*)*" [online]. Available at: http://thediasporadiva.tumblr.com; E. Dabiri (2014), "Why I'm Not an Afropolitan" [online], *Africa Is a Country*. Available at: http://africasacountry .com.

2 S. Ogbechie (2008), "Afropolitanism: Africa without Africans (II)" [online]. *AACHRONYM*. Available at: http://aachronym.blogspot.co.uk.

3 S. Bosch Santana (2013), "Exorcizing Afropolitanism: Binyavanga Wainaina Explains Why "'I Am a Pan-Africanist, Not an Afropolitan,'" at *ASAUK 2012* [online]. Available at: http://africainwords.com.

4 B. Bwesigye (2013), "Is Afropolitanism Africa's New Single Story? Reading Helon Habila's Review of "'We Need New Names' by Brian Bwesigye," *Aster(ix) Journal* [online]. Available at: http://asterixjournal.com.

5 M. Tveit (2013), "The Afropolitan Must Go" [online], *Africa Is a Country*. Available at: http://africasacountry.com.

6 Carli Coetzee (2015), "Introduction," *Journal of African Cultural Studies*, DOI: 10.1080/13696815.2015.1105129.

7 Aaron Bady and Taiye Selasi "New African Fiction," *Transition*, No. 117 (2015), 148–65, DOI: 10.2979/transition.117.148.

8 Taiye Selasi, "Bye-Bye Babar" [online], *The Lip*. Available at: http://thelip .robertsharp.co.uk.

9 T. Makhetha (2007), *Africa Remix* [Johannesburg, South Africa], Johannesburg Art Gallery.
10 M. Salami (2013), *Can Africans Have Multiple Subcultures? A Response to "Exorcising Afropolitanism"* [online], *MsAfropolitan*. Available at: http://www.msafropolitan.com.
11 F. Fanon and R. Philcox, *The Wretched of the Earth* (New York: Grove Press, 2004).
12 Salami, *Can Africans Have Multiple Subcultures?*
13 P. Gilroy, *After Empire* (London: Routledge: 2004).
14 E. Dabiri and C. Gabay, *Sanctioned Blackness* (forthcoming, 2017).
15 Fanon and Philcox, *The Wretched of the Earth*.
16 Gilroy, *After Empire*.
17 Ogbechie, "Afropolitanism: Africa without Africans (II)" [online].
18 T. Selasi, "Taiye Selasi on Discovering Her Pride in Her African Roots." Available at: http://www.theguardian.com/books.
19 E. Hobsbawm and T. Ranger, *The Invention of Tradition* (Cambridge: Cambridge University Press, 1983), 249.
20 David C. Conrad and Barbara E. Frank, *Status and Identity in West Africa: Nyamakalaw of Mande* (Bloomington: Indiana University Press, 1995), 11–12.

PART V

Spaces

16

City of Youth and Mellow Elusiveness

Accra's Cosmopolitan Constellations

ATO QUAYSON

The evidence of material on African cities does not inspire confidence. They are increasingly overcrowded with no clear plan for matching population growth to available facilities. Sewage and garbage disposal are perennial problems. Laboring street children are everywhere. The hope some five decades ago when many countries gained freedom from their former colonial masters was that these cities would act as engines of growth and development. It was also hoped that they would act as the crucibles within which heterogeneous identities could be merged into a national template. Now the progressive politicization of ethnic and religious identities in places such as Nairobi and Kano has quickly disabused observers of that hope.

And yet it appears also that the dominant crisis-management discourse, heavily enamored of international financial agencies, is actually helping to obscure more pressing questions. I have often wondered to myself, for instance, what it would really take to engage with the mundane and apparently ephemeral details of the African city. I think here of the spontaneity of street life, the slogans, mottoes, and inscriptions on lorries and passenger vehicles, the appropriation of official spaces for nonofficial uses, and all in all, the blatant insertion of local social imaginaries into the public discourses that attempt to define the city. But it would not be adequate either to settle for a simple inventory of subaltern urban forms. That can only lead to a brute numerology; there are countless statistics already that tell us everything we need to know about the crisis confronting the African city.

Issues of method arise. How does one keep focused on the mundane and the apparently ephemeral and from this construct a viable understanding of the African city? More pressingly, how does one tie cosmopolitan impulses to the constellations in which they arise? For in Accra, as in many other African cities, the constellations must be taken to include ethnicity, as well as the long history of how groups of strangers contribute to cosmopolitan impulses within the ethno-temporalities of such cities. Whether we are looking at Accra, or Jos, or Nairobi, or Luanda, or Johannesburg, the structure of multiethnic societies raises issues that cannot be easily passed over in discussions of cosmopolitanism.

Part I: Cosmopolitanisms Now

In January 2013 the *New York Times* listed Accra as the fourth most desirable destination in the world out of forty-six places surveyed. Accra came hard on the heels of Rio de Janeiro, Marseilles, and Nicaragua, respectively. What this confirms is something long known to casual observers: it has been a hub for West African businessmen for well over two decades, at least since the inception of the successful and continuing democratic experiment of 1992. And at least in the past decade-and-a-half almost every major American university has sent their students on various programs to Ghana and routed them through Accra. These include Harvard, Princeton, Michigan, Rutgers, and Colorado, to name just a few of the better known ones. The nine-campus University of California system has been running year-abroad programs in Ghana since the early 1990s while NYU has gone beyond all the others by buying a large property in Accra that plays host to regular cohorts of students and professors from their campus in New York. This is not counting the many students who come to Accra from Europe, including the United Kingdom, Holland, Sweden, Italy, and several others. There are literally hundreds of North American and European students in Accra at any given time during the course of the year studying, doing research, or just helping out on various projects.

Now, if some North American youths were to visit Accra today for research, activism, or pleasure, what kind of things would they be likely to experience? They might be invited to a Facebook beach party. A Facebook beach party is basically an event put together by anyone on Facebook to get all their FB friends to come together and have fun, whether these are real friends or just of the FB variety. If they are in town in August, these lucky students might be invited to go to the Chale Wote Festival at Jamestown, the long-standing neighborhood near the old and disused harbor and now a magnet for heritage tourism. The Festival has been running since 2012 as a way of bringing together a variety of artists, musicians, and other street entertainers in celebration of street life. It is a heady mix of the local and the foreign, with a large dollop of eccentricity for good measure. If feeling so inclined, our visiting youths might instead join a roller skating team that meets at Jamestown on Saturdays and Sundays for roller skating competitions. If our students were in Accra between 2006 and 2013, they might have found themselves at the Coconut Grove Hotel dancing alongside the two thousand others around the hotel's grand swimming pool. The highly popular salsa night was held every Wednesday from 7 to 10 p.m. and also simultaneously beamed live on CitiFm in their Salsa Mania program. Free classes were offered to beginners, but in reality the distinction between beginners and aficionados was thoroughly and systematically obscured because, as is commonly asserted, *asa bone nkum asaase* (i.e., bad dancing never killed the earth). At Oxford Street, roller skaters double as drug couriers, readily distributing marijuana, cocaine, and other hard drugs to willing buyers in the evening.

Or our young visiting folk might be confidently informed by their local friends over copious amounts of beer about various mayoral races in Toronto, London, or Sydney, New York, with full-scale analyses of the merits or demerits of different arguments about forms of public transport, or water conservation, or cycle routes, or whatever might be most prominent in these elections elsewhere. This is not entirely surprising, for since the expansion of the Ghanaian diaspora beginning in the 1980s people in the country have taken to making sure that they know as much as possible about happenings anywhere that Ghanaians are to be found. If our visiting youth were especially interested in soccer (locally called by its proper name, football) they might enter into a heated argument with Manchester United, or Chelsea, or Barcelona fans who would be able to give them detailed team sheets of their favorite teams in European Champions League games since the early 2000s.

If our visitors are in any way observant about their environment, they would also quickly notice the Ghanaian penchant for slogans on vehicles and indeed on other surfaces as well: "One Man No Chop"; "Shoes are

Repairing Here"; "May Allah Rain His Blessings Upon Me"; "Ashawo." A bit of investigation would reveal that these slogans have diverse sources of inspiration and cover everything from sexual innuendoes, religious sentiments, and translations from local-language wisdom traditions, to the candidly fabricated from a personal context. "Observers are Worried. Why?" inscribed on a house or lorry is a nose-thumbing gesture at people who might be questioning the source of the wealth used to build the said house or purchase the said lorry. Other slogans of variant vintage solemnly declare: "I No Be Like You"; "Mama Chocolate"; "A Short Man Is Not a Boy" (which has subtle sexual innuendoes), "Belly Never Know Vacation", "You Too Can Try" (a subtle challenge/insult translated from local languages); "Envy Never Lights a Fire", "Still, It Makes Me Laugh"; "And Jesus Wept"; "Enye Easy" ("It Is Not Easy"); "Insha'Allahu"; "Gold Never Rust"; "Mammy Watta", "Fear Man and Take Snake"; and "Kwaku Ananse" (the last three inspired by folktales); and, simply "Auntie Akos," as tribute to the person who helped procure the vehicle.

The slogans and inscriptions are also often translations of globalized signifiers onto the local cultural scene. "Nike," with a barely recognizable "swoosh" beside it on the back of a passenger vehicle signals the global reach of the sportswear company. A barbershop display depicting haircuts of Barack Obama alongside Mike Tyson suggests that they both pack a mean punch while also enticing customers in for a similarly "powerful" haircut. Images of Kofi Annan, erstwhile President Rawlings, and Princess Diana may also be placed together on the same sign-art poster to suggest that they were all three "of the people, by the people, and for the people," problematic as this might seem to ignorant skeptics. Fascinatingly, both sets of images might also double as artwork on passenger lorries, with appropriate inscriptions "for the road," as it were. Read correctly, then, each signifying surface defines a dramatic scene, where the writing plus any added images are the nodal points of much wider discursive propositions. In their own distinctive ways they all invite viewer participation in the improvised scene laid out, whether the scene be exclusively textual or a combination of writing and images. The participation indexed by these slogans, sayings, and mottoes differs markedly from that implied in the inscriptions and images to be found on the advertising billboards of multinational corporations.

This is just a modest sampling of how well Accra might tickle the fancy of young visitors in alliance with their local friends, but it is by no means all that it has to offer. Such mobile slogans are a distinctive feature of Accra and of many African urban environments. The central feature of these mottoes and slogans is an elusively inventive and improvisational character that installs writing ambiguously between literacy and orality. Thus the urban scriptural economy is often shaped around items that draw simultaneously from repertoires of both orality and literacy. This is evident in areas as diverse as funerary and obituary notices, popular performances and literary texts that draw on oral discursive traditions, concert party and film posters, and the sayings, slogans, and inscriptions on walls, print cloths, canoes, lorries, cars, and various other surfaces across the urban landscape. Each of these items extends from a domain of oral performativity and reaches into the domain of writing, such that the process of reading them requires an innovative understanding of their mixed genres and the orality/literacy spectrum from which they draw their meaning(s).

There are two quick points to be extracted from what has been laid out about Accra so far, the first fairly obvious and even banal and the second more significant and profound. The first is that given the vast interconnectedness of today's world, the heart of darkness has ceased to exist. This is despite all the evidence to the contrary that we get in the media. And this interconnectedness has been going on for a very long time. Whether with the arrival of the Afro-Brazilians (the Tabon) of Otublohum in the nineteenth century or the return of the demobilized soldiers from World War II who played such a signal role in the decolonization movement, Ghana and Accra, its capital, have been socially integrated into the global world. The world of Facebook, Twitter, and Gollywood is but one installment of this continuing transnationalism. The second point I want to make is that despite all the negative news that comes from the continent, the imagination of Ghanaians and indeed Africans is not limited by circumstance. Despite wars and rumors of war, famines, poor water and sanitation, political corruption, and fragile states, people in Africa have the same capacity for reimagining the world as do people born in Mississauga, or New Jersey, or Bromley, or Leiden. The challenge is not just how to acknowledge this fact, but how to identify and nourish the sources of the African imagination.

And what we might term the African imagination is more complex than might first appear.

Part II: Hybridity and the Process of Becoming Ethnic

Given the many tastes and satisfactions that can be had in today's Accra, it is easy to succumb to the temptation of seeing it in ahistorical terms, as though it were merely the iteration of cosmopolitanism everywhere else in the world. Two reminders from Accra's variegated history are important for curbing such enthusiasm. These pertain to the city's absorption of stranger groups—the manner by which they have been required to be incorporated into the ethnohistory of the indigenous Gas—and the implications that this raises for contrasting multiethnicity and multiculturalism.

When Saidiya Hartman went to spend two years in Ghana as a Fulbright Fellow in the late 1990s, she was astounded to be called obroni, a term which roughly translates as "white person." Her astonishment arose from the fact that the claims on her identity as an African American woman made her a consciously black person. What she appears not to have realized in her riveting account of doing research on the trajectories of slave identities in Ghana was the fact that she had been inserted into a completely different racial economy in which to be fair-skinned was to automatically have a form of privilege. Indeed, the word obroni is also a term of endearment applied, say, between lovers to suggest something precious and ineffable. While in such instances completely detached from race, it is still possible to discern in it the liminal valence of the racial economy. What we might then describe as a pigmentocracy has not got the same social effects as in the Caribbean, in India, or in the United States, and yet still carries a social valence. The source of this social valence may be traced to the period of transatlantic slavery, where, as I have noted elsewhere, the increasing numbers of mixed-race children whose fathers were officers in the European trade forts and castles ensured that skin hue went through various gradations of insurance against being enslaved. Typically, being mulatto (as the term was then) signified an automatic connection to the white European world exemplified in the European trading outposts.

But it is the fate of another set of slaves, this time the returnee Afro-Brazilians (Tabon) from Bahia in the mid-nineteenth century, that most readily reveals the dynamics of social hierarchy tied to race. Crucially, the Afro-Brazilians were in the space of two generations to be completely assimilated to Ga social and political culture, despite maintaining their Brazilian names and a number of cultural traits brought over from Portuguese Brazil.

As Lorand Matory has pointed out, as many as eight thousand manumitted slaves from Bahia returned to West Africa from 1822 to 1899, with many of these settling in colonial Lagos. Among the reasons for the resettlement of returnee Afro-Brazilians in Lagos was the active British interest in freeing slaves who had been ensnared in the residual slave trade after its abolition in 1807.[1] Since British West Africa in the nineteenth century included several other territories in the region, Lagos must not be taken as an isolated focus of British antislavery or indeed of resettlement efforts.[2] The administrative connections between Sierra Leone, the Gold Coast, and Lagos were to prove highly significant for the dynamic settlement patterns in the period of returnee stranger groups from the New World to West Africa, raising significant implications about hybridity and intercultural exchange beyond the Bahia-Lagos nexus Matory traces in his excellent study. Indeed, as we shall see presently, the returnee Afro-Brazilians to Accra in the nineteenth century did know of their fellow Afro-Brazilians in Lagos and Porto Novo and actively sought to establish commercial and cultural networks with them.

Strictly speaking, however, the Tabon arrived in Accra in three different stages between 1829 and 1836, with the arrivals of 1836 comprising the largest group and the ones that were to have the greatest impact among their hosts.[3] The name Tabon derives from the form of greeting they exchanged amongst themselves and with their hosts ("como esta?"; "esta bom"). The numbers attributed to the 1836 group vary, but scholars generally agree that they were in the region of two hundred persons and represented at least seven separate family groups. Given that the Malê (Muslim) slave rebellion had taken place in Bahia in 1835, and that the returnees constituted distinct family groups, it has been surmised that at least some if not all the Tabon of 1836 may have been deportees from that rebellion.[4] Scholars of the Tabon have also noted that it is they who introduced Islam to the Accra coast, originally at Otublohum, where they had initially settled. The group arriving in 1836 were led by Nii Azumah Nelson I and included the Vialla (Viera), Manuel, Gomez, Peregrino, Mahama Nassu (or Nassau), and Zuzer families.[5] Other Tabon names common in today's Accra and traceable to later arrivals are Ribiero, Morton, Olympio, Nelson, Da Costa, Da Rocha, Fiscian, Maslieno, and Da Silva.

The warm reception extended to the Afro-Brazilians by the Dutch makelaar (trading agent) Kwaku Ankra ensured that the Tabon were quickly extended special Dutch protection on their arrival. Not long after their arrival they were given large tracts of land in present-day Asylum Down, Adabraka/Kokomlemle, and North Ridge, on which they cultivated vegetable crops including tomatoes, potatoes, and okra, along with the staple cassava. This continued until the early part of the twentieth century, when intense urban pressures forced the conversion of these lands from agrarian to urban uses.[6] The conversion of lands generated a number of significant tensions within the Tabon community and between them and their Ga hosts.

In 1860 the Basel Missionary Trading Company opened a shop for blacksmiths at Christiansborg, where students were taught to make wheels and produce barrels and carts for exporters of palm oil, palm kernels, coffee, and later cocoa.[7] It would not be hyperbolic to assert, however, that it was the Tabon who first introduced such skills with a specifically urban inflection into the general local economy. When they first arrived the Tabon were already very skilled at shoemaking, carpentry, metal forging, architecture, and tailoring; they were also highly experienced farmers, skilled in irrigation techniques, and in the location and digging of wells.[8] This confirms Reis's observation about the sophisticated occupational characteristics of the African slaves who filled the streets of Salvador in Bahia. As he notes, they "worked in the open air as artisans, washerwomen, tailors, street vendors, water bearers, barbers, musicians, artists, masons, carpenters, stevedores, and sedan chair porters."[9] The digging of wells and the availability of good drinking water was especially useful to their Ga hosts, as potable water was not to be generally available until the 1920s with the opening of the Weija Waterworks, and even then after serious disagreements about water rates between the Ga chiefs and the colonial administration.[10]

If the Ga of nineteenth-century Accra were focused predominantly on the occupational specializations of fishing, fish processing, salt making, and trade, the Tabon came to contribute early forms of urban livelihood diversification that were later to strongly resonate with the large numbers of migrants arriving from other parts of the Colony and West Africa. Unlike company artisanal slaves (cooks, carpenters, blacksmiths, etc.) who worked in the European forts and castles from the seventeenth century and whose allegiance was primarily to their masters, or the converts to early Christianity who fell under the aegis of the Basel Missionaries, the Tabon gave their allegiance to no one, regarding themselves as a distinct sociocultural group forging a place within a new urban environment.[11] Their urban skill set must then be interpreted as a crucial element of urban exchange value, tied neither to the residual slave economy of the European forts and castles nor to the normative religious implications of the Christian missions. Their early access to tracts of land both close to the Jamestown harbor and further inland also meant that they were quickly able to occupy the upper entrepreneurial echelons of society, since they not only owned significant means of agricultural production but also had the requisite skills to establish highly valued craft industries such as tailoring and blacksmithing.

The Tabon possessed skills that became increasingly significant for negotiating urban life and, given the circumstances under which they first arrived, implied a significant resource for their integration into Ga society. By the 1930s the burgeoning town came to be defined very much along the lines of the urban skills represented by the Tabon, with the opportunities for working in the expanding colonial civil service, in the labor and building industries, and in commerce fully altering the nature of the urban assimilation of variant migrants to the town. Gradually, success in the town ceased to be linked to the goodwill of either the European trading enterprises or to the indigenous Gas as collective owners of the lands where migrants sojourned. Furthermore, with greater urbanization Accra became more and more dependent on agricultural produce from outlying areas, which also shifted the nature of the networks that fed the town. While early Tabon agricultural enterprise played a central part in the feeding of Accra, later migrant groups also came to make a decisive contribution. At Tudu the community of Muslim merchants drawn from Yoruba, Hausa, and the Northern Territories contributed cattle, milk products, shea butter, kola, and other important items to the diversification of Accra's diet.[12] But even in the diversification of urban diets the Tabon seem to have led the way.

At the same time, the Tabon were undergoing a slow but steady process of becoming Ga. With this in mind, we are able to conclude that the Tabon were not only assimilated to the Ga, but that their assimilation proceeded through their conversion into an ethnicity, the terms of which were partly shaped by their adoption of Ga ways and partly by the processes enjoined by colonial rule. What we described as the Tabon's heritage from Bahia must also be understood as having been formed recursively by the African retentions in the New World that were constantly augmented by cultural flows from Africa itself and then subsequently returned to Africa.

As Price and Mintz and Matory have instructed us, the New World was a crucible for the formation of creolized cultures that were at various times augmented by freshly arriving Africans, and, perhaps more importantly, returned back to Africa in a lively transnational cultural exchange that made Africa coeval with the New World and not an ahistorical motherland.[13] Whether with the much celebrated religions of santeria and candomblé, or with the cuisines, hair styles, and dress codes that are commonly shared between West Africa and the New World, cultural interchange must be understood as having been standardized by the nineteenth century. While the first cohort of Afro-Brazilian returnees to West Africa in the nineteenth century included people of first-generation slave descent, the point is not so much to establish that they had returned "home" to their original cultures. Rather, "home" and its cultures were coconstituted by the recursive relays of cultural details that played out between the West African subregion and Bahia, such that it was very difficult by the mid-nineteenth century to speak of any straightforward origins of, for example, the culinary habits they brought back with them. More important than any notion of return was the process of progressive ethnicization into which the Tabon were inserted and which converted them into Gas.

The process of becoming ethnic involved in the first instance adapting to aspects of Ga political and ritual practice. While the Ga Mantse (king) is normally selected from two of the oldest quarters, the choice of the Tabon Mantse involved the nomination of a leader by the heads of all the original seven Tabon families. The Tabon have followed this more democratic principle to this day, and yet have also absorbed large portions of Ga chiefly ritual attributes, including their chiefly regalia and installation rites. The Tabon also actively participate in the Homowo festival and also practice male circumcision, two key signifiers of being a Ga. By the beginning of the twentieth century the Tabon Mantse had succeeded in being elevated to the seat of benkumhene of the Ga Mantse, in other words, the wise counselor who sits to the left of the principal chiefly overlord.[14] The designations of nifa (right) and benkum (left) are also military designations, and imply that in times of war the relevant chief will provide soldiers for the right or left flank. The ascension of the Tabon Mantse to the position of benkumhene was no ordinary feat of assimilation into the Ga political order. The early twentieth century saw the eruption of internecine conflicts within the Tabon community with respect to whether the Tabon Mantse was comparable to an indigenous Ga chief and thus had the same right to dispense lands as the Ga hosts.[15]

At the same time the process of becoming Ga did not completely obliterate certain features brought from Bahia that have been incorporated into Ga ritual, thus making the Tabon variants essentially hybrids of memorialization. With respect to the Homowo festival, the ritual celebrations see the Ga Mantse sprinkling *kpoikpoi* (ground and slightly fermented maize mixed with palm oil) for the benefit of the ancestors, while the Tabon for their part sprinkle *akara/koose, waakye, massa, pinkaso*, and a variety of special Tabon foods. Yet each of the foods just mentioned has a mixed West African and New World provenance, with a suggestive Muslim marking for *akara/koose* (black-eyed beans ground, seasoned with chilli, then fried; this food being common to Muslim communities in both Nigeria and Ghana); and *waakye* (rice and beans, varieties of which are found both in Brazil and the Caribbean, as well as among Ghanaian Muslim communities). Also significant for ritual hybridities are Tabon outdooring (child naming) and marriage ceremonies, where despite close similarity between theirs and those of their host community, the copious chewing of kola nut suggests a clear reference to Muslim heritage, even if this is now expressed in an exclusively ritual form.[16]

Perhaps the one element that ensured their ultimate ethnicization is that the Tabon never managed to retain a grasp of the Portuguese language. Their small overall numbers, the pressure of conversion of a large part of their number to the dominant religion of Christianity, and the fact that they were among the first to take to Western-style education meant that within two short generations they had all but lost their mastery of the Portuguese language. The loss of Portuguese did not, however, prevent them from retaining their Afro-Brazilian names, something they use to this day as a means of signaling their special genealogy *and* of retaining a continuing sense of viability as a community. If we learn anything from the Tabon for our understanding of Accra it is that they represent a mode of cultural hybridity that is easy to bypass due to their degree of apparent assimilation into Ga culture. But the example of the Tabon also teaches us that despite being no more than a group of returnee Africans from the faraway lands of enslavement, the process of settling into their new "homeland" was far from straightforward. It involved a long process of ethnicization that helps to distinguish them from other stranger groups that came to settle in West Africa. Strictly as part of a future research agenda, it would be instructive to compare the Afro-Brazilians of West Africa to the African American returnees to Liberia in the nineteenth century, for example, or the Black Nova Scotians of Sierra Leone in the late eighteenth and early nineteenth centuries, all of whom seem to have been assimilated to their local African backgrounds and yet have retained significant signifiers of their diasporic provenance. Each instance raises significant questions about ethnicity, multiculturalism, and hybridity and the processes by which a group becomes African.

The case of the Tabon, along with many other stranger groups that came to settle across Africa (the Syro-Lebanese of West Africa and the Indians of East and South Africa come readily to mind) help to raise the fraught question of ethnicity and how this relates to cosmopolitanism. For it might be argued, somewhat polemically, that much of Africa is multiethnic and not multicultural, and that cosmopolitanism depends fundamentally on an explicit embrace of multiculturalism rather than multiethnicity. For even the horrible pogroms against black Africans that took place in South Africa early in 2015 were a sign of the problem that country has with ethnicity. Much of the violence started in the predominantly male urban hostels, which in the apartheid era were segregated according to different ethnicities and by the early 1990s were deployed as devices for ethnic mobilization. Like many such pogroms all over the world, the victims were people who were not of the correct ethnicity, in this case other foreign Africans. I would even like to suggest that in Africa xenophobia is shorthand for ethnic resentment rather than the hatred of foreigners.

So what does this imply for cosmopolitanism today? Perhaps the truth of the matter is that in multiethnic cities like Accra and others like it, cosmopolitanism is an experience of elusive potential enjoined for the middle-class elites and their transnational cohorts and that this experience must be understood alongside other identity formations, some deeply ethnic, that completely contradict the cosmopolitan impulse. It is the precise constellation within which a local cosmopolitan impulse takes shape that we are challenged to understand. If cosmopolitanism is not to be taken as a mere typology of tastes and fashions, but as a choice of identity among others, then the constellation within which this choice is exercised is as important as the choice itself.

NOTES

1 J. Lorand Matory, *Black Atlantic Religion: Tradition, Transnationalism, and Matriarchy in the Afro-Brazilian Candomblé* (Princeton: Princeton University Press, 2005), 53.

2 When the Gold Coast was fully taken over by the British government in 1821 it was first placed under the control of the government of Sierra Leone. After a hiatus from 1828 to 1843, when a committee of London merchants ran the administration of the two colonies, Sierra Leone resumed control again until 1850. The two colonies were then separated until 1866 when they were again put under the control of Sierra Leone. However, in 1874 the Gold Coast and Lagos were joined together to become the Gold Coast Colony, with Lagos gaining full autonomy some twenty years later.

3 For a fuller account of the Tabon of Accra, see Ato Quayson, *Oxford Street, Accra: City Life and the Itineraries of Transnationalism* (Durham: Duke University Press, 2014), chapter 2, "Ga Akutso Formation and the Question of Hybridity: The Afro-Brazilians (Tabon) of Accra."

4 Marco Aurelio Schaumloeffel, *Tabom: The Afro-Brazilian Community in Ghana* (Bridgetown: Schaumloeffel, 2009); Alcione M. Amos and Ebenezer Ayesu, "'I Am Brazilian': History of the Tabon, Afro-Brazilians in Accra, Ghana," *Transactions of the Historical Society of Ghana*, ns. (2003): 35–58.

5 Schaumloeffel, *Tabom*, 26.

6 Hermann von Hesse points out that the acquisition of lands for agricultural cultivation by the Tabon was really a measure to solve a looming crisis that

threatened the early returnees. While some such as Aruna Nelson were content to stay at Otublohum, others such as Mama Nassu had originally been farmers in Bahia and were keen to enter into agricultural production. While the acquisition of lands was performed on behalf of all the Tabon as a collective, only a section of them ended up cultivating the lands. By the beginning of the twentieth century and with the increasing urbanization of Accra lands, the outlying areas of Asylum Down, Kokomlemle, and Adabraka, where they had procured their lands, began to generate strong interest from non-Tabon. This in its turn led to disagreements amongst the Tabon community itself about who could properly be allowed to sell them. Several cases were brought by Gas against the Tabon and amongst the Tabon themselves. See Hermann von Hesse, "A Brief History of the Afro-Brazilian Community of Accra." B.A. thesis, University of Ghana (2010); also Marco Aurelio Schaumloeffel, *Tabom: The Afro-Brazilian Community in Ghana* (Bridgetown: Schaumloeffel, 2009); and Samuel S. Quarcopoome, "The Impact of Urbanization on the Socio-Political History of the Ga Mashie People of Accra: 1877–1957." Ph.D. dissertation, University of Ghana (1993).

7 Peter A. Schweizer, *Survivors on the Gold Coast: The Basel Missionaries in Colonial Ghana* (Accra: Smartline Publishers, 2000), 85.

8 Schaumloeffel, *Tabom: The Afro-Brazilian Community in Ghana* (Bridgetown: Schaumloeffel, 2009), 28–29.

9 João José Reis, *Slave Rebellion in Brazil: The Muslim Uprising of 1835 in Bahia*, translated by Arthur Brakel (Baltimore: John Hopkins University Press, 2005), 160.

10 The Accra Water Rate Bill of 1925, revised several times subsequently, draws some very strong criticism from residents of Accra, including the chiefs. Some of the lively arguments are captured on the pages of the *Gold Coast Spectator*, November 29, 1930.

11 On the mentality and peculiar cosmology of company slaves brought on by their circumstances, see Ray Kea, "'But I Know What I Shall Do': Agency, Belief & the Social Imaginary in Eighteenth-Century Gold Coast Towns," *Africa's Urban Past*, eds. David M. Anderson and Richard Rathbone (Oxford: James Currey, 2005), 163–188.

12 Samuel Ntewusu provides an exhaustive and fascinating account of the contribution of the Yoruba and northern merchant communities of Tudu to Accra's urban formation. See his "Settling In and Holding On: A Socio-Economic History of Northern Traders and Transporters in Accra's Tudu: 1908-2008," Ph.D. dissertation, Leiden, University of Leiden (2011). The argument about shifts in food dependency for Accra and other urban centers in the Gold Coast in the long durée is put forward persuasively by Ray A. Kea in his *Settlements, Trade, and Polities in the Seventeenth Century Gold Coast* (Baltimore; John Hopkins University Press, 1982). There is also speculation that the name Tudu may itself have been of Brazilian origin. The Tabon had opened shops around the area, and on being asked what they had on offer often replied "tudoo," meaning everything; this word was later used by the locals to designate the entire area. No other explanation has thus

far been provided for this unusual place name, which does not seem to derive from Ga or any other local language. Thus its Brazilian provenance seems as likely as any.

13 Richard Price and Sidney Mintz. *The Birth of African-American Culture: An Anthropological Perspective* (New York: Beacon Press, 1992).

14 Schaumloeffel, *Tabom*, 81.

15 An example of such a land dispute, which almost caused irreparable damage to the Tabon community, was that brought in 1938 by J. E. Maslieno against J. A. Nelson, representing two established Tabon families. See Schaumloeffel, *Tabom*, 35–36; and also Quarcopoome, "Urbanization, Land Alienation and Politics in Accra." *IAS Research Review, New Series*, 8.1&2, (1992), 40–54.

16 See von Hesse, "A Brief History of the Afro-Brazilian Community of Accra," 12, 14, 32–34.

17

The Cosmopolitanisms of Citizenship

JEREMY WALDRON

It is appropriate to begin this essay by reflecting a little bit on the cosmopolitanism of the university and the various ways in which universities
can represent, bear witness to, nourish, and advance the cosmopolitan
strain in our civilization. Consider this quotation from Jacques Verger,
the French medievalist and specialist in the study of universities in the
Middle Ages. Reflecting on the role of university institutions in Paris,
Oxford, Bologna, and other European cities in the thirteenth century,
Verger said this in his contribution to the *New Cambridge Medieval
History*:

> Unlike both other urban professions and the schools of the preceding
> century, the universities were not institutions that were purely local.
> They may have been located in a given city, but they were simultane-
> ously institutions belonging to the whole of Christendom. Their range of
> recruitment was not limited by administrative or ecclesiastical boundar-
> ies but extended as far as their power of attraction, which in itself was
> solely determined by the influence of their teaching. Their freedoms and
> privileges, whose main purpose was to remove them from the control of
> the local authorities, were confirmed by the papacy, the universal power
> par excellence. The knowledge conveyed by the universities was itself
> conceived as universal knowledge, exempt from any particular locality,
> unique and valid in all of Christendom (which was demonstrated by the
> exclusive use of Latin). Consequently the degree conferred by the univer-
> sity was valid everywhere.[1]

Now if we were describing the mission of the university today in universal terms, we would perhaps not use the word *Christendom*—"institutions
belonging to the whole of Christendom," "universal knowledge valid in

all of Christendom." (I will come back to this below). Still, the quotation reminds us that the cosmopolitan approach of our work and our institutions today is not a novelty. If anything, it is the recovery of a much older cosmopolitanism, a much older universalism in the university that used to inform the way our predecessors in these traditions completed their work and approached the body of knowledge and scholarship for which they were responsible.

This cosmopolitanism is evident to me in the way I think of my own discipline, law. It is easy to think of law as tied to a particular jurisdiction, a particular country: American law, English common Law, Islamic law, and so on. People sometimes ask me, "How come you teach law in New York when you earned your law degree in Dunedin, New Zealand, and your doctorate in jurisprudence at Oxford? How that can that qualify you to teach law in the United States?" The question is predicated on a parochial view of the study of law that perhaps makes some sense today but would have made little sense in the era of which Verger was writing. In that era, law was conceived as a universal discipline, not one tied to particular legal systems. Jurists at Oxford did not just study English law; medieval law professors in Paris did not just study French law; and legal scholars in Bologna did not study just the law of some particular Italian city. They simply studied *the law*, the body of thought and knowledge—legal science—that was associated with the enterprise of governing human activities and transactions and associated with the rule of law as such. Of course, each community had its customs and some idiosyncratic laws of its own. But not until the jurisprudence of the beginning of the nineteenth century do we see the representation of distinctive custom, local or parochial, being treated as the essence of law, as much a peculiar identity of each particular society as its language or its culture. We see that in the work of people like Savigny as a reaction against the universalist pretentions of the Napoleonic Codes.[2]

Before that, societies that insisted on the distinctiveness of their own parochial legal folkways were seen as aberrations—not as the norm— rather like a society insisting on its own physics or its own chemistry. As late as 1842, in a decision involving a bill of exchange written in Maine but negotiated in New York City, the U.S. Supreme Court invoked the idea of the law as a universal discipline, saying that the case was to

be settled by the general principles and doctrines of commercial jurisprudence as such. (I emphasize that this was a tough decision in commercial law, not some fancy jurisprudential theory.) The Court said this:

> The law respecting negotiable instruments may truly be declared in the
> language of Cicero to be in a great measure, not the law of a single coun-
> try only but of the whole commercial world. *Non erit alia lex Romae, alia*
> *Athenis, alia nunc, alia posthac, sed et apud omnes gentes, et omni tempore,*
> *una eademque lex obtinebit.* (Not just in Rome or in Athens, but through-
> out the whole world and among all peoples and at all times, one and the
> same law obtains).[3]

Not until 1928, under the corrosive skepticism of Justice Oliver Wen-
dell Holmes, did the Supreme Court turn decisively against that idea,
holding that law could not float free in the world at large but had to be
tied down to a particular jurisdiction, to the sovereignty of a particular
country. This was the great case of *Erie Railroad v. Tompkins*,[4] in which
the Court rejected the idea of a federal version of general common law.
"Law," said Justice Holmes, "in the sense in which courts speak of it
today does not exist without some definite authority behind it," and the
definite authority must be that of a particular state.[5] I think it is fair to
say that ever since that case was decided, a great many legal scholars,
among whom I count myself, have been trying to confine it to its facts
and claw back a sense of law as a cosmopolitan institution and a universal subject of study.[6]

In some ways the idea of cosmopolitan law is easy to understand.
We understand the idea of international law. We understand the idea
of human rights law. We understand the laws of armed conflict and
the principles referred to in the prosecution of the Nazi war criminals,
"principles which had been entrenched and rendered sacred and which
had become the heritage of all civilized peoples."[7]

We understand the idea of the law of nations, referred to in Article
I, Clause 8, of the U.S. Constitution.[8] Maybe, as some scholars suggest,
we need to come to terms with the idea of global common law.[9] Those
are more or less obvious cases, and they do not occasion much concern.
Less obvious is the routine development of law as a transnational enterprise, facilitating global commerce, protecting property and person in

transactions and migrations all over the world. The law of international trade is something that you can perhaps understand as the outward projection of the commercial law of particular societies. But it can also be understood like the old mercantile law, *lex mercatoria*, as a body of customs that evolved along the trade routes and lived in the caravans of the traders as they moved between societies, something that was then only partially incorporated into the municipal law of particular countries.[10] Even if we focus on law enforced within each particular country, the life of the law has always involved copying, imitating, and boilerplating from one society to another as societies look at each other and take advantage of the best—sometimes the worst—but mostly the best that they can find in each other's legal culture and legal science.

Even to the extent that we associate law with national sovereignty, we still think of sovereignty itself in a cosmopolitan way as a feature of a network or community of nation-states,[11] recognizing one another, maintaining regular channels of contact and consultation on issues of common concern, respecting one another's passports, maintaining treaties of legal comity on everything from extradition to child custody, applying one another's laws where appropriate to problems that lawyers call conflicts of laws, facilitating and sustaining international treaties that make possible travel around the world—for example, travel and telecommunications from New York to Abu Dhabi—all the effortless connections and connectedness between continents that we take for granted. This is cosmopolitan law woven into the fabric of ordinary experience.[12]

I am not saying that there are no differences. Of course there are. But even on the parts of the law that we are most particularly (and particularistically) attached to—our own constitution, for example—we see the cutting and pasting of language from one country to another. Our Eighth Amendment forbidding "cruel and unusual punishment" is cut and pasted from the English Bill of Rights of a hundred years before.[13] Exactly the same language, cut and pasted by the drafters of the Canadian Charter of Rights and Freedoms, surfaces in that country in 1982,[14] almost two hundred years after Americans adopted the language of "cruel and unusual" from the very country we had revolted against. By the same token, our constitution serves as a template for others around the world. Countries copy one another, not because they are plagiarists or unoriginal, or because they cannot do the work themselves; they copy because they value the common enterprise of legality and human rights. They value what they have in common with other countries, in the constitutionalist tradition, more than they value their national distinctiveness.

I have drawn on examples of law because that is what I know about. Everything I have explored could be applied to other academic disciplines, particularly this theme of recovering the sense of an older cosmopolitanism. No one believes there is a distinctive physics and chemistry that differs from one side of the world to another, so that U.S. physicists study the way particles move in this part of the world while physicists at the European Organization for Nuclear Research study the way that particles move in Switzerland. Scientific study is, by definition, universal. I have long been intrigued by what one might call the effortless cosmopolitan community of scientists. When scientists talk about what "we" know, what "we" do not yet know—"We think the Big Bang happened some 10 or 20 billion years ago, but there are one or two observational anomalies that we haven't figured out" or "We have a pretty good account of what causes AIDS and how to mitigate its progress, but we don't yet have anything in the way of a vaccine"—the term *we* does not just refer to me, the scientist, and my chums in my particular laboratory. It does not even just refer to me and my conationals or scholars in the same university. The *we* refers to the consensus of the community of scientists in the world—scientists who read the same literature, are aware of one another's findings, check and recheck each other's results, and grapple with the same problems in roughly the same terms.

It is a wonderful notion, because it is a cosmopolitan conception of community. An effortless community—well, perhaps not completely effortless as people do have to work at it—but a civilization-wide community taken for granted among humans working together in their ordinary lives in the pursuit of knowledge. When you think of it, this is true not just of the disciplines studied in universities. There is a similar pervasive cosmopolitanism in everyday life. It would be tedious to count the mundane ways, whether it is trade or consumer goods. I mean things like the jeans we wear, the electronic devices we listen to, the music we groove to, the food we eat—all these artifacts by which we are connected effortlessly to thousands of workers, manufacturers, and producers around the world, bound to one another in a vast and densely entangled web of trade, commerce, and consumption.[15]

I wrote earlier that the reference to Christendom in Verger's statement about medieval universities made his conception of the universal mission of the university seem less cosmopolitan than perhaps we are comfortable with. Today, we might want to think well beyond the boundaries of what used to be called Christendom to embrace the Islamic world (and others) as well. But it is still worth reflecting on the fact that both great world religions work as cosmopolitan entities, as religions that inhabit the world. Think for a moment about Christendom. We may think of it as located in Rome or in the site of a particular cathedral or in a city like Jerusalem or the towns in Galilee where its founder grew up, or the cities in Asia Minor where the apostles preached the gospel before the religion became politicized under Constantine. But basically, Christianity exists in the world. Even Catholic Christianity's location in Rome (*Roman* Catholicism) is not a matter of a religion or a sect having put down cultural roots in a particular community; it is a base of operations for a cosmopolitan enterprise in what was at the time the most cosmopolitan city in the world. And so it exists today, exercising pastoral leadership over a billion people, many of whom regard their involvement in that vast global enterprise as the most profoundly important feature of their lives. The same is true of Islam. It arose in a particular time and place, and it has its holy and sacred sites in Mecca and Jerusalem. But it exists now, if it exists anywhere, *in the world*. In this world-cosmopolitan character, it may again be the fact about their lives that people take most seriously in what are otherwise the most disparate communities.[16]

This brings me to an important point of about social perception. There is a kind of optical illusion or fallacy that it is important to avoid when we think about culture and cosmopolitanism. I call it "the grade school teacher's fallacy." When grade school teachers in the United States want to introduce the children in their classrooms to other cultures—to the culture of the Dominican Republic or Mexico, the Netherlands or India—they will show the children things that are *different* about these cultures (I mean different from ours). The teachers may give their pupils the impression that the most important thing about each particular society—each cultural or ethnic community—is its distinctiveness, the practices and customs, foods and costumes, that distinguish it from others. But this may be a serious misconception, both as a description of the consciousness of the communities in question and as a prescription about what it is to show respect for the members of a given community.

For example, a man in Djakarta and a woman in Damascus may believe (quite rightly) that they have much more in common in their shared commitment to Islam than anything the U.S. grade school teacher would say was useful for illustrating the distinctiveness of Indonesian or Syrian society. Similarly, a woman in the Philippines, a man in Brazil, and a teenager in Ireland may all think of the teachings and sacraments of the Roman Catholic Church as the most important aspects of their culture in regard to the way their lives are actually lived. And it is not just religion but science, trade, and everything. The most important things that people value may be woven into their culture as cosmopolitan strands, not particularistic strands. I am not arguing that people do not value the distinctiveness of their societies. I am trying to highlight the point that when we actually look at what matters most to people in their lives without any preconceptions about distinctiveness, we may well find that cosmopolitan or worldly or global strands matter more than anything else.

When we talk about the cosmopolitanism of the university, we are not necessarily talking about something that divides the elites who inhabit an academic institution from the lives of ordinary men and women of various societies around the world. When philosopher Martha Nussbaum spoke of cosmopolitan responsibility a few years ago in an article written for the *Boston Review*, she quoted the old Stoic adage that each of us dwells in two communities, the local community of our birth and the community of human aspiration in which we look neither to this corner nor to that but measure the boundaries of our nation by the sum. She also quoted the saying of Marcus Aurelius, "It makes no difference whether a person lives here or there, provided that wherever he lives, he lives as a citizen of the world."[17]

When she quoted those propositions, Nussbaum's critics responded that "you can not be a citizen of the world unless there is a world government. You can not be a citizen of the world unless there's a world polity, political system to be a citizen of."[18] It was also said, "teaching a child to be a citizen of the world is teaching the child to be a citizen of an abstraction."[19] That argument, I think, is thoughtless. It rests on too tight a connection between citizenship and civic responsibility on the one hand, and state and government on the other hand. A citizen, a good citizen, is somebody who takes responsibility for a collective enterprise. When there is no government to rule that enterprise, the responsibilities of the citizens may matter even more. When we use the phrase "good citizen" in academic life, we use it in relation to institutional responsibility— again, without any sense that its use is inappropriate, unless there's an overarching mechanism of control. A good citizen is one who shoulders his or her burdens of departmental life and departmental administration, is available to help in crises, and so on.[20]

To push the point a little further, one can imagine there was the distinction between good citizens and bad citizens even among the members of the underground universities and their departments in, say, Czechoslovakia in the early 1980s. Precisely because they did not have formal structures of governance, precisely because they did not have presidents and department chairs, they had to, as it were, run that cosmopolitan part of their lives themselves. The distinction makes sense despite the absence of formal ruling structures for the departments in question. Indeed, it became important precisely because of their absence. So the analogous phrase "citizen of the world" should not be regarded as meaningless in the absence of world government. If anything, the absence of such a coercive institution to secure, nourish, and sustain the structures of life and practice at a global level places a greater burden on individual men and women and on the initiatives that they undertake voluntarily. It makes it all the more important for us to use "citizen of the world" as an idea to regulate and discipline our actions. The absence of any organization that can do that work for us provides a greater reason for thinkers not to reject peremptorily Martha Nussbaum's proposal that people must be educated to this cosmopolitan dimension of their civic responsibilities.

My argument has been about the pervasive presence of cosmopolitan strands woven into the fabric of everyday life, just as they are woven into the understanding—a proper understanding—of the university and the scholarly and scientific enterprises. That these cosmopolitan strands are pervasive does not mean that they can be taken for granted. It does not mean that they will continue to subsist resiliently, no matter what we do. They can be nourished, or they can be subverted, occluded, and undermined. I take it that when we talk of global citizenship, we are talking about a duty to take care of the cosmopolitan side of our institutions. Cosmopolitanism is an ethically weighted concept. We have a responsibility to respond to the ethical values that the term embodies and make sure that these are not overwhelmed or disparaged in the name of particularistic attachments. Most of all, we have a responsibility simply to bear witness to and participate in the cosmopolitan life of the world.

NOTES

1 Jacques Verger, "The Universities and Scholasticism," in *The New Cambridge Medieval History: Vol. V: 1198–c.1300*, ed. David Abulafia (Cambridge: Cambridge University Press, 1999), 256, 263.

2 See, for example, Frederick Charles von Savigny, *Of the Vocation of Our Age for Legislation and Jurisprudence* (1828), trans. Abraham Hayward (Bethesda, Md.: Legal Classics Library, 1986).

3 *Swift v. Tyson*, 41 U.S. 1 (1842), citing Lord Mansfield in *Luke v. Lyde*, 2 Burr. 883, 887, 97 Eng. Rep. 614 (K. B. 1759).

4 *Erie Railroad Co. v. Tompkins*, 304 U.S. 64 (1938). In this case, Justice Holmes relied on his own earlier dissent in *Black & White Taxicab Co. v. Brown & Yellow Taxicab Co.*, 276 U.S. 518 (1928).

5 Ibid., at 533 (Holmes J., dissenting).

6 See, for example, Craig Green, "Repressing Erie's Myth," *California Law Review* 96 (2008): 595; Jeremy Waldron, "Foreign Law and the Modern Ius Gentium," *Harvard Law Review*, 119 (2005): 129; and Jack Goldsmith and Steven Walt, "Erie and the Irrelevance of Legal Positivism," *Virginia Law Review* 84 (1998): 673.

7 This is a quotation from Attorney General Gideon Hausner in the trial of Adolf Eichmann in Jerusalem in 1962. For the relevant part of the Eichmann transcript, see www.nizkor.org.

8 U.S. Constitution, Article I.8: "The Congress shall have power to . . . define and punish piracies and felonies committed on the high seas, and offenses against the law of nations."

9 See, for example, Wayne R. Barnes, "Contemplating a Civil Law Paradigm for a Future International Commercial Code," *Louisiana Law Review* 65 (2005): 677.

10 See Wyndham Anstis Bewes, *The Romance of the Law Merchant* (London: Sweet & Maxwell, 1923).

11 The idea of a society of states as the basis of international order is best known from Hedley Bull, *The Anarchical Society: A Study of Order in World Politics* (New York: Columbia University Press, 1977).

12 I have pursued this further in Jeremy Waldron, "Cosmopolitan Norms," in *Another Cosmopolitanism* (2005 Tanner Lectures by Seyla Benhabib), ed. Robert Post (Oxford: Oxford University Press, 2006), 83–101.

13 The English Bill of Rights of December 16, 1689, provided as follows: "The . . . lords spiritual and temporal, and commons . . . do in the first place (as their ancestors in like case have usually done) for the vindicating and asserting their ancient rights and liberties, declare . . . that excessive bail ought not to be required, nor excessive fines imposed; nor cruel and unusual punishments inflicted."

14 Canadian Charter of Rights and Freedoms (Part One of Canada's Constitution Act, 1982), Article 12: "Everyone has the right not to be subjected to any cruel and unusual treatment or punishment."

15 I have pursued this theme at length in Jeremy Waldron, "Minority Cultures and the Cosmopolitan Alternative," *University of Michigan Journal of Law Reform* 25 (1992): 751, reprinted in *The Rights of Minority Cultures*, ed. Will Kymlicka (Oxford: Oxford University Press, 1995).

16 See also the discussion of religion in Jeremy Waldron, "Teaching Cosmopolitan Right," in *Education and Citizenship in Liberal-Democratic Societies: Teaching for Cosmopolitan Values and Cultural Identities*, ed. Kevin McDonough and Walter Feinberg (Oxford: Oxford University Press, 2003), 31–33.

17 See Martha Nussbaum, "Patriotism and Cosmopolitanism," *Boston Review* 19 (October/November 1994); and Martha Nussbaum with others, *For Love of Country? Debating the Limits of Patriotism*, ed. Joshua Cohen (Boston: Beacon Press, 1996). Her quotations are from Seneca, *De Otio,* and Marcus Aurelius, *Meditations.*

18 Amy Gutmann, "Democratic Citizenship," in *For Love of Country?* 68.

19 Michael McConnell, "Don't Neglect the Little Platoons," in *For Love of Country?* 81.

20 This paragraph and the next are adapted from Waldron, "Teaching Cosmopolitan Right," 39–44.

18

Afropolitan Style and Unusable Global Spaces

ASHLEIGH HARRIS

While African studies is a thriving discipline across the Anglophone academy, we might, along with Achille Mbembe and Sarah Nuttall, note the "overwhelming neglect of how the meanings of Africanness are made."[1] The readings of African spaces that dominate the discipline— for example, Africa in crisis, Africa at war, Africa as running before the temporality of modernity—produce a significant problem for the development of a cosmopolitan theory that is truly global in reach. Indeed, we may well ask ourselves whether cosmopolitanism has, despite its intrinsic claims to the contrary, perpetuated a global knowledge economy in which Africa is a regular site of analysis and application of theory, but not a space of knowledge and theory production itself. We might read the fact that the word "Afropolitan" has been lexicalized in both academic and popular contexts as an indication of cosmopolitanism's failure to address this problem.

Even the origin of the term "Afropolitanism" is entangled in this politics of knowledge production. Taiye Selasi first coined the term in an article entitled "Bye-Bye Babar" in *Lip Magazine* in 2005, which was reproduced, with much wider critical impact, in *Callaloo* in 2013. Selasi's Afropolitanism is, at first glance, a welcome rejection of the "quasi-equivalence . . . between race and geography"[2] that has pervaded African nationalism. Selasi's Afropolitanism describes, rather, a young mix-culture that is "redefining what it means to be African."[3] Yet despite her clear rejection of autochthonous Africanness, Selasi's Afropolitan is, on closer inspection, little more than African expatriate and diaspora culture in a world quite radically dissociated from African everyday life. Her article begins with a description of young Afropolitans dancing to a Fela Kuti remix at the Medicine Bar in London:

Like so many African young people working and living in cities around
the globe, they belong to no single geography, but feel at home in many.
They . . . are Afropolitans—the newest generation of African emigrants,
coming soon, or collected already, at a law firm/chem lab/jazz lounge
near you.[4]

Throughout her article, Selasi only observes the remix cultures of
these Afropolitans in non-African spaces, with the implication that the
redefinition of "what it means to be African" is the onus of this "newest
generation of African *emigrants*" (my emphasis). She even ruminates
on a time when the "talent" of Africa will "repatriate", insinuating that
Africa's talent is, by definition, elsewhere.

Kenyan author Binyavanga Wainaina ardently rejects the terms of
this form of Afropolitanism. For him, "Afropolitanism has become the
marker of crude cultural commodification—a phenomenon increasingly 'product driven,' design focused, and 'potentially funded by the
West.'"[5] I would take this further to argue that these economic patterns
that Wainaina reads behind Afropolitan style are not disconnected from
the broader issue of Africa's omission from global knowledge production per se. As John Comaroff and Jean Comaroff have put it, the global
knowledge economy has "treated [African spaces] less as sources of re-
fined knowledge than as reservoirs of raw fact: of the minutiae from
which Euromodernity might fashion its testable theories and transcendent truths. Just as it has long capitalized on non-Western 'raw materials'
by ostensibly adding value and refinement to them".[6] Even Afropolitanism, with its rejection of nationalist identity and its ambition of reading
Africa in and of the globe, remains troubled by the persistence of such
unidirectional knowledge economies.

We may well ask, then, whether we need the term "Afropolitanism" at
all. In short, I argue that we need a name for that which cosmopolitanism often neglects precisely because that neglect is invisible to itself. That
is, without Afropolitanism, the routine ways in which Africa remains
only an object (rather than a producer) of knowledge for the metropolitan and academic gaze of the global North are unlikely to be made
visible. Beyond glib observation that the underdeveloped South is part
of a single, but unequal, globe, Afropolitanism requires us to account for

how that economic inequality shapes Africans' experiences of worldliness. If Africans do not assimilate into the privileged economies of
trendy, metropolitan remix cultures, they will not enjoy equal cosmopolitan freedoms as citizens of the world. As such, the phenomenology
of being African in and of the world requires its own terminology. In
this essay, I begin to theorize the contours and illustrate the usefulness
of that terminology through a discussion of Zimbabwean author Brian
Chikwava's 2009 novel, *Harare North*.[7] Chikwava's novel is Afropolitan
in style and form insofar as it dramatizes the cosmopolitan experience
and phenomenology of being African in the world. Ultimately, it is the
condition of homelessness[8]—or the attenuation of global space for the
African body—rather than the possibility of being at home in the world
that Chikwava's Afropolitanism articulates.

Given that my focus is on Afropolitanism as literary style, Rebecca
Walkowitz's well-known elaboration of a theory of cosmopolitan style,
which emphatically resists a Eurocentric conception of modernism, is a
good starting point to illustrate how easily Africa can be circumvented
when theorizing cosmopolitanism. Even Walkowitz's title, *Cosmopolitan
Style: Modernism beyond the Nation*, emphasizes her aim to establish a
critical cosmopolitanism that relocates modernist aesthetics and style
across multiple global contexts. Nonetheless, the book describes this
cosmopolitanism almost entirely outside Africa's contribution to that
style. The omission is all the more remarkable given that Walkowitz acknowledges, in her Introduction, that it was in Jean Paul Sartre's essay
"Black Orpheus"[9]—where he argued for the revolutionary value of negritude poetry—that he began to form "a nascent theory of cosmopolitan style."[10] While this suggests that Walkowitz reads negritude poetry as
a major influence on Sartre's thinking—and thereby on the consequent
formation of cosmopolitanism—the rest of her book includes only one
passing reference to African literature: a broad gesture not toward African writing and theory itself, but rather toward the politics of "postcolonial fiction and criticism by Ngugi wa Thiong'o, Chinua Achebe,
Frantz Fanon, Edward Said, and Gauri Viswanathan".[11] I would argue
that Walkowitz's omission is symptomatic of a much longer critical tradition that has transposed active African participation in the philosophy
and aesthetics of modernity into a passive register of influence. Even
Léopold Sédar Senghor himself, whose anthology of negritude poetry

Sartre's essay introduced, battled with these lines of influence. Senghor first endeavored to prove the centrality of African art in the modernist tradition by citing symbolism, surrealism, nabism, expressionism, fauvism, and cubism as some of the forms that drew on what he calls the "Negro revolution." Yet in the same breath he hedges the significance of negritude in twentieth-century modernism, awkwardly admitting that "without the discovery of African art, the revolution would still have taken place, but probably without such vigor and assurance."[12]

Simon Gikandi discusses the lines of influence between postcolonial literatures and modernism from the African—rather than the European—perspective: "[I]t was primarily . . . in the language and structure of modernism," he writes, "that a postcolonial experience came to be articulated and imagined in literary form." That is, for Gikandi, the "archive of early postcolonial writing in Africa, the Caribbean, and India is dominated and defined by writers whose political or cultural projects were enabled by modernism even when the ideologies of [European modernists] were at odds with the project of decolonization."[13] Modernist style not only suited the politics of anticolonial literature, but was also an obvious influence on early African postcolonial literary style, since, as Gikandi notes, the styles of modernism coincided with the advent of written and published literature in Africa.

But, in affirmation of Senghor's uncertain hope that negritude was "a [universal] humanism of the Twentieth Century,"[14] we now know that this influence was neither unidirectional nor limited to the anthropological curiosity of a few avant-gardists and surrealists. As Gikandi goes on to argue: "[M]odernism represents perhaps the most intense and unprecedented site of encounter between the institutions of European cultural production and the cultural practices of colonized people. It is rare to find a central text in modern literature, art, or ethnography that does not deploy the other as a significant source, influence or informing analogy."[15] Despite this, scholarship on modernist style has largely obscured African writers' participation in twentieth-century aesthetics and continues to overlook the ongoing role that African writing plays in constituting cosmopolitan style today.

In an attempt to correct this scholarly trend, Achille Mbembe began articulating a conception of Afropolitanism (just a year or so after Selasi first used the term). Citing the multiple and sustained movements of people into, out of, and across Africa in both precolonial and colonial times, Mbembe insists that the "cultural history of the continent can hardly be understood outside the paradigm of itineracy, mobility and displacement." Furthermore, he writes:

> Awareness of the interweaving of the here and there, the presence of the elsewhere in the here and vice versa, the relativisation of primary roots and memberships and the way of embracing, with full knowledge of the facts, strangeness, foreignness and remoteness . . . it is this cultural, historical and aesthetic sensitivity that underlies the term "afropolitanism."[16]

For Mbembe, Afropolitanism is, then, "an aesthetic and a particular poetic of the world." This aesthetic is deeply resistant to nativist politics and to negritude style, both of which suggest autochthonous articulations of African being. Yet, while Afropolitanism acknowledges that "part of African history lies somewhere else, outside Africa" it is not only an aesthetic, like Selasi's, for an African diaspora. Indeed, Mbembe's Afropolitanism is as much a tracing of Africa in the world as it is a history of the world in Africa.[17] If Afropolitanism is to get political purchase on the circumvention of Africa in cosmopolitanism, then it surely has to begin from this premise: Africa is, and has always been, an active participant in modernity, not merely a site of "raw" and premodern culture, in need of processing into the value-laden objects of a global market economy.

Brian Chikwava's novel *Harare North* presents a deep and sustained writing of Africa onto the cartography of the foreign city in ways that exemplify Mbembe's Afropolitan style. In the novel, London is narrated in the idioms, grammar, and psychology of an unnamed Zimbabwean in such a way that its streets become pervaded with what we might call the phenomenologies of Zimbabwe. London thus becomes the idiomatic, witty title of Chikwava's novel: *Harare North*. Our sense of London is mediated so entirely by the perspective of the unnamed narrator that it is more a substratum of the condition of the poor Zimbabwean in the globe than an objective space determined by its own history. Our sense of this rewriting of London into the phenomenology of the narrator is such that the city he reveals to us is one of his own making: this is not

London, but Harare North, a city catalogued through distinctly Zimba-bwean idioms and vocabularies.

This is evident from the outset, as Chikwava has his narrator speak both ungrammatically and in an idiom heavily inflected with chiShona proverbs and linguistic play. The result is not infantilizing, as is often the effect of written vernaculars. Rather, the grammatical errors (per-sonal and possessive pronoun confusion, the dropping of the definite ar-ticle, subject-verb agreement errors, and number errors), which remain consistent throughout the novel, reveal an impression of the narrator's unwritten and unspoken mother-tongue, chiShona, on—or under—the English language that only tenuously covers the surface of the text. As such, language haunts the pages of *Harare North*.

English and its varied and various reappropriations have, of course, been widely debated and discussed across postcolonial scholarship and we needn't rehearse that debate here. A germane example, however, can be found in Dambudzo Marechera's seminal work of African modern-ism: *The House of Hunger*, a novel that also prefigures the structural de-vices of Chikwava's text. Marechera's narrator articulates the problem of learning and writing in the English language thus: "I was being severed from my own voice. . . . It was like this: English is my second language, Shona my first. When I talked it was in the form of an interminable argument, one side of which was always expressed in English and the other side always in Shona."[18]

The consequence of this "interminable argument" is a kind of stut-tering, one that may appear similar to the "stutters or stammers" of modernist writers that Rebecca Walkowitz argues were used "to reg-ister antagonisms within a civic rhetoric that claims to be uniform and consistent." The stutter, she writes, "represents the discrepancies within collective assertion; it registers a protest that is otherwise prohibited."[19] Yet, as Marechera's narrator discovers, his stammer does not always register protest. Indeed, in an attempt to articulate his protest against a Catholic priest, he complains: " 'It's people like you who're driving us mad!' I wanted to say more, but I began to stammer and [the priest] took advantage of that to say 'It's the ape in you, young man, the heart of darkness.' "[20] In Walkowitz's analysis the stuttering of Whiskey Sisodia in Salman Rushdie's *The Satanic Verses* is a strategy of "mix-up," which is used to articulate the "new experiences of contemporary immigration and also to distinguish between the cosmopolitanism of exploitative fusion, on the one hand, and the cosmopolitanism of tactical syncretism, on the other."[21] Yet, whereas Rushdie's "mix-up" might certainly be said to introduce a productive level of disorder between these two oppositions, I tend, rather, to agree with Timothy Brennan's assessment of Rushdie's cosmopolitanism as insufficiently antagonistic, and thus "convenient."[22] Marechera's stammering narrator, on the other hand, is sufficiently antagonistic, but his awkwardness in formulating himself reinscribes him in the racist rhetoric of the colonial episteme: as an inarticulate "ape."

Chikwava also emphasizes the stutter of a key character in his novel, Shingi—the narrator's best friend, who despite having his papers in order and thus living and working legally in the United Kingdom, spirals into drug addiction and, after a brutal attack, is left struggling for his life in hospital. Shingi's stutter does not produce the linguistic play or double entendres of the sort that Walkowitz finds in Rushdie's stuttering Sisodia; rather, Shingi's stutter is a marker of various irreconcilables in his life: the most significant being the incommensurability of his Zimbabwean family's economic need and what he can reasonably earn and send back to them. Shingi's stutter becomes a marker of the schizophrenic nature of his everyday life, where he exists on the tightrope between the reality of economic desperation and a desperate fantasy of wealth and economic security.

Chikwava is at pains to illustrate the distance between those, like Shingi, who fail to cross this economic chasm, and those privileged immigrants, such as the narrator's cousin Paul and his wife Sekai, who live a comfortable middle-class, émigré life. The chasm is wide: unlike Sekai—a nurse—who can afford to pay the narrator a significant sum of money when he blackmails her after discovering she is having an affair, we are introduced to Tsitsi, whose only source of income, being a minor, is to rent out her baby to people claiming parental benefits. Assimilation—or successful immigration—is primarily dependent on economic factors. Yet, according to the narrator, the cost of Sekai's assimilation is that she has become a "lapsed African" who "don't really know about things going on in Zimbabwe because she have been in England for too long. She buy all the propaganda that she hear from papers and TV in this country. . . . She don't even know Comrade Mugabe." Sekai, who no longer follows the protocols of Shona society, is indeed at a remove from everyday life in Africa, a distance that is further marked by her detachment from under-privileged African émigré life in London. Tsitsi, on the other hand, who "sing old Shona song about bird that don't want to come play because it want to fly high into clouds so it can be like them clouds," fails to inte-grate into English social behavior entirely. Just like the language of the narrator, Tsitsi's mode of being—which the narrator describes as "just rural mother"—fits awkwardly in the context of London. When her baby falls ill (as a result of salmonella caused by his diet of cheap milk powder), we read: "Tsitsi now start wailing in proper native way, wrapping them arms around she head and throwing sheself about on the hospital floor in disorderly way and frightening English people." The scene later prompts the narrator to lecture the other immigrants he shares a squat with: "We have to acquire what they call culture" and "ease down some of they na-tive behaviours so they don't frighten all them important English people". If assimilation is an economic process, access to the formal economy is oiled by cultural commonality and linguistic fluency.[23]

The line between the formal and informal economies falls precisely in the space between Paul and Sekai's middle-class lives and the lives of those living in the squat. The narrator, who is an illegal in London, can-not work in the formal economy and thus quickly crosses over that line, finding work illegally under Shingi's name and looking for any opportu-nity in the informal economy to make a living. Ato Quayson illustrates the pervasiveness of such improvisations within the informal economy in African social life. He elaborates this in the Ghanaian context through the figure of the kòbòlò, who "is defined primarily as a good-for-nothing street lounger [but] turns out on closer inspection to be a much more complex sociological category that encapsulates a transitional state of urban existence at the intersecting vectors of space, time, and longing."[24] As Quayson points out, the scale and complexity of informal economies across Africa result in this figure being a commonplace in most African cities: "Akin to the area boy in Lagos popular lore, the term 'kòbòlò' also has resonance with the Dakarois fakhman, a term that designates a good-for-nothing street loiterer and potential criminal."[25] Chikwava's London-based narrator draws on this pervasive figure in African street life and literature,[26] thereby enabling the phenomenology of African street life in the spaces of London.

Chikwava's street hustler is, like the kòbòlò, "on a quest to escape the vagaries"[27]—and, I would add, violence—of the informal economy. The narrative form that shapes this quest is determined by the success or failure of the protagonist to assimilate. A successful assimilation narrative would fit the easy form of the Bildungsroman, with economic, rather than moral, aspiration as its driving force. Yet, in *Harare North*, the protagonist's hustle fails, and the result is a narrative form that becomes entropic. Chikwava consciously resists anodyne and harmonious closure, activating awkwardness as a strategy for dislocating the event of reading itself. Indeed, after a series of betrayals and failures to discover a sense of belonging in London, the narrator takes to the street: completely dispossessed of all but his suitcase, which eventually breaks open, scattering his last possessions through the streets of London before he notices: "Nothing is left inside suitcase except the smell of Mother . . . it's full of nothing."[28]

Quayson provides a nuanced reading of how, in the African city, an incoherent economy produces free time for the street hustler. This is not to say that the hustler enjoys free movement in the city, as the flâneur might. Rather, he/she feels an "obligation to do something as a way of combatting the vagaries of free time."[29] In Chikwava's novel, the narrator's homelessness takes the phenomenology of free time even further. With his psyche, suitcase, and time equally "full of nothing," the narrator's homelessness exposes him to incoherent and persistently arduous time. As Steven VanderStaay puts it in *Street Lives*, "Homeless people with nowhere to go are often forced to spend their day getting there. Walking, remaining upright, and endlessly waiting become all-consuming tasks, full-time work."[30] In "The Homeless Body," Samira Kawash describes the problem thus: because "there is no place in the contemporary urban landscape for the homeless to be . . . the itinerant movement of the homeless is a mode of movement peculiar to the condition of placelessness." Rather than the temporality of waiting, then, in which the anticipation of an event of ingenuity or improvisation is, whilst precarious, still emplaced, the homeless "exist in a perpetual state of movement."[31]

The narrator of *Harare North* now inhabits London in this condition of restless placelessness, without hope or purpose: "I'm feeling like umgodoyi—the homeless dog that roam them villages scavenging until brave villager relieve it of its misery by hit its head with rock. Umgodoyi have no home like winds. That's why umgodoyi's soul is tear from his body in rough way. That's what everyone want to do to me, me I know."³² The temporal dimension of this sort of wandering, without dignity and community, becomes as diffuse as the winds. The phenomenological dimension of time is not simply one of waiting, but one of temporal collapse. All times get compressed into a single flow in what we can only describe as psychosis. The narrator's ensuing loss of self is indicated in the last paragraph of the novel, rendered in a second-person narrative address:

> Half naked, you turn left into Electric Avenue and walk. You start to hear in tongues; it feel like Shingi is on his way back to life. You can tell, you know it; Shingi is now coming back. Already there's struggle over your feeties; you are telling right foot to go in one direction and he is telling left foot to go in another direction. You tell the right foot to go in one direction and he is being traitor shoe-doctor and tell left foot to go in another direction. You stand there in them mental backstreets and one big battle rage even if you have no more ginger for it.³³

The narrator's spiral toward homelessness is accompanied, then, by a narrative structure that spirals outward—scattering the account that he gives of himself until even the personal pronoun "I" is abandoned in his de-realization of self. Chikwava's careful attention to the process by which this already vulnerable global subject crosses into the hinterland of homelessness draws our attention to the broader significance of this figure when contemplating cosmopolitan space. As Kawash writes of the homeless body:

> Stories recounting the events that precipitate an individual into homelessness emphasize an inexorable chain of loss that spirals inward towards the body: loss of job, loss of welfare, loss of friends and family, loss of health. This tumult of dispossession leaves the homeless with little intact but the body. Without a safe place to leave things, one's possessions must be reduced to whatever one can carry. Even that is always at risk of dispossession; both the shelters and the streets pose the constant threat of violence and theft.³⁴

Kawash's description of the condition of homelessness might be read as a plot outline of *Harare North*: at the close of the novel, the narrator is left "half-naked," with a suitcase "full of nothing," trapped in an unrelenting stasis (which is not the same as stillness), and faces starvation and violent attack in the "mental backstreets." "It is because it is paradoxically positioned as simultaneously excluded and present," writes Kawash, "that the homeless body appears as a limit-figure in relation to the public." The narrator's stasis, which encapsulates the phenomenology of passing time without taking up space produces just such a limit-figure. Here, we are no longer concerned with the comparatively trivial concerns of dislocation or homesickness as experienced by the privileged migrant, but with a homeless figure that in turn figures its psychological correlate: the uncanny. Kawash argues:

> The public view of the homeless as "filth" marks the danger of this body as body to the homogeneity and wholeness of the public. The desire or ambition for such wholeness thus faces an obstacle that may be ideologically disavowed but that always returns as an irreducibly material challenge. The solution to this impasse appears as the ultimate aim of the "homeless wars": to exert such pressures against this body that will reduce it to nothing, squeeze it until it is so small that it disappears, such that the circle of the social will again appear closed.[35]

Chikwava's narrative traces this compression as his narrator's body is increasingly, violently, squeezed out of public spaces. His body is the material reminder, the abject return, of the repressed of a contemporary economic order that disavows him as no more than the waste it produces. It is not incidental that Chikwava is dramatizing this figure as an African émigré, a trace of the seismic scale of this economic violence and the geographies of vulnerability it produces.

Chikwava's novel registers these phenomenologies of free, and violently entropic, time on the stylistic and formal level. The awkwardness of the narrator's tale, language, and body—as homeless—mark the limit of cosmopolitanism in the global North (the successful abjection of the homeless body would, as Kawash suggests, make the social circle appear "closed"). Perhaps the word "awkwardness" is too insipid to capture the discomfort of being that is rendered on the level of syntax, grammar, and style, and also in the spiral toward entropy that structures this novel. Where Walkowitz sees stuttering as a charged style of (privileged) immigrant cosmopolitan fictions, the irresolvable bind between placelessness and the inexorability of time forces Chikwava's style and form into far more uncomfortable places. In a time in which the homeless are being increasingly, violently, compressed into a nonspace (outopia) of the utopian dream of market capitalism, Chikwava's novel seeks a style and form for that condition.

It is worth noting that Rebecca Walkowitz draws on the following passage from Michel de Certeau's *Practice of Everyday Life* to illustrate the cosmopolitan strategies that emerge in creative improvisations that constitute the "small degrees of resistance" in the everyday life of immigrants.

Thus a North African living in Paris or Roubaix (France) insinuates into the system imposed on him by the construction of a low-income housing development or of the French language the ways of "dwelling" (in a house or a language) peculiar to his native Kabylia. He superimposes them and, by that combination, creates for himself a space in which he can find ways of using the constraining order of the place or of the language. Without leaving the place where he has no choice but to live and which lays down the law for him, he establishes within it a degree of plurality and creativity. By an art of being in between, he draws unexpected results from his situation.[36]

The passage fits Walkowitz's theory of the stammer well. But for de Certeau, this frisson of being, which brings with it a "degree of plurality and creativity," follows the same logic as that I have described above: the European city demands an assimilation that effaces African phenomenologies of being. If this is the starting point of how we negotiate Africa's place in contemporary cosmopolitanism, then the Afropolitan can be nothing more than Taiye Selasi's young mix-culture. Yet, in the extreme space of homelessness depicted by Chikwava, where the conditions of "dwelling" in both language and space are severely compromised and even violently denied, such "small degrees of resistance" are not only impossible, but grotesquely inadequate. Chikwava's narrator is not "in between" two systems at the end of this novel: he is entirely compressed into public space in ways that make that space unusable in de Certeau's sense. In negotiating ways of depicting this impossible dwelling, this unusable space, Chikwava begins to articulate, to recall Mbembe's words, "an aesthetic and a particular poetic of the world" that—despite its ultimate dramatization of its own impossibility and erasure—we might call Afropolitanism.

NOTES

1 Achille Mbembe and Sarah Nuttall, "Writing the World from an African Metropolis," *Public Culture* 16.3 (Fall 2004): 352.

2 Achille Mbembe, "African Modes of Self-Writing," *Public Culture* 14.1 (Winter 2002): 256.

3 Taiye Selasi, "Bye-Bye Babar," *Callaloo* 36.3 (2013): 529.

4 Selasi, "Bye-Bye Babar," 528.

5 Stephanie Bosch Santana, "Exorcizing Afropolitanism: Binyavanga Wainaina Explains Why 'I Am a Pan-Africanist, Not An Afropolitan,'" (2013): n.p. Available http://africainwords.com. See also Binyavanga Wainaina, "I Am a Pan-Africanist, Not an Afropolitan," unpublished plenary address at the Biennial Conference, 6–8 African Studies Association of the U.K., September 2012, Leeds University, United Kingdom.

6 John Comaroff and Jean Comaroff, "Theory from the South: Or, How Euro-America Is Evolving toward Africa," *Anthropological Forum: A Journal of Social Anthropology and Comparative Sociology* 22.2 (2012): 114.

7 Brian Chikwava, *Harare North* (London: Random House, 2009).

8 Unlike the forms of homelessness in exile, critiqued by scholars like Rob Nixon in "London Calling: V. S. Naipaul and the License of Exile," *South Atlantic Quarterly* 87.1 (1988): 27, the homelessness of the Afropolitan is not created by virtue of national displacement. Instead, I will argue that this homelessness is rooted in economic conditions: the homeless figure here is not the exile, with all his attendant nostalgia for home, but is rather, simply, the dispossessed.

9 Sartre's text originally prefaced Leopold Senghor's canon-forming text *Anthologie de la nouvelle poésie nègre et malgache de langue français* (1948). See Jean-Paul Sartre [1948], "Black Orpheus," *Massachusetts Review* 6.1 (Autumn 1965): 13–52.

10 Rebecca L. Walkowitz, *Cosmopolitan Style: Modernism beyond the Nation* (New York: Columbia University Press, 2006), 24.

11 Walkowitz, *Cosmopolitan Style*, 11–12.

12 Léopold Sédar Senghor [1970], "Négritude: A Humanism of the Twentieth Century," in Tejumola Olaniyan and Ato Quayson, eds., *African Literature: An Anthology of Criticism and Theory* (Malden, Mass.: Blackwell Publishing, 2007), 200.

13 Simon Gikandi, "Preface: Modernism in the World," *Modernism/Modernity* 13.3 (September 2006): 420.

14 Senghor, "Négritude," 196.

15 Gikandi, "Preface," 421.
16 Achille Mbembe, "Afropolitanism," trans. Laurent Chauvret, in Simon Njami, ed., *Africa Remix: Contemporary Art of a Continent* (Johannesburg: Jacana Media, 2007), 27–28.
17 Mbembe, "Afropolitanism," 28.
18 Dambudzo Marechera, *The House of Hunger* (Oxford: Heinemann, 1978), 30.
19 Walkowitz, *Cosmopolitan Style*, 136.
20 Marechera, *House of Hunger*, 35.
21 Walkowitz, *Cosmopolitan Style*, 132.
22 See Walkowitz, *Cosmopolitan Style*, 133; and Timothy Brennan, *At Home in the World: Cosmopolitanism Now* (Cambridge, Mass.: Harvard University Press, 1997), 306.
23 Chikwava, *Harare North*; 5, 8, 59, 98–99, 112, 146, 147.
24 Ato Quayson, *Oxford Street: Accra: City Life and the Itineraries of Transnationalism* (Durham: Duke University Press, 2014), Kindle edition, location 3885.
25 Quayson, *Oxford Street*, Kindle location 3885.
26 In *Oxford Street* Quayson also notes the prevalence of this figure across various sub-Saharan African writing, citing Wole Soyinka's *The Road* and *The Beautification of the Area Boy*, Ben Okri's short stories, Dambudzo Marechera's *House of Hunger*, and Zakes Mda's *Ways of Dying* (Kindle location 5763) as some examples of African fictions that rely on this figure.
27 Quayson, *Oxford Street*, Kindle location 3908.
28 Chikwava, *Harare North*, 228.
29 Quayson, *Oxford Street*, Kindle location 4837.
30 Samira Kawash, "The Homeless Body," *Public Culture* 10.2 (Winter 1998): 327, cites Steven Vanderstaay, *Street Lives: An Oral History of Homeless Americans* (Philadelphia: New Society Publishers, 1992), 2.
31 Kawash, "The Homeless Body," 326–328.
32 Chikwava, *Harare North*, 226.
33 Chikwava, *Harare North*, 229–230.
34 Kawash, "The Homeless Body," 331.
35 Kawash, "The Homeless Body," 329.
36 Walkowitz, *Cosmopolitan Style*, 134, cites Michel de Certeau [1974], *The Practice of Everyday Life*, trans. Steven Rendell (Berkeley: University of California Press, 1984), Kindle edition, location 612.

19

Other Cosmopolitans

YAN HAIPING

"桥梁是自古有之, 最普遍而又最特殊的建筑物."
—茅以升[1]

Bridges have been there since the ancient times, and are at once the most ordinary and most special architectures of the life world.
—Mo Yisheng

The idea of cosmopolitanism in the Chinese context, evoking an imaginary of a world in great harmony and peace, was cross-culturally produced at a time of total turmoil and extreme violence.[2] *Book of Great Harmony* by Kang Youwei, the leading figure of the abortive 1890s Reform, appeared in 1935, when the Japanese imperial military, having occupied the old Manchuria since 1931, was poised to attack and penetrate north—and soon south—China. A founding document in what was later defined as Chinese utopianism, the book brings to light a state of plenitude where the earth's human inhabitants are living together as free equals without cultural, national, racial divides. Completed in 1902 but hidden from public view for thirty-three years,[3] the book is cognizant of European thought traceable to Kant and others,[4] and at the same time cites directly the Confucian classic *Book of Rites*. It takes up in particular its chapter on "workings of the great Tao" in actualizing a harmonious lifeworld as the ancient origins of and new destination for a reimagined human community.[5] The cross-cultural impetus potently active throughout the book is as striking as the worldwide rise of ethnocentric violence that surrounded its untimely publication. Against the backdrop of escalating violence, which seems to decree its subordination or eradication, *Book of Great Harmony* appears to be the unintelligible hieroglyph for an impossible insistence on a humanly transformative way of being and becoming.

Cross-cultural impulses like these, appealing to or evoking what the historical conjuncture seems to present as impossible, are recurrent phenomena in contemporary Chinese culture. Appearing amidst proliferating historical genres of representations in literature, the arts, and media, they are often predicated on revisiting the tumultuous China of the 1930s and 1940s. Arranging a few instances of these historical representations into a new constellation, the present essay tries to come to terms with the cross-cultural impulse at work in them and suggests that their boundary-crossing vibration may be critically relevant to current discussions on the need to reenvision "emerging communities" of various kinds,[6] in an era of radical economic globalization laden with abiding ethnocentric conflicts.

Actual Bridges, or Imaginary Rainbows

One such representation is *Memory: A Cultural Documentary*, which first aired in 2001 and became an instant success with a record-making number of viewers. Another text that deserves a place in the canon of Chinese cosmopolitanism, the film comprises twenty-four episodes that retell the life stories of a group of "modern pioneers" in the fields of science, literature, the arts, education, journalism, studies of religion and commerce, and more.[7] Among its magnificently reenacted figures, Mo Yisheng, a civil engineer renowned for the bridges he built during and after the 1930s, is perhaps paradigmatic. A graduate of Tangshan Polytechnic[8] in China with further training at Cornell University and the Carnegie Institute of Technology in the United States, Mo completed a tremendous project in 1934, namely the Qiantangjiang Bridge, the first of its kind in China. The bridge enabled trains and road vehicles as well as humans to move across the Qiantang River, a river flowing through two provinces, including the affluent Yangtze Delta, leading to the Pacific Ocean via the East Sea. As one of the earliest specialists in Chinese civil engineering, Mo over the years not only built actual bridges but also loved writing about them as "imaginative stories of world arts and sciences" for the general public in China and as "Chinese arts and cultural history" for "friends beyond" China. In one of the pieces on "world arts and sciences" for a Chinese readership, for instance, he wrote of Leonardo da Vinci as a "human bridge leading to peace-making":

> In an age where the power of religion dominated human life, da Vinci's creative work in both arts and sciences opens up imaginative new horizons, and enables human beings to break free from the grips of dogmatic powers to move beyond perceived absolute boundaries and travel long and far with their resilient human capabilities. Da Vinci's time was ravaged by endless religion-driven wars. He opposed all such wars which, as he put it, were "catastrophes of inhuman madness." Between the road to build peace and the dead-end of making wars, he chose peace with unwavering resolve and infinite imagination.[9]

In another piece on "five ancient bridges in Chinese history" for international readers, he depicts those "straight bridge[s], suspension bridge[s], arch bridge[s]" with nuanced care in the style of Chinese classical poetry, and concludes with a description of their attributes in relation to all bridges around the world as follows:

> [B]ridges across the world are of infinite variety in style, formation, and structure; they are always different and yet always in intimate dialogues with one another. They can crisscross with one another in semi-ring shapes in endless extensions reaching the horizons. . . . [W]hen we step onto such semi-rings, we reach where they reach, connect where they connect, arrive where they arrive, namely, to all corners of heaven and earth, and across all and any humanly made divides or boundaries. Bridges deserve our genuine respect. They offer others their bodies to support life-enhancing journeys across boundaries and limitations, while taking difficult challenges upon themselves. Those who build bridges during rainy days and times of storms are builders of the finest elements of humanity. Bridges are earthly creatures in tune with the rainbows in the sky, as brilliant, full of strength and enchanting. Rainbows in the sky are bridges on earth.[10]

It was in stormy times that Mo completed his first actual bridge project, inscribing these stories of "bridge-builders for life" in his memory. The cosmopolitan impulse, palpable in these writings, is characteristic of what is historically called the May Fourth generation, China's first generation of publicly educated men and women coming of age at the turn of the last century and leaving their distinct imprint in the fluid making of modern Chinese cultural consciousness throughout the twentieth century.[11] *Memory: A Cultural Documentary*, an influential model for numerous other series with increasingly enlarged scales and different perspectives, revisits many of these figures.[12]

Building bridges between the modern world's different codes, classes, and components, be they material, cultural, or spiritual, is a complex struggle. In 1937, one year after Japan attacked the Lugou Bridge in the north and launched a total war with China, Japanese military legions were about to storm across Qiantang Bridge to penetrate the south. As masses of refugees were crowding across the bridge with the Japanese military at their heels, Mo found that his bridge built for connecting human needs was in danger of turning into part of an apparatus designed to destroy human lives and their connections. Saying nothing of his feelings, Mo revealed a surprising detail in his plans for the bridge. He had built into the body of the Qiantang Bridge one centrally located rectangular hole as well as a line of evenly distributed sites where explosives could be set off, triggering the swift and complete destruction of the bridge.[13] And as Japanese troops advanced, this is what was done. Decades later, Mo wrote of the destruction of the bridge with a measured scientific clarity but still haunted by a touch of pain: "[That] we built the bridge with pre-calculated sites for explosives in order to destroy it in totality is a sign of an inauspicious time, writ large therein, however hidden."[14]

As formulated by Kant and in many subsequent variations, the cosmopolitan idea is predicated on universal rationality and the promise of eternal peace. It was received by Mo Yisheng and his generation via Kang Youwei's ideal of Great Harmony as the moral call of progress in, by, and for modernity. But it appears to invite both rainbows in the sky and explosives on the ground.[15] Habermas tries to support rationality by distinguishing "a strategic use of language" from "a genuinely communicative use of language,"[16] but his aid is ineffectual, for the explosives placed by the builders in the body of the bridge involve more than the norms of communication. Nor does Rawls's procedure for attaining morality and universal justice—the expansion of the "human faculty" of "reasonableness"—seem any more capable of warding off injuries and suffering in this explosive history. These historical conditions raise conceptual questions and personal conundrums. How might Mo and his fellow bridge builders have come to terms with the very fact that they had to destroy with their own hands the "rainbows" they had internalized in their minds' eye and then actualized in their lifeworlds as materializations of their lives "in harmonious relation to all other beings in the world"? How can anyone be or become a "citizen of the world," free to travel anywhere, when the prevailing force fields of such a world stop her from even inhabiting it, let alone being a free spirit among equals?[17] How might the bridge builders, obliged to blow up the bridge that materialized their labor, their work, and their meaningful action (in Hannah Arendt's sense), even gain access to an ethic of cosmopolitan care about "people and the world as a whole," much less become its champions?[18]

The Diasporic in the Homeland, or the Insistence of the Impossible in History

The Mo Yisheng episode in *Memory: A Cultural Documentary*, like most televisual representations of history, does not delve further into the consequences of the conundrums it registers. It ends on a conciliatory note, stating that Mo was to rebuild the bridge. The fact remains that the kind of self-implosion of their lifework that Mo and his fellow builders carried out tends to extend to all aspects of their lifeworlds including, in extreme junctures, their own lives. A profusion of what is currently called "life-writings" in recent decades (the genre of "biography"), similarly focused on the 1930s and 1940s, provides immense material evidence, no less mediated but more intricate and detailed, of the extremity of those historical predicaments. "Suddenly April: Remembering My Mother Lin Huiyin," a nuanced account of the life and work of China's first female architect, is a case in point. Drafted in the late 1980s and expanded in the 1990s by Lin Huiyin's son Liang Congjie, "Suddenly April" brings a long underestimated artist to the center of public attention, serving as the introduction to *A Collection of Lin Huiyin's Works* published in 1999, the first collection of its author's literary and architectural writings.[19] "Suddenly April" tells us how Lin Huiyin, born into an elite family, traveling in England and Europe at a tender age, and studying art and architecture at the University of Pennsylvania and Yale University, was cross-culturally cultivated in her social formation, becoming a gifted vernacular poet and an astute critic of literature and the arts. While Mo Yisheng was blowing up the Qiantang Bridge in the south, Lin Huiyin was leaving the Japanese-occupied city of Beiping in the north. The period of 1941–1945 saw her and her family living as war refugees in Lizhuang, a village in Sichuan Province. Suffering from severe lung disease, Lin Huiyin and her husband Liang Sicheng, the leading architect of China, persisted in their research while writing *A History of Chinese Architecture* in Chinese and *An Illustrated History of Chinese Architecture* in English, both of which became classics in academic historiography. In his memoir *Chinabound*, John Fairbank recalls his visit in 1942 to Lin and Liang, his "best friends in China, or anywhere in the world." Fairbank was as stunned by Lin's poor health conditions as by the couple's impossible perseverance and dedication to their research under such harsh conditions.[20] More relevant to the discussion here is the account of Lin Huiyin's casual chat with her children in 1944, which discloses her view on "self-eradication" in extreme times:[21]

> In Li Village, we were isolated. Mother had no one to chat with but us. So she talked to us about Shakespeare, Goethe, Turgenev, Michelangelo. All of that was incomprehensible to us. In retrospect, it was as if mother was playing the lute to a cow; we were the calves. Finally, one day, I could not help but ask: "Mom, what if the Japanese army finally comes here?" "For [some] of us, there is always the Yangtze River," she replied contemplatively, "Mom will go there." "But what about me?" I cried out. "Should this really happen," Mom held my hands gently but tightly, said apologetically, "Mom won't be able to take care of everything!" I was tongue-tied.[22]

A detail from a long past recollected by a loving son, this memory is no doubt personally inflected. Yet the sense of being shaken to the core by his mother's willingness to contemplate self-eradication is palpably real. And the rivers across the Chinese landscape did receive human bodies along with the bodies of other species, dead or alive, on a massive scale, in its modern chronicles of structured catastrophe. Many memories have been repressed or erased, many details are beyond quantifiable measurement, and yet the archival evidence is there.

Given such a decisive detail, would we have to call Lin Huiyin, however cross-culturally cultivated in her personal and social formation, a China-centric "nationalist" after all? Are Mo Yisheng and his fellow builders essentially "nationalistic" in their blowing up of the Qiantang Bridge regardless of their well-articulated concern for peace and "harmonious relations" among the world's peoples? Why or why not? These are questions arising from the conundrums with which Mo, Lin, and their generation struggled in the turbulent China of the 1930s and the 1940s. Their struggles are both subtly and sharply registered in all the genres and mediums of cultural rewriting today. However, they have yet to find adequate cognitive space in current China Studies. Indeed, scholars and critics have long noted how a mental habit of Eurocentrism, long established in China Studies, has forced modern Chinese history into the rubrics of English, French, German, or Japanese histories and in particular into the supposedly universal paradigm of modern "nation building."[23] Distorted by such rubrics and paradigms, the living history of modern China becomes one more variation of, or merely a footnote appended to, the logic of the nation-state. And Chinese cosmopolitanism can only appear as ethnocentric nationalism. Aligned with such a logic, figures of the tumultuous 1930s and 1940s like Mo, Lin, and others either find no significant or intelligible place therein or are assigned ideological labels like radical or conservative. All political categories stay within the possibilities or probabilities permitted by an overriding category of "nation building" or "national identity." "They are all Chinese," as a U.S. senior China specialist summed "them" up in the early 1980s, signaling his willingness to end the Cold War image of China and render "the Chinese" bioethnically-cum-"universally" intelligible again.[24] But are they?

Or on the contrary, can they be thought of as cosmopolitans? Here some recent articulations on nationalism and cosmopolitanism come as a timely aid, especially Craig Calhoun's insight about how "statements of cosmopolitanism as universalism echo rather than transcend nationalism." Following this thought through, one might argue that Mo Yisheng's "conundrums" sound a cautionary note about Eurocentrism and its claim to universality—indeed that they demand critical reflection on its limitations. Evoking Spivak's classic question "can the subaltern speak?" one may ask whether the ethnocentrically marked body, as targeted object for aggression, subjugation, exploitation, and manipulation in world history, has some as yet unarticulated way of countering the ethnocentric operations of such a world in history? Could Mo's act of "self-implosion" or Lin's will to "self-eradication" be considered a life-affirming passage toward becoming non-ethnocentric Chinese—a historically embodied enunciation of being and becoming a Chinese cosmopolitan? Might Lin Huiyin and her fellow Chinese counter and foil their putatively structured destiny as the disaporic within the homeland by putting their comfort, education, social or class-based privileges, labor, health, and life in the service of "an appeal to and insistence on the impossible" in times of extreme violence governed by the logic of bioethnic politics? And if so, what might be the implications of such a countering beyond the definitions of "national loyalty" or "national identity" as understood in the normal vocabulary of the "modern nation-state" and its standard history?

In 1937, on the eve of Japan's declaration of total war against China, Lin Huiyin, Liang Sicheng, and their assistants traveled to Mount Wutai in search of ancient Chinese temples and other historic architecture. A photograph was taken of Lin Huiyin at work. In it, she wears a simple traditional Chinese blouse and a round wide-brimmed soft straw hat, and is sitting under the arched roof of a brick kiln while taking notes from her field research. These notes and more constitute the foundation of *A History of Chinese Architecture* in Chinese and *An Illustrated History of Chinese Architecture* in English,[25] the first such histories in the world. A ray of sunshine lights up the kiln and illuminates the contours of her body with a sense of luminous intelligence in a specific earthly existence.[26] What kind of trans-social time and cross-cultural space is needed for us to enter into dialogue with such an existence? Further, in what kind of time and space will such dialogue be possible? Could this existence serve as a cross-cultural gift or an opening, and if so, how might one prepare to receive such a gift and take advantage of such an opening? This may be the right moment to remember Lin Huiyin's best known poem, written in 1934, titled "You Are the Tender Month of April." Her son, decades later, cites it in his account of the life and work of his mother "Suddenly April":

> You are the tender month of april
> your laughters dance in Aeolus's call

and swiftly change your steps in ripples of spring.
you are, resilient clouds writing in the sky

in murmurs of dusky air, stars sparkle
casually, when misty rain falls, upon flowers.
so radiant, so gently, and you, in these fairy hours
are crowned in Flora's honor, innocence embodied

yet majestically, like a bright full-moon night,
or the newly thawing snow. And an aqua sprout
shooting in all suppleness, you are. Rejoice of seeing
the lotus flower upon the expanse of water shimmering.

You are blooming buds of trees across miles of miles vastness,
or a swift swallow, whispering at all windows of the humanly dwellings,
you are love, and a lyrical music in the worldly,
you are tender april on earth, enchanting plenitude of poetry.[27]

A poem penned in Chinese, it has been translated into twenty or so
other languages, followed by many subsequent translations. As an
architect, Lin Huiyin designed some of the most enduring memorials in
China after the founding of the PRC in 1949. After her death in 1954, one
of her designs was carved on the marble stone of her grave: a garland
made of peonies, lotus flowers, and daisies—symbolizing the magnifi-
cent, the transcendent, and longevity in classical China—surrounded
by resilient olive leaves representing the hope for peace in the Western
tradition. The caption goes as follows: "Symbols originating from different civilizations are here coherently intertwined with one another, which
amounts to a celebration of the harmonious interconnection between
peoples in the world as well as poetic art and human history."[28] Might
such a "celebration" be a momentary homecoming for the other cosmopolitans, as an embodied appeal to and insistence on the impossible?

Other Cosmopolitans, in China and Beyond

In his comments on Kang Youwei, Mao Zedong famously asserts that
"Kang Youwei wrote *Book of Great Harmony*, but he did not and was

unable to find a viable way of arriving at such a great harmony." Such a task of way-making, Mao argues, will be accomplished by revolutionary transformations of China led by the CCP.[29] How well Mao succeeds where Kang Youwei fails, as Mao puts it, or whether Mao and his peers succeeded or failed, as intensely argued or debated by so many over the years, or what constitutes "great harmony" and its "success" or failure" itself—this is a series of topics for other occasions. Suffice it to say here that Mao Zedong was not alone in appealing to the imaginaries of "great harmony" and in translating such appeals into practice, be it a modus vivendi or anything else, especially amidst the crises and catastrophes of 1930s and 1940s China. The unfathomable wealth of past praxis has been explored once again in present-day China with escalating intensity and deepening critical sophistication; there is yet no end in sight, given the unfolding results and potential consequences. The cultural documentary *Memory* and the life-writing "Suddenly April" are two examples of a duet from this wealth currently being retraced, recuperated, investigated, and represented in different mediums. *East Wind Rain*, a film that premièred in 2010,[30] makes this duet into a trio.

A historical film predicated upon the lives of the citizens of Shanghai in wartime, *East Wind Rain* brings to light, for the first time in Chinese cinema history, a multinational constellation of those active in the resistance movements against the Japanese War of Invasion in China. The film opens with the execution of Ozaki Hotsumi by the Japanese. A core member of the Richard Sorge Spy Ring, centered in Shanghai and consisting of people of German, Japanese, Russian, and American nationality, Ozaki Hotsumi was gathering information about the Japanese military government's strategy and conveying it to the Third International between 1929 and 1941, at considerable personal risk—ultimately a fatal one. He was arrested by Japanese special higher police in 1942 and was sentenced to death for "crimes of treason" in 1944.[31] This ending differs from Mo Yisheng's blowing up of the Qiantang Bridge and Lin Huiyin's will to eradicate her own life in an extreme situation, yet it resonates fundamentally with them both. Nakanishi Masahiro, another Japanese national depicted in the film, was based on the historical figure of Nakanishi Tsutomu, a Japanese member of the Chinese Communist Party who worked in a Sino-Japanese intelligence group—which was also a part and parcel of—the resistance activities of the CCP-led

Shanghai-Nanjing Underground. A range of other nationalities cross the screen, displaying different social formations and a profoundly convergent concentration on a goal that seemed most untimely or impossible: to be and to become non-ethnocentric citizens of a human world in a time of rising bioethnic violence.

In a rainy scene at a lakeside where Nakanishi meets An Ming (the Chinese field figure in the Underground) to decide how to deliver information to prevent another catastrophe from happening, for otherwise "more people will die," both are aware of the consequences that such a decision entails for themselves. The succinct scene ends with An Ming, offscreen, quietly remembering in Chinese Rabindranath Tagore's line, "let life be beautiful like summer flowers," and Nakanishi's low voice finishing the line in Japanese: "death like autumn leaves."[32] This is the spirit of cosmopolitanism.

Presented as "drama," "suspense," "war," and "historical film," respectively, *East Wind Rain* draws on the life writings (individual histories) of these historical figures of diverse nationalities while also imaginatively reproducing them on the cinematic screen as an epic of non-ethnocentric community, mobilizing the capacity of the audience to imagine a humanity beyond modern bioethnic codifications. A visualization of other cosmopolitans of China and beyond, offers up for recognition and cognitive reflection the otherwise largely unknown transnational genealogies of actual or imagined human praxis inherent in the history and memories of the city of Shanghai.

That such an epic of non-ethnocentric community and its genealogies of a humanity beyond bioethnic codifications are uncovered in the city of Shanghai is consequential not only in terms of the film's genre, its period-specific aesthetic style, and its cinematic grandeur. As one of the crucial and most transformative urban nodes of China in the 1930s and the 1940s, the city is more than a material and symbolic focal point through which China was coerced into modernization with all the concomitant trials and tribulations, crises and catastrophes, as is mostly the case in contemporary Chinese cinema. Indeed, of the exponentially growing number of cinematic works on the Chinese lives of the 1930s and 1940s, especially with war thematics, the best in terms of aesthetic quality or the most powerful in cultural signification are primarily or entirely located in or merged with rural China. *Evening Bell* (1988), *Devils on the Doorstep* (2007), and *The Year 1942* (2012), to mention the most obvious, are ample evidence.[33] Renditions of modern China in contemporary Chinese films, in other words, draw their cultural strength largely from the rural world and its imaginaries. The result is a sense of locality lodged in a largely reactive resistance to the modern workings of universalizing ethnocentricism without the capacity to claim or transform that universalism. In *East Wind Rain*, on the other hand, the city is rearticulated as a crucible in which "other cosmopolitans" can appear and display their transnational significance, where they can move, engender, and reengender themselves, be and become representatives of a "China modern" or a "Chinese modernity." The film's Shanghai is pregnant with alternatives to the ethnocentric rubrics of the modern. In the fluid space of this Shanghai, world history is repopulated and rewritten.

Scholars and historians have long defined Shanghai's fluidity in the 1930s and 1940s as "cosmopolitan," but they have often done so without adequately specifying its "cosmopolitan" attributes or critical implications. Some ascribe this status to its political form as a city "antithetical" to that of the modern nation-state, indicating the fragmented sovereignty of semi-colonial China as embodied by the extraterritoriality of the French Concessions and International Settlements. Others focus on its "cultural hybridity" resulting from its mixed and fluid multinational populations. In 1936, according to Rhoads Murphey's early work, there were approximately 60,000 "foreigners" in Shanghai. Among them were 20,000 Japanese, 15,000 Russians, 9,000 British, 5,000 Germans and Austrians, 4,000 Americans, and 2,500 French.[34] Such features, emblematic of a city in flux and a struggling country at a most brutal juncture of its modern history, do not go unnoticed in *East Wind Rain*. But *East Wind Rain* does not rest content with these features. It also pays close attention to what has been called "an intellectual class" whose formative trajectories within overseas education afforded them cross-cultural experiences in personal learning and social knowledge production, as well as expanded connections for transnational alliances. It is important to note that such an "intellectual class" is composed of both "Chinese" and "non-Chinese" figures, including Ozaki Hotsumi, Nakanishi Tsutomu, and many others of different nationalities. These figures navigated extensive semi-professional Chinese cultural associations such as the Creation Society, the League of Left-Wing Writers, and the Japan-China Struggle League, making connections with key Chinese intellectuals such as Lu Xun, Tao Jingsun, Yu Dafu, Feng Naichao, Feng Keng, Ding Ling, and others who constitute the center of gravity for modern Chinese culture in critical transition. A mutual activation of a profound kind was at work when, for instance, Lu Xun, Ding Ling, and their Chinese peers mounted protests in 1933 on the streets and in writing against the torture of a Japanese Marxist Kobayashi Takiji by the Japanese Imperial government because of Tajiji's antiwar activism.[35] Such details run through modern Chinese literary and cultural history and require us to be cognizant of their transnational signification. The founding congress of the CCP in 1921 also included "non-Chinese" intellectuals, another detail the far-ranging implications of which have yet to be recognized. Literary and cultural scholars have generally viewed the ideological composition of such an "intellectual class" as, in the words of Leo Ou-fan Lee, "a loose alliance of the left-wing against Japanese imperialism in Asia and fascism in Europe," motivated further by an international impetus of Marxist origin at work across the world.[36] *East Wind Rain* goes much further and is much more specific. It locates in such intellectuals the concrete "other cosmopolitans" who put their comfort, education, social or class-based privileges, labor, health, and possibly their lives in the service of "an appeal to and insistence on the impossible" in a time of extreme violence governed by the putatively invincible logic of bioethnic politics. In so doing, they turn themselves into humanly embodied bridges that connect specific lives and daily life struggles, including their own, with a critical imperative to care about "the world as a whole," putting their bodies on the line as it were in the search for a modern world capable of opening itself up to the yet-to-be-reckoned-with possibilities for making and remaking "great harmonies."

In this time of global sea change and the flux of radical realignment, such humanly embodied bridges are as imperative as they have ever been since the dawn of human history. In the words of Mo Yisheng decades before, "[B]ridges have been there since the ancient times, and are at once the most ordinary and most special architectures of the life world. They offer others their bodies to support life-enhancing journeys across boundaries and limitations. Bridges are rainbows on earth."[37]

NOTES

1 Mo Yisheng, "Rainbows in the Human World," *Mutual Arriving* (Tianjin: Baihua Literature and Art Publishing House, 2009), 25.

2 "The Enforcement of Great Tao Is Great Harmony," in *Book of Rites* (Shanghai: Shanghai Classics, 1987).

3 See Li Zehou, *Modern Chinese Intellectual History* (Beijing: People's Publishing House, 1997).

4 N. G. D. Malmqvist, "On the Similarities and Differences between Chinese and Western Utopians," *21st Century* (Reshiyi shiji), June 1991, 11–16. In his *Chinese Socialism to 1907* (Ithaca: Cornell University Press, 1976), Martin Bernal traces Kang Youwei's book to an influence from Edward Bellamy's *Looking Backward, 2000–1887* (Oxford: Oxford University Press, 2007) and its argument for social-ism, or what one may call a "left cosmopolitan."

5 "The Enforcement of Great Tao," in *Book of Rites*.

6 The problem of the (re)making of "human communities" underlines much of the current theoretical debate, with issues ranging from cosmopolitan propositions to interspecies advocacy. For a recent reference, see the 2013 October special issue of *Theatre Journal* titled "Interspecies Performance" (Baltimore: Johns Hopkins University Press, 2013).

7 *Memory* (Jiyi), a documentary directed by Zhou Bing and produced by the "Time and Space in the East" Program hosted by one of the most popular media figures, Bai Yansong, at CCTV, first aired in August 2001. It is an early example of the era of "cultural documentaries." Ever increasing in length, with 150 or even 200 epi-sodes as of 2014, these documentaries—which have grown in quantity and aired over a long duration—have not only changed the field of visual representation in the country but the landscape of cultural memory itself.

8 One of the earliest modern institutions in Chinese higher education, it was established in 1896 in response to the need to build a Chinese railway system and industries.

9 Mo Yisheng, *Mutual Arrivals* (picide dida) (Tianjing: Baihua Literature and Art Publishing House) (Baihua wenyi chubanshe), 293.

10 Mo Yisheng, ibid., 25–26. Mo was born in 1896 and came of age during the high moment of the May 4th Movement when an important contingent of Chinese intellectuals embraced the idea of the humanistic individual, along with its inher-ent universalist logic of a Kantian lexicon. One of the leading philosophers of contemporary China in Shanghai, Li Zehou, is in fact presently teaching a very select seminar on Kant and the idea of cosmopolitan morality.

11 See Leo Ou-fan Lee, *The Romantic Generation of Modern Chinese Writers* (Cambridge: Harvard University Press, 1973).

12 *Entering Their Worlds* (zoujin tamen, Shanghai Media Group, 2009), *Masters* (dashi, Shanghai Media Group, 2011), and *The Distinguished in Literary China* (dajia, CCTV, 2012), are but a few of the more influential series in this genre.

13 Eight years later the bridge was rebuilt. It was fully functioning in 1949 when the PRC was founded.

14 Mo Yisheng, "On the Building of Qiantangjiang Bridge," in *Mutual Arrivals*, 305–50.

15 While important in its complex historical ramifications, the distinction between Japan's way to modernity and European rubrics of modernity is not central to the argument of this essay. Suffice it to note here that Japan's colonial militarism is inherent in the Meiji Project. Its principle of disassociating itself from Asia and reassociating itself with (modern) Europe is part and parcel of the kind of "modernity" we have known in world history. See Stefan Tanaka, *Japan's Orient: Rendering Pasts into History* (Berkeley: University of California Press, 1993).

16 Richard Rorty, "Justice as a Larger Loyalty," in *Cosmopolitics*, ed. Pheng Cheah and Bruce Robbins (Minneapolis: University of Minnesota Press, 1998), 55.

17 In a historical review of the life and work of Hu Shi, one of the "liberal cosmo-politan intellectuals" of the first half of the twentieth century, a critic defines him as an "idealist who ended up being in the service of the imperialist forces that ravaged China and its citizens." Huang Jisu, *Waves of a Century* (bainianchao), June 1999.

18 It has been noted that Martha Nussbaum, Anthony Appiah, and Seyla Benhabib, among others, seem to regard the idea of cosmopolitanism as a cognitive vehicle for making a direct connection between the individual and the world as a whole. David Held's notion of "cosmopolitan democracy" does not specify alternatives to such a direct connection. Ben Anderson, on the other hand, has long argued that, in complex and differential contexts such as that of South Asia, for instance, "cosmopolitans" can be or historically have also been "indigenous." The conun-drums suggested here are related but distinct from the problematics of the above-mentioned explorations predicated upon the binary between the transcendental or global "cosmopolitan" and the embedded or local "indigenous." Rather, they point to the historical content—rather than the scale—of difficult but unavoid-able relatedness across national boundaries in world history, a topic that requires extensive and sustained analysis which is beyond the scope of this essay.

19 Liang Congjie, "My Mother Lin Huiyin" (edited by Wu Wanru), in *Waves of Youth* (qinchun chao), September 2000. Liang Congjie, Introduction, "Suddenly April: Remembering My Mother Lin Huiyin," in *A Collection of Lin Huiyin's Writings* (Tianjing: Baihua Publishing House, 1999). Such "life-writings" of the cultural figures who came of age in the 1930s and 1940s, as a rapidly ascending genre in contemporary China, encompass a growing range of literature. The following are among the most notable works: Xu Renhua and Li Lu, eds., *On the Twentieth of May* (Beijing: People's Publishing House, 1995); Yan Liang et al., eds., *Stormy Lives*, 4 vols. (Nanjing: China Culture Publishing House, 2008); Wang Lianjie, *Nameless Heroes* (Beijing: Tuanjie Publishing House, 2008); Li Jiefei, *Paradigmatic Cases of the Literary World* (Wuhan: Hubei People's Publishing House, 2008); Dong Xiao, *July in Exile* (Wuhan: Changjiang Publishing House in Arts and Literature, 2013).

For an important forthcoming series with a more self-aware cross-cultural focus, see Liu Jialin et al., eds., *Journeys Overseas* (Shanghai: Jiaotong University Press); Yan Haiping and Cao Li, eds., *Circum-Pacific.*

20 John King Fairbank, *Chinabound: A Fifty-Year Memoir* (New York: Harper & Row, 1982).

21 Liang Congjie, "My Mother Lin Huiyin," edited by Wu Wanru, in *Waves of Youth* (qinchun chao), September 2000.

22 Liang Congjie, Introduction, "Suddenly April: Remembering My Mother Lin Huiyin," in *A Collection of Lin Huiyin's Writings* (Tianjing: Baihua Publishing House, 1999).

23 See, for instance, the observations in Naoki Sakai's works on the subject of "Asia theory," and on the recent "historical turn" in studies of Chinese women's history by a new generation of Chinese scholars, including Song Shaocheng, Zhang Lianhong, Dong Liming, and Liu Jing. Such observations are applicable to the evolving field of China Studies within geographically defined China proper as well as the long-standing institutions of established area studies in the United States or Europe. For instance, Jonathan Spence, an outstanding historian based in the United States who specializes in modern China and whose monumental work, *The Search for Modern China* (New York: W. W. Norton, 1990) is a mark of achievement, nonetheless begins his *Search* with a comparison that evokes a Eurocentric logic: "Comparing with Japan or Germany" (let alone England or France), he writes, "modern China has still not achieved its sense of identity." In the growing scholarly discourse of the past three decades that claim to be opening up new spaces for rethinking modern China, including its literary history, the "deconstruction" turn that focuses on unpacking the politics of ethnocentric nation-building or of the teleologically predicated idea of the "nation-state" in its omnipresent operation, often reinscribes what is being "unpacked" by fixating on the universal omnipresence of such an idea and its total power. Such a fixation, however critical, leaves little room for thinking beyond the very centrality of this "omnipresence." Adequate explications of this observation constitute a large topic beyond the scope of the present essay.

24 A guest lecture series on "Modern Chinese Culture and Society," October 5 to November 5, 1983, Uris Hall, Cornell University.

25 *A History of Chinese Architecture* was completed in 1944. See "Preface: On the new edition," *A History of Chinese Architecture* (Tianjing: Baihua Publishing House, 2005). *A Pictorial History of Chinese Architecture* in English was completed in 1946 and published by MIT Press in 1984.

26 I used the photograph in my book. See the image on the front cover of Yan Haiping, *Chinese Women Writers and the Feminist Imagination, 1905–1948* (Oxford: Routledge, 2006),

27 Translated by Zheng Songyun, unpublished manuscript.

28 Chen Xueyong, *The Life of Lin Huiyin* (Beijing: People's Literary Publishing House, 2008).

29 Mao Zedong, "On People's Democratic Dictatorship, June 30, 1949," in *A Selection of Works by Mao Zedong*, vol. 4 (Beijing: People's Publishing House, 1991),1468–82.

30 Liu Yunlong, dir., *East Wind Rain* (produced by Shanghai SMG, Beijing East Union Film, TV and Communications Corporation, and Hangmei Communications Corporation, 2010).

31 His position as a special advisor and private secretariat for Prime Minister Fumimaro Konoe gave him special access to top policy information, which he passed on to the Communist International.

32 Rabindranath Tagore, *Stray Birds*, trans. Xu Hanling (Tianjing: Education Press, 2007). The original Chinese translation of this line was rendered by literary and art historian Zheng Zhenduo, "生如夏花之绚烂, 死如秋叶之静美," and has become part of the modern Chinese language.

33 Wu Xiniu, dir., *Evening Bell* (1988); Jiang Wen, dir., *Devils on the Doorstep* (2007); Feng Xiaogang, dir., *The Year 1942* (2012).

34 Rhoads Murphey, *Shanghai: Key to Modern China* (Cambridge: Harvard University Press, 1953), 23. The statistics need to be updated, given recent research on and about the city and the regions.

35 Yuan Liangjun, ed., *Materials for Ding Ling Research* (Ding Ling yanjiuziliao, Tianjing: Tianjing People's Publishing House, 1982).

36 Leo Ou-fan Lee, *Shanghai Modern: The Flowering of a New Urban Culture in China, 1930–1945* (Cambridge: Harvard University Press, 1999), 322.

37 Mo Yisheng, "Rainbows in the Human World," in *Mutual Arriving* (Tianjin: Baihua Literature and Art Publishing House, 2009), 25.

AFTERWORD

KWAME ANTHONY APPIAH

Last month I went to a wedding in Namibia, in a village of two hundred people just south of the Angolan border. The bride was a young
Ovambo woman. She was born in Moscow, where her father, who was
a member of the liberation movement that freed Namibia from South
African colonial control, had been posted at the time she was born.
And she had studied economics in South Korea. Still her lineage was
local on both her mother's and her father's side for many centuries. The
bridegroom's lineage was a little more complicated. He was the son of a
Norwegian father. But he too is at least in part a child of Africa, because
his mother's father was a Ghanaian politician, who, like his bride's father,
was involved in the anticolonial struggle. His grandmother, though, was
British. So the bridegroom's family gathered in this small African vilage
from Norway, England, and Ghana; and also from America and Nigeria,
since one of his aunts had married a Nigerian and his uncle was married to an American. I could add that one of his uncles has a Chinese
brother-in-law. Or that he has cousins in Kenya and the United States,
as well as Ghana, Norway, and Nigeria. But the point is that this is a
modern family, connecting people from many nations into a network of
relationships that will endure through generations.

In a world like this, the idea that we can live in isolated moral cultures
makes no sense, so far as I can see. Even if we grow up in places with
different ideas about manners and cuisine and religion and even if, in
part as a result, we disagree about some moral questions, the problem of
how to share the world with people who have different views about these
matters is not a theoretical but a practical one. Among the people at the
wedding party were some who were ethical vegetarians: the proper food
at a grand Ovambo wedding is a series of cows slaughtered and cooked
for the occasion. Something had to be prepared for the vegetarians: they
had to agree to join a party where most people were eating meat. Male

circumcision was once an Ovambo tradition: and if it had still been, then the bride and groom, if they had a son, would have had to decide whether to do it, since most Norwegians think nonmedical circumcision is wrong.

Those who have read my book on cosmopolitanism may recall that I think we will usually find the answer to these questions best if we are in regular conversation with one another across the boundaries of race, religion, tribe, and nationality. You will also know that I think the heart of a conversation is not about the search for agreement. It is about getting to know each other in ways that mean we can share the world precisely without agreement. We do not converse in order to convert, though we may be passionately argumentative. The right model for talk aimed at conversion is the sermon or the lecture. And lecturing across societies, far from being helpful for peaceful coexistence, probably threatens it. Conversation, then, as I say, is not about coming to agreement, so to take up the metaphor of conversation across cultures is not to urge a search for agreement.

Nor do we converse in order to establish or sustain relationships with our interlocutors. Of course, conversation, if it goes on long enough, usually does both these things. But it only does them if that is not seen as its point. Conversation is a way of being together with others that has no further aim than the rewards of being together: it is a reflection of our deep human sociability.

Now people who are in regular conversation with each other may or may not know much about each other's lives. But it does mean that they are used to being together. So to take up the metaphor of cross-cultural conversation is not to recommend a search either for cross-cultural intimacy or a simple pursuit of cross-cultural knowledge or understanding.

Of course, cross-cultural conversations will yield some agreements and some mutual knowledge and mutual understanding. These are commendable in and of themselves, and are a useful background to peaceful cohabitation. But the real virtue of conversation across cultures is that it allows people to get used to spending time together in a way that is rewarding despite their misunderstandings and disagreements. Conversation partners are used to one another, in all their mutual strangeness. They can disagree without being disagreeable.

I mentioned at the start that in a globally interconnected world, there are practical problems about how we should decide things like whether to circumcise your son. Because these are practical problems, sensible people solve them practically. (I am not one of those philosophers who says, "I know, I know. It works in practice. But does it work in theory?") Let me give you a fictional example.

In the British television series, *Skins*, which is about a group of students in the English town of Bristol, one of the characters is Anwar, an English teenager of South Asian ancestry, whose father is a devout Muslim. In one episode, he has a birthday party and invites his best friend, Maxxie, who happens to be gay. Now Maxxie's been waiting for Anwar to tell his parents, which Anwar has been afraid to do. So Maxxie is standing outside, refusing to come in to the party until Anwar tells them, as he's promised. While they're talking, Anwar's father comes out and invites Maxxie in: his wife has made a spicy curry just for him. As Anwar's father talks, Anwar, in the background, finally says "Dad, Maxxie's gay." But his father ignores him. So then Maxxie himself says "I'm gay, Mr. Kharral. I always have been." There's a long silence and Anwar waits anxiously to hear what his father will say.

And then Mr. Kharral says this: "It's a . . . stupid messed-up world. I've got my God, he speaks to me every day. Some things I just can't work out. So I leave them be, okay, even if I think they're wrong. Because I know one day He'll make me understand. I've got that trust. It's called belief. I'm a lucky man. Right. Come Maxxie, the food's ready."

This is how things are with people who are in conversation with one another. They do not have to agree. They have only to accept each other. And they can do that without a theory or a principle, because being together has generated commitments that can transcend even serious disagreement. This kind of cosmopolitan cohabitation is something we all know how to do. But we are only going to bother to take this step if we are already in conversation with one another. And, as I say, that means sharing our thoughts about the things we agree about and about the things we disagree about. Big things and small things. Politics, religion, television shows, movies, the gossip about other people in the dorm.

This is not the advice of a relativist. I'm not saying that you can accept anything at all: if Mr. Kharral had wanted to kill Maxxie or have him locked up; if Maxxie had wanted to curse the Prophet for being a homophobe; they would each have crossed a boundary that made cohabitation impossible, at least until one of them changed his mind. But

Mr. Kharral begins in exactly the right place: with an admission that he can't work out everything. That the world is hard to understand and he may not be right about everything. He doesn't abandon his belief that homosexuality is wrong: he lays it aside as something to work out later. Right now what matters is celebrating his son's seventeenth birthday with his son's best friend. This works in practice. It doesn't need a theory. I am a philosopher. I like theories. But theory isn't the only thing that matters. And sometimes it doesn't matter at all.

And I know this not just because I have thought about these things for a long time but because the family I began with is my family: the bridegroom was my sister Isobel's son Kristian.

Kwame Anthony Appiah is Professor of Philosophy and Law at New York University. Among his many works are *The Ethics of Identity* (2005) and *Cosmopolitanism: Ethics in a World of Strangers* (2006).

Thomas Bender is Professor of History and University Professor of the Humanities at New York University. He is the author of many works, which include *A Nation among Nations: America's Place in World History* (2006) and *The Unfinished City: New York and the Metropolitan Idea* (2002).

Homi K. Bhabha is Anna F. Rothenberg Professor of the Humanities at Harvard University. His books include *The Location of Culture* (1994) and *Nation and Narration* (1990).

Elleke Boehmer is Professor of World Literature in English at the University of Oxford. Her most recent books include *Indian Arrivals 1870–1915: Networks of British Empire* (2015) and *Stories of Women: Gender and Narrative in the Postcolonial Nation* (2005).

Craig Calhoun is the Director of the London School of Economics. His many works include *The Roots of Radicalism: Tradition, the Public Sphere, and Early Nineteenth-Century Social Movements* (2012) and *Nations Matter: Culture, History and the Cosmopolitan Dream* (2007).

Emma Dabiri is a Teaching Fellow at the Department of the Languages and Cultures of Africa at the School of Oriental and African Studies at the University of London.

Magdalena Edwards is a Chilean-born writer whose work has appeared in the *Los Angeles Review of Books, Paris Review Daily, Boston*

Review, The Millions, and *El Mercurio.* Currently she is translating Clarice Lispector's novel *The Chandelier* for New Directions.

Jean Bethke Elshtain was Laura Spelman Rockefeller Professor of Social and Political Ethics at the University of Chicago Divinity School and also held joint appointments in the Department of Political Science and the Committee on International Relations. She was a prolific author, and some of her most famous works include *Women and War* (1987), *Democracy on Trial* (1993), and *Sovereignty: God, State, and Self* (2008).

Leela Gandhi is John Hawkes Professor of Humanities and English at Brown University. She is the author of several works, including *The Common Cause: Postcolonial Ethics and the Practice of Democracy, 1900–1955* (2014), and *Affective Communities: Anticolonial Thought and the Politics of Friendship* (2006).

Ashleigh Harris is Associate Professor of English at Uppsala University. Her recent work includes "Facing/Defacing Robert Mugabe: Land Reclamation, Race and the End of Colonial Accountability," in *What Postcolonial Theory Doesn't Say* (2016).

David A. Hollinger is Preston Hotchkis Professor Emeritus at the University of California, Berkeley. His many books include *After Cloven Tongues of Fire: Protestant Liberalism in Modern American History* (2013) and *Cosmopolitanism and Solidarity: Studies in Ethnoracial, Religious, and Professional Affiliation in the United States* (2006).

Paulo Lemos Horta is Assistant Professor of Literature at New York University Abu Dhabi. His books include *Marvellous Thieves: The Secret Authors of the Arabian Nights* (2017) and the *Arabian Nights: An Anthology* (2014; coedited with Wen-Chin Ouyang).

Achille Mbembe is Research Professor in History and Politics at the Wits Institute for Social and Economic Research, University of the Witwatersrand in Johannesburg, South Africa. His works include *De La Postcolonie, essai sur l'imagination politique dans l'Afrique contemporaine* (2000), translated as *On the Postcolony* in 2001.

Walter Benn Michaels is Head of the English Department at the University of Illinois at Chicago. He has authored such works as *The Beauty of a Social Problem: Photography, Autonomy, Economy* (2015), and *The Shape of the Signifier: 1967 to the End of History* (2004).

Phillip Mitsis is Alexander S. Onassis Professor of Hellenic Culture and Civilization at New York University. Among his works are *Epicurus' Ethical Theory: The Pleasures of Invulnerability* (1988) and the *Encyclopedia of Classical Philosophy* (1997), for which he was co-associate editor.

Ato Quayson is University Professor of English and Director of the Center for Diaspora Studies at the University of Toronto. He is the author of many works, including *Oxford Street, Accra: City Life, the Itineraries of Transnationalism* (2014) and *Aesthetic Nervousness: Disability and the Crisis of Representation* (2007).

Bruce Robbins is Old Dominion Foundation Professor in the Humanities in the Department of English and Comparative Literature at Columbia University. He is the author or editor of several volumes, including *Perpetual War: Cosmopolitanism from the Viewpoint of Violence* (2012) and *Feeling Global: Internationalism in Distress* (NYU Press, 1999).

Silviano Santiago taught at Pontifícia Universidade Católica do Rio de Janeiro and Universidade Federal Fluminense. He is the author of, among other works, *The Space In-Between: Essays on Latin American Culture* (2002) and the noir novel *Stella Manhattan* (1994).

Jeremy Waldron is University Professor at New York University School of Law. His most recent works include *Political Political Theory: Essays on Institutions* (2016) and *One Another's Equals: The Basis of Human Equality* (2017).

Yan Haiping is Professor of Crosscultural Studies, Chair of the Department of Foreign Languages and Literatures, Vice Dean for International Affairs, School of the Humanities, and Dean, Institute for World Literatures and Cultures (IWLC), Tsinghua University. She is the editor of *Other Transnationals* (2005) and the author of *Amidst Landscapes of Mobility* (forthcoming).

Robert J. C. Young is Dean of Arts and Humanities at New York University Abu Dhabi and Professor of English and Comparative Literature at New York University. Among his many influential works are *The Idea of English Ethnicity* (2008) and *White Mythologies: Writing History and the West* (1990).

INDEX

Abdullah, Mirza, 155, 157–58
Abu Dhabi, 138–39
Accra, Ghana, 15, 228n10; agriculture in,
  223–24, 227n6; as business and academic hub, 216; hybridity in, 220–27;
  political and military designations in,
  224–25; popular culture in, 216–19;
  slogans and advertising in, 217–19;
  Tabon and Ga relations historically in,
  222–26, 227n6, 229n15; Tabon settlement in, 221–22
acculturation, 31
Addams, Jane, 117–18
Adorno, Theodor, 84
advertisements, 110, 218
Africa, 95, 271–72; arts and culture
  centers in, 106–7; Burton on, 159;
  colonialism in, 104, 221, 224, 227n2;
  colonial/postcolonial readership in,
  108–13; diasporas from, 103–4, 202,
  210; ethnic assimilation in, 224–27;
  globalization in, 107; hybridity in,
  104, 220–27; immigrant populations
  in, 104–5; Muslim populations in,
  223, 228n12; nationalism in, 106;
  pre-colonial, 209–10; Tabon return
  to, 15, 219–22, 227n6; urban center
  crisis in, 215–16, 248. *See also*
  Accra; Ghana; Gold Coast; Nigeria;
  South Africa; West Africa;
  Zimbabwe
African/Africans: artists, 107, 206, 243;
  culture in London, 244–45, 247–49;
  émigrés, 246–47, 250; identity for,
  102–3, 209–10; immigrants, 246–52;
  literature, 242, 253n26; modernism

influence from, 242–43, 244; solidarity
  violence for, 106
African Americans, 12, 91, 94–95
"Africa Rising," 206–7
Africa Writes Festival, 201
Afrikaners, 103, 104
Afro-Brazilians, 11, 35–36, 226, 228n12.
  See also Tabon
Afropolitanism, 10, 12; in academia, 240;
  in art world, 206; consumerism of,
  203, 204–5, 241; critique of, 201–10;
  defining, 207–8; diasporas and, 103–4;
  homelessness and spaces of, 15, 242,
  251–52, 252n8; identity in, 208–9; ideology of, 106; immigrant populations
  and, 104–5; imperialism and, 14; for
  Mbembe, 102–7, 243–44, 252; media
  on, 205–6; paradigms of, 102; Salami
  on, 203, 204–5, 207–8; Selasi on, 202,
  208, 240–41, 244, 251; solidarity in,
  102; style of, 203, 204–5, 242; transnational culture of, 107; wealth and
  elitism with, 203–8, 241
Agamben, Giorgio, 142
agencement, 71
agrarian reform, 26, 38n3
agriculture, 26–28, 223–24, 227n6
ahimsaic historiography, 84, 85
AIDS. *See* HIV/AIDS
Alencar, José de, 31
Alexander the Great, 5, 14, 68, 79, 179–83
alien (*meteco*), 22, 23, 25, 38n2
Amado, Gilberto, 23
Amado, Jorge, 31
Ambedkar, B. R., 81
American Indians. *See* Native Americans

immigrants, 117, 125; in Africa, 104–5; African, 246–52; from Asia, 98; black, 94–95, 97–98, 101n12; difference of circumstance among, 98–99; exile/émigré, 22–25, 73–74, 119, 163, 246–47, 250, 252n8; in France, 22–25, 151; Hispanic American population as, 98; identity for, 28–29, 97; Indian, 111–12; language loss for, 11, 25, 28–29; in London, 246–47; nation-state principles and, 31–32; from Portugal, 22–25; rural to urban labor shift for, 26–28; in Salt Lake City, 161; slavery with colonial, 31–32; spaces for, 250–51; U.S. historical approach to, 98–99. *See also* diaspora
imperfection, 16, 70–71
imperfectionism, moral, 70, 80, 83–84
imperialism, 4, 6, 9, 13; Afropolitanism and, 14; British, 72–73, 80–81; Burton on, 158; counter measures to, 70, 76; defense of, 68; sovereignty and, 67. *See also* anti-imperialism; British Empire; Ottoman Empire; Roman Empire
India, 46, 49–50, 111–12, 115n12, 174
India, colonial, 46–53; anti-colonialism in, 114; Burton in, 154–55; racial segregation in, 119; reading and readership of, 12, 108–13
indifference, 5, 75, 106
indigenous populations, 35, 38, 140, 174–75, 268n18. *See also* Gas
individual, 23, 33
Industrial Revolution, 25–28
inequality, 10–11, 62; Afropolitans and economic, 203; in global citizenship, 258; global neoliberalization and, 61; Orwell on, 40–41, 44–47, 49–50, 56n1; post-Industrial Revolution, 27, 28; utilitarianism and, 55–56; utopian socialism on, 73; war and economic, 42
infinite self-extension, 67–68
infinitude, horizontal, 33, 34, 68–69, 71–72, 76, 81–82

injustice. *See* justice
institutionalization, 138
intellectuals, 23, 266; African, 106–7; multiculturalism role for, 37–38
interconnectedness, 8, 191; digital, 12; horizontal infinitude and, 33, 34, 68–69, 71–72, 76, 81–82; problem solving in, 273–74
internationalism, 135–36, 140
Ireland, 202
Islam, 128, 143, 196, 197, 235

James, William, 68–69, 81, 117, 118–19, 158
Japan, 15, 254, 257, 263–64, 268n15
Jerusalem, 165, 235
Jews, 116, 128, 200n12; Burton on European, 164–65; diaspora for, 7, 9; pluralism and, 95–96
jingoism, 73
Johannesburg, 107
journalism, 108, 109
Judaism, 128, 200n12
justice, 142, 191, 195; gender, 174; redistributive, 11, 41–45, 54–56, 144–45; universal idea of, 137. *See also* global justice

Kang Youwei, 16, 254–55, 257, 262–63
Kant, Immanuel (Kantian), 5, 130, 138, 179, 183; peace as aim for, 42; on reason, 67; on self autonomy, 69; universalism of, 135, 194, 199n5, 257, 267n10
Kapur, Manju, 108, 113
Kawash, Samira, 248–50
Kennan, George F., 40–41, 44, 54
Kennedy, Dane, 159, 165
Kepler, Roy, 82
Kierkegaard, Søren, 66
Kingsolver, Barbara, 53
kinship, 176–78, 187n8, 271–74
Kipling, Rudyard, 22, 153, 166
Kizomba, 36
Kobayashi Takiji, 266

kòbòlò, 247–48
Koestler, Arthur, 69
koinos nomos, 182–83
Kojève, Alexandre, 68
"kosmo-polites," 2
Krishnaswamy, Mahesh, 193
Kristeva, Julia, 147–48
Kundera, Milan, 10, 127

labor migrants, 9
labor movement, 74
Lagos, 221, 227n2
laicité, 128–29
language, 22; of affection, 29; appropria-
    tion in Brazil, 23, 38n2; commerce
    and role of, 15; loss of, 11, 25, 28–29,
    226–27; postcolonial use and as-
    similation of, 245–46; preservation of,
    60, 105, 130; universal, 130. *See also*
    Portuguese
Latour, Bruno, 116
law and legality: of global commerce,
    232–33, 238n8; historical view of,
    231–32; universalism of, 231–34,
    239nn13–14. *See also* common law
Lawrence, T. E., 157, 166
Levinas, Emmanuel, 77
Lévi-Strauss, Claude, 37
Liang Congjie, 258–62, 263, 268n19
Liang Sicheng, 259
liberalism, 8. *See also* neoliberalism
Liberal Party (Britain), 80
Linebaugh, Peter, 9
Lin Huiyin, 258–63
Linton, Ralph, 31
literacy/literariness, 10, 145, 219
literature, 23; African, 242, 253n26; An-
    glophone, 111–13; bridges in, 255–58;
    Chinese, 256, 259, 266; colonial/
    postcolonial, 12, 108–13, 243; on eco-
    logical virtue, 53
locality, 2–3, 194–95
London, 73–75, 109–11, 244–49

loyalties, 10; historical, 138; multiple and
    overlapping, 43–44; prejudice and,
    195–96; to whole over locality, 2–3,
    194–95

Macaulay, Thomas, 108
madeleine experience, 23
magic, 69–70, 75
Maitland, Edward, 78
major globalism, 66–69, 86n2
"Malta Forum," 128
Mannheim, Karl, 117
Mao Zedong, 262–63
map, world, 93, 94, 95
Marechera, Dambudzo, 245, 246
Margalit, Avishai, 13, 142, 151
marriage, 99–100, 161
Marx, Karl (Marxism), 72, 73–74, 84, 102,
    136, 266
materialism, 84
Matory, Lorand, 221, 224
May Fourth generation, 257
Mbembe, Achille, 102–7, 203, 205, 209,
    243–44, 252
Mead, Margaret, 30–31
Mecca, 155, 235
media, 205–6, 217, 219
medieval era, 6, 15, 230–31, 235
Medina, 155, 160
Meirelles, Fernando, 38
Melville, Herman, 120, 122
memory, 13, 149–51
meteco (alien), 22, 23, 25, 38n2
metropolis. *See* urban centers
Mexican Americans. *See* Hispanic
    Americans
middle class. *See* social class
Middle East, 138–39
Mignolo, Walter, 7
migrants, 3, 144, 198; in Dubai, 141; iden-
    tity for, 13; labor, 9; multiculturalism
    and, 34
Mill, John Stuart, 73

Lightning Source UK Ltd.
Milton Keynes UK
UKHW01f2007240518
322824UK00037B/213/P